AF471089

FERRIES 2003
BRITISH ISLES AND NORTHERN EUROPE EDITION

ISBN 1 871947 71 5

Ferry Publications, PO Box 33,
Ramsey, Isle of Man IM99 4LP

Email: ferrypubs@aol.com   Website: www.ferrypubs.co.uk

europe's **leading** *guide to the ferry industry*

contents

© Ferry Publications 2003

Mont St Michel *(Brian D. Smith)*

europe's **leading** *guide to the ferry industry*

introduction

THIS is the sixteenth edition of this book, which first appeared in 1983 as the 24 page 'home published' *'Car Ferries from Great Britain and Ireland'*. The book aims to list every passenger/vehicle ferry in Great Britain and Ireland, ro-ro freight vessels which operate regular services between Great Britain and Ireland and to nearby continental destinations and major passenger/vehicle ferries in other parts of Northern Europe. The coverage of Northern Europe is not fully comprehensive (to make it so would probably triple the size of the book) and does not include freight-only operations and vessels-although for the first time some freight-only vessels have been included where the operators also run passenger services. Also, ro-ro vessels engaged in 'deep sea' and Mediterranean trade and those operated solely for the carriage of trade cars are not included.

Each operator is listed alphabetically within sections - international and Northern Ireland routes, domestic services, freight-only operations, chain, cable and float ferries, passenger only ferries, other North European passenger operators and vehicle/passenger vessels owned by companies not currently engaged in operating services. After details relating to each company's management, address, telephone numbers, email, web site and services, there is a fleet list with technical data and then a potted history of each vessel with previous names and dates.

The war in Iraq has caused complications in the freight ferries sections with several ships departing from their usual routes on charters to the Gulf for the MoD or the US Defense Department. By the time this book is published some or all may have returned; meanwhile the vessels continue to be listed under their usual operator along with the ships chartered as temporary replacements.

We are pleased this year to feature the *Mont St Michel* as our theme ship in this title. Finally my thanks to Superfast Ferries for their sponsorship of this book.

Whitstable, Kent   **Nick Widdows**

April 2003

europe's **leading** *guide to the ferry industry*

foreword

O nce again there have been more radical changes in the ferry industry during 2002 and a further consolidation of operations. Some long associated companies have been absorbed into other organisations or have disappeared completely. The industry continues to explore the development of the conventional fast ferry and also the use of Ro-pax vessels.

Possibly the most radical change in the UK during the last twelve months has been the reorganisation of the ferry group of P&O. Under a reorganisation package, P&O North Sea Ferries and P&O Portsmouth was absorbed into the operations at Dover under a new marketing company of P&O Ferries. P&O Irish Sea have retained their identity operations to Ireland for the moment but major changes were due on the horizon as we went to press between Stena Line and P&O on the Irish Sea. Meanwhile, P&O lost its long association with the ferry services to Orkney and Shetland, when Northlink Ferries took over the operations to these islands following the decision of the Scottish Assembly to appoint this new group to run the ferry services. The new group, part of the Royal Bank of Scotland and Caledonian MacBrayne brought a new style and standard of ferry operations to Shetland and Orkney plus a new multi million infrastructure at all the ports to accept the three new vessels. The new fast ferry operation between Rosyth and Zeebrugge appears to have attracted good levels of passengers but the anticipated freight levels, we understand, have not yet been achieved.

In 2002 Brittany Ferries announced the construction of a new cruise-ferry for their Spanish and Irish services, which will bring a new style and standard of operations when the *Pont Aven* enters service in April 2004.

DFDS have also undergone radical changes during 2002, with new tonnage in both their Esbjerg and Cuxhaven services. Meanwhile, further changes within the DFDS group are enhancing their operations in Scandinavia. New tonnage came on line for Gotland Line and further orders for ships have been made by other Scandinavian companies, including that of Color Line.

Further improvements have been undertaken by the author to this title again this year and we sincerely hope that you will enjoy it, not only as an invaluable reference book but as a further insight to the ever-changing ferry industry in Northern Europe. The title was joined in 2002 by its sister title covering Southern Mediterannean operations and between both titles we are able to offer a comprehensive study to the industry within Europe.

Miles Cowsill
Director
Ferry Publications Ltd
Isle of Man, British Isles

Superfast IX *(Miles Cowsill)*

a **guide** *to*

using this book

Sections Listing is in seven sections *Section 1* - Services from Great Britain and Ireland to the continent and between Great Britain and Ireland (including services to/from the Isle of Man and Channel Islands), *Section 2* - Domestic services within Great Britain and Ireland, *Section 3* - Freight only services from Great Britain and Ireland and domestic routes, *Section 4* - Minor vehicle ferries in Great Britain and Ireland (chain and cable ferries etc), *Section 5* - Major passenger only operators, *Section 6* - Major car ferry operators in Northern Europe, *Section 7* - Companies not operating regular services possessing vehicle ferries which may be chartered or sold to other operators.

Order The company order within each section is alphabetical. Note that the definite article and words meaning 'company' or 'shipping company' (eg 'AG', 'Reederei') do not count. However, where this is part of a ship's name it does count. Sorting is by normal English convention eg 'Å' is treated the same as 'A' and comes at the start, not as a separate character which comes the end of the alphabet as is the Scandinavian convention. Where ships are numbered, order is by number whether number is expressed in Arabic or Latin digits or words (eg SUPERSEACAT TWO comes before SUPERSEACAT THREE).

Company information This section gives general information regarding to status of the company ie nationality, whether it is public or private sector and whether it is part of a larger group.

Management The managing director and marketing director or manager of each company are listed. Where these posts do not exist, other equivalent people are listed. Where only initials are given, that person is, as far as is known, male.

Address This is the address of the company's administrative headquarters. In the case of some international companies, a British and overseas address is given.

Telephone and Fax Numbers are expressed as follows + [*number*] (this is the international dialling code which is dialled in combination with the number dialled for international calls (00 in the UK, Ireland and most other European countries); it is not used for calling within the country), ([*number*]) (this is the number which precedes area codes when making long distance domestic calls - it is not dialled when calling from another country or making local calls (not all countries have this)), [*number*] (this is the rest of the number including, where appropriate, the area dialling code). In a few cases free or local call rate numbers are used for reservations; note that these are not available from overseas. Telex numbers are also included where applicable; it should be noted that many operators no longer use this service, its role having largely been taken over by fax and email.

Internet Email addresses and Website URLs are given where these are available; the language(s) used is shown. Note that use of the Internet is increasing quickly and new sites may come into use during the currency of this book. If a web site is not shown for a particular operator, it may be worth trying one or more search engines to see if a new site has opened. In a few cases Email facility is only available through the Website. To avoid confusion, there is no other punctuation on the Internet line. All these addresses can be accessed from www.ferriesoftheworld.com and this will be updated at regular intervals as new web sites come on line. It should be noted that some sites are not always up to date and it is disappointing that few operators use this facility for 'real time' data showing day by day service changes. However, the standard is generally much higher than a few years ago and many operators now allow on-line booking, often at a discount over other methods. It is also often possible to find times for freight only sailings.

Routes operated After each route there are, in brackets, details of *1* normal journey time, *2* regular vessel(s) used on the route (number as in list of vessels) and *3* frequencies (where a number per day is given, this relates to return sailings). In the case of freight-only sailings which operate to a regular schedule, departure times are given where they have been supplied. Please note that times are subject to quite frequent change and cancellation.

Winter and Summer In this book, **winter** generally means the period between October and Easter while **summer** means, Easter to October. The **peak summer period** is generally June, July and August. In Scandinavia, the summer peak ends in mid-August whilst in the UK it starts rather later and generally stretches into the first or second week of September. Dates vary according to operator.

Spelling The convention is used in respect of town and country names is that English names are used for towns and areas of countries where such names exist (eg Gothenburg rather than Göteborg) and English names for countries (eg Germany rather than Deutschland). Otherwise local names are used, accented as appropriate. In a few cases, English names have slipped out of common usage and the local name is more commonly used in Britain, ie Dunkerque not Dunkirk, Helsingør not Elsinore and Vlissingen not Flushing. Many towns in Finland have both Finnish and Swedish names; we have used the Finnish name except in the case of Åland which is a Swedish speaking area. In the case of Danish towns, the alternative use of 'å' or 'aa' follows local convention. For technical reasons it is not possible to express some Polish names with the correct accents. The following towns, islands and territories are expressed using their English names; the local name is shown following: Antwerp - Antwerpen/Anvers, Fyn - Funen, Genoa - Génova, Ghent - Gent, Gothenburg - Göteborg, Jutland - Jylland, Copenhagen - København, Ostend - Oostende, Oporto - Porto, Seville - Sevilla, Sealand - Sjælland, Venice - Venezia.

Terms The following words mean *'shipping company'* in various languages Redereja (Latvian), Rederi (Danish, Norwegian, Swedish), Rederij (Dutch), Reederei (German), Zegluga (Polish). The following words mean *'limited company'* AB - Aktiebolag (Swedish) (Finnish companies who use both the Finnish and Swedish terms sometimes express it as Ab), AG - Aktiengesellschaft (German), AS - Aksjeselskap (Norwegian), A/S - Aktie Selskabet (Danish), BV - besloten vennootschap (Dutch), GmbH - Gesellschaft mit beschränkter Haftung (German), NV - naamloze vennootschap (Dutch), Oy - (Finnish), Oyj - (Finnish (plc)), SA - Société Anonyme (French).

Types of Ferry

These distinctions are necessarily general and many ships will have features of more than one category.

Car Ferry Up until about 1970, most vehicle ferries were primarily designed for the conveyance of cars and their passengers and foot passengers. Little regard was paid to the conveyance of lorries and trailers, since this sort of traffic had not began to develop. Few vessels of this type are still in service.

Multi-purpose Ferry From about 1970 onwards vehicle ferries began to make more provision for freight traffic, sharing the same ship with passengers and cars. Features usually include higher vehicle decks, often with retractable ramps enabling two levels of cars or one level of freight and coaches, and separate facilities (including cabins on quite short crossings) for freight drivers.

Cruise Ferry In the 1980s the idea of travelling on a ferry, not just to get from A to B, but for the pleasure of the travel experience became more and more popular and ferries were built with increasingly luxurious and varied passenger accommodation. Such vessels also convey cars and freight but the emphasis is on passenger accommodation with a high level of berths (sometimes providing berths for all passengers).

Ro-pax Ferry A vessel designed primarily for the carriage of freight traffic but also carry a limited number of ordinary passengers. Features generally include a moderate passenger capacity - up to about 500 passengers - and a partly open vehicle deck. Modern ro-pax vessels are becoming increasingly luxurious with facilities approaching those of a cruise ferry.

Ro-ro Ferry A vessel designed for the conveyance of road freight, unaccompanied trailers and containers on low 'Mafi' trailers. Some such vessels have no passenger accommodation but the majority can take up to 12 passengers - the maximum allowed without a passenger certificate. On routes where there is a low level of driver accompanied traffic (mainly the longer ones), ordinary passengers, with or without cars, can sometimes be conveyed. On routes with a high level of driver accompanied traffic, passenger capacity will sometimes be higher but facilities tend to be geared to the needs of freight drivers eg lounge with video, high level of cabins on routes of three hours or more. Technically such vessels are passenger ferries (having a passenger certificate) but are included in the freight section when exclusively or largely conveying freight drivers.

Fast Ferry Streamlined vessel of catamaran or monohull construction, speed in excess of 30 knots, water jet propulsion, generally aluminium built but some have steel hulls, little or no freight capacity, no cabins.

Timescale Although the book goes to press April 2003, I have sought to reflect the situation as it will exist in summer 2003 with regard to the introduction of new ships or other known changes. Vessels due to enter service from September 2003 are shown as 'Under Construction'. The book is updated at all stages of the production process where this is feasible - although major changes once the text has been paginated are not possible; there is also a 'Late News' section at the back for changes which cannot be incorporated into the text.

List of vessels

NO (A)	GROSS TONNAGE (B)	SERVICE SPEED (KNOTS)	NUMBER OF PASSENGERS	VEHICLE ACCESS DECK (D)
1 NAME	‡26433t 87	22k	150m 290P 650C 100L	BA2 UK
NAME	YEAR BUILT	LENGTH OVERALL	VEHICLE (C) DECK CAPACITY	FLAG (E)

(A) » = fast ferry, • = vessel laid up, F = freight only vessel, p = passenger only vessel

(B) '‡' = not measured in accordance with the 1969 Tonnage Convention; c = approximate.

(C) C = Cars, L = Lorries (**15m**), T = Trailers (**13.5m**), r = can also take rail wagons, - = No figure quoted.

(D) B = Bow, A = Aft, S = Side, Q = Quarterdeck, R = Slewing ramp, 2 = Two decks can be loaded at the same time, C = Vehicles must be crane loaded aboard, t = turntable ferry.

(E) The following abbreviations are used:

AT = Antigua & Barbuda	ES = Estonia	LT = Lithuania	RO = Romania
	FA = Faroes	LV = Latvia	RU = Russia
BA = Bahamas	FI = Finland	LX = Luxembourg	SI = Singapore
BB = Barbados	FR = France	MA = Malta	SP = Spain
BD = Bermuda	GI = Gibraltar	NA = Netherlands Antilles	SV = St Vincent & Grenadines
BE = Belgium	GR = Greece		
BZ = Belize	GY = Germany	NL = Netherlands	SW = Sweden
CI = Cayman Islands	IM = Isle of Man	NO = Norway	UK = United Kingdom
CR = Croatia	IT = Italy	PA = Panama	
CY = Cyprus	IR = Irish Republic	PL = Portugal	
DK = Denmark	LB = Liberia	PO = Poland	

In the notes ships are in CAPITAL LETTERS, shipping lines and other institutions are in *italics*.

Capacity In this book, capacities shown are the maxima. Sometimes vessels operate at less than their maximum passenger capacity due to reduced crewing or to operating on a route on which they are not permitted to operate above a certain level. Car and lorry/trailer capacities are the maximum for either type. The two figures are not directly comparable; some parts of a vessel may allow cars on two levels to occupy the space that a trailer or lorry occupies on one level, some may not. Also some parts of a vessel with low headroom may only be accessible to cars. All figures have to be fairly approximate.

Ownership The ownership of many vessels is very complicated. Some are actually owned by finance companies and banks, some by subsidiary companies of the shipping lines, some by subsidiary companies of a holding company of which the shipping company is also a subsidiary and some by companies which are jointly owned by the shipping company and other interests like a bank, set up specifically to own one ship or a group of ships. In all these cases the vessel is technically chartered to the shipping company. However, in this book, only those vessels chartered from one shipping company to another or from a ship owning company unconnected with the shipping line, are recorded as being on charter. Vessels are listed under the current operator rather than the owner. Charter is 'bareboat' (ie without crew) unless otherwise stated. If chartered with crew, vessels are 'time chartered'.

Gross Tonnage This is a measure of enclosed capacity rather than weight, based on a formula of one gross ton = 100 cubic feet. Even small alterations can alter the gross tonnage. Under old measurement systems, the capacity of enclosed car decks was not included but, under a 1969 convention, all vessels laid down after 1982 have been measured by a new system which includes enclosed vehicle decks as enclosed space, thereby considerably increasing the tonnage of vehicle ferries. Under this convention, from 1st January 1995, all vessels were due to be re-measured under this system; despite there, there are a number of vessels which have either not been re-registered or the details of the new measurements were not obtainable. All vessels measured by the old system are indicated with a double dagger '‡'. Tonnages quoted here are, where possible, those given by the shipping companies themselves.

The following people are gratefully thanked for their assistance with this publication many people in ferry companies in the UK and abroad, Gary Andrews, Cees de Bijl, Dick Clague, Erik B Jonsen, Barry Mitchell, The Ostend Ferry Crew, Jack Phelan, Pekka Ruponen, Christian Schrandt, Michael Speckenbach (FERRYinformation), Henk van der Lugt, Ian Smith (Camrose Organisation), Foto Flite, Haven Colourprint and Pat Somner (Ferry Publications).

Whilst every effort has been made to ensure that the facts contained here are correct, neither the publishers nor the writer can accept any responsibility for errors contained herein. We would, However, appreciate comments from readers, which we will endeavour to incorporate in the next edition which we plan to publish in spring 2004.

Pride of Canterbury
DOVER
Say yes to the best
Say yes to the best

Pride of Canterbury (Miles Cowsill)

Brittany Ferries'
mont st michel

Was she worth the wait? That is surely the question on everyone's lips. A decade after the arrival of Brittany Ferries' previous new build, 2002 saw the debut of the £80 million *Mont St Michel* on the flagship Portsmouth – Caen route. Displacing the veteran *Duc de Normandie*, the *Mont St Michel* brings much-needed parity to the 6-hour route, which from humble beginnings in 1986 has risen to become Brittany Ferries' most popular service.

The *Mont St Michel's* arrival was not without problems however – launched on 16th March 2002 she was originally scheduled to arrive from Dutch builders Van de Giessen de Noord on the 4th July. Her final completion and fitting out was beset by seemingly endless delays, forcing Brittany Ferries to substitute the veteran *Quiberon* in her place. Initial concern that the summer season would be missed soon turned into question marks over whether she would even arrive that year as the delays pushed her delivery date later and later. Ultimately, she turned into an early Christmas present, finally sailing majestically into Caen for the first time on 12th December and entering service with the 15.05 sailing from France on 20th.

In terms of appearance, the *Mont St Michel* clearly shows her Van de Giessen genes. While she certainly has an imposing presence, there is no doubt that she lacks the elegance of her elder running mate, the much-admired, 1992-built *Normandie*. Upon boarding the *Mont St Michel*, however, regular travellers may well be struck by the striking similarity of her internal layout to that of the *Normandie*. Indeed, internally, such is that similarity that they could almost be considered as half-sisters. Perhaps this will lead people to question why Brittany Ferries reused a design already ten years old. The answer is that the layout of the *Normandie* has been such a success that it did not need to be significantly altered – instead it has been slightly evolved with the benefit of experience and fitted out with an impressive level of detail.

The heart of the ship is the central atrium, spanning three decks, each linked by a black marble staircase that rises up from her reception hall on Deck 7. The Information Desk and Bureau de Change are found in this hall, which features black-marble flooring and boasts deep chaise-long style sofas in bright purple. Her atrium itself is filled with a stunning abstract sculpture of the real Mont St Michel in glass, which evolves in colour from blues and greens at the bottom to bright reds, yellows and pinks at the top. Large plasma screens hang in the reception hall and in strategic locations around the vessel offering travel, safety and shopping information.

COMPLEX

The entrance to the Monts and Merveilles shopping complex is located forward in the reception hall. In addition to the standard products on offer, the complex boasts a Beauty Cafe, a delicatessen and a dedicated wine cellar. Illuminated by fluorescent white lighting, the Beauty Cafe provides a spacious alluring retail environment and details such as a display of sculpture or the armchairs provided for customers to relax while sampling the products are indicative of the quality of outfitting found throughout the vessel. Passageways curve around the Monts and Merveilles leading to the two 66-seat cinemas, complete with their own ticket office. Two small conference rooms are also located here, while five recliner lounges, each individually named, occupy the forward section of Deck 7 offering seats for

Seating area on Deck 8 *(Brittany Ferries)*

Blue Note Piano Bar *(Brittany Ferries)*

La Galerie Self Service Restaurant *(Brittany Ferries)*

Le Kiosque and the atrium *(Brittany Ferries)*

458 passengers. Set aside for pre-booked passengers, the forward Tombelaine lounge, seating 124, is complete with panoramic views over the bow and a dedicated lounge area with complimentary newspapers. Happily, the *Mont St Michel* boasts a forward viewing platform, although whether the majority of passengers will ever find it is questionable. Access is awkward, from two service stairwells on either beam of the Tombelaine lounge, but in its favour, the platform does offer wooden benches and teak decking.

The decorative theme of the *Mont St Michel* is the arts of Normandy, and each of her four main public rooms has been styled around one of four key subjects - painting, literature, music and cinema. To quote Brittany Ferries, her interior decor is a "celebration of Normandy, with each space conceived as a meeting between travellers and works of art". As with other members of the fleet, each main saloon is equipped with individual menus bearing the names of both the facility and the vessel. In the case of the *Mont St Michel*, these menus are used as a medium to explain the themes of the decor to her passengers.

Her restaurant deck, Deck 8, commences forward with La Gallerie self-service. Styled around the art of painting, La Gallerie is completed in bright yellows and oranges, creating a light, positive atmosphere. With a capacity for 374 diners, dividers are used to split the seating area into more intimate spaces, and both the dividers and the bulkheads are lined with impressionist art, including several works depicting the Mont St Michel. To starboard, a separate 90-seat ro-ro drivers' restaurant is found, while as on the *Normandie*, a passenger arcade portside leads aft to the atrium. At this level, her smaller retail outlets - La Vitrine and Le Kiosque - are arranged around the central stairwell to starboard, while to port there is a lounge seating area. Complete with wooden flooring and filled with chunky leather-upholstered sofas and armchairs, this is the perfect location for watching shipboard life pass by. The passenger arcade continues aft into Les Romantiques - her impressive formal restaurants promoted by Brittany Ferries as 'three restaurants in one'.

At the entrance of Les Romantiques is her small restaurant boutique, which tempts passengers with a tantalizing selection of local Norman produce such as oils, spices and linens. The arcade walkway continues aft leading to her open decks, passing through Les Comptoir des Saveurs, while the main Les Romantiques buffet and a la carte restaurant is found to starboard, divided from the walkway by transparent glass panels. The location of the promised third restaurant - Table d'Hotes - is hence rather a mystery – physically there are just two distinct areas. Perhaps Table d'Hotes refers to the boutique?

OPEN PLAN

The open-plan Les Comptoir des Saveurs, best described as an upmarket French bistro, offers an open bar together with several small table areas. The space certainly exudes an upscale atmosphere - with the prices to match - but whether a public walkway through the centre will be conducive to creating a premium-dining venue is questionable. This space may have been better as a wine bar, as is found adjacent to the Les Abers restaurant on board the *Bretagne* of 1989. Back on the *Mont St Michel*, the main Les Romantiques restaurant to starboard is filled with deep armchairs in blood red with wooden trim, and also offers al fresco dining in summer months on a dedicated terrace with teak decking and wooden furniture.

Les Romantiques as a whole has a literary theme and successfully re-creates the ambiance of a library with wooden flooring throughout and bulkheads panelled with warm woods or lined with bookcases. Once again, it is the strength of the detail that impresses – for example, in Les Comptoir des Saveurs, the baby grand piano or the trio of antique artists sketchbooks displayed in individual cases. The story of these notepads is told in accompanying plaques, which reveal that they were found washed up on an St Malo beach at the turn of the 19th century. Worthy of note are also the WC facilities for Les Romantiques, where male and female amenities share a square sink with division achieved only by a mirror suspended above - further evidence of the thought that characterises her interior design.

Perhaps the biggest failing of the older *Normandie* is the layout of Deck 9, where Le Derby Bar is too

MONT ST MICHEL
CAEN
Brittany Ferries

Mont St Michel *(Miles Cowsill)*

small and there is insufficient division between the bar area and the adjacent vienoisserie - resulting in the latter space often simply becoming a noisy, smoky overflow for the bar. Although both facilities remain on Deck 9 on board the *Mont St Michel*, this problem has been resolved with the configuration of the bar and viennoisserie altered from a port/starboard layout to a fore and aft layout. Much greater separation is thus achieved, creating in two distinct, individual spaces – Le Blue Note Bar forward and Le Café du Festival aft.

Le Blue Note Bar itself is divided into two spaces – the main bar area and the smaller Blue Note Piano Bar to starboard. The Piano Bar features wooden flooring, funky blue armchairs and deep sofas upholstered in white leather, and is clearly intended to be a separate feature - a quieter, more intimate area. However, the whole Blue Note Bar area is open plan and there is minimal distinction between the two spaces - except in terms of fittings. Without any physical division from the main area, the Piano Bar will be neither quiet nor intimate when the main bar is even moderately busy, thus recreating the problem found on board the *Normandie*, just in a different arena! Both bars share the forward V-shaped servery, behind which her video games arcade has been discreetly hidden away. The lounge area for the main Blue Note Bar is filled with circular tables surrounded by clusters of blue chairs, and contains a circular stage/dance floor aft. As could be guessed, the theme of the bars is music. In particular, the Piano Bar appears to be styled around jazz, with paintings of jazz scenes on the bulkheads and showcases displaying genuine instruments – a trumpet and a saxophone for instance.

Moving aft, the 160-seat Le Cafe du Festival is an extremely light and airy space, benefiting from floor to ceiling windows on two sides. The bright nature of the cafe is accentuated by the vivid colour scheme in place, which sees the chairs upholstered in fluorescent pink, yellow and green. The centrepiece of the cafe is a circular table on which stands a sculpture of a tree – a unique, eye-catching feature indicative of the small, individual touches which can be seen throughout the vessel. As the name suggests, the theme here is cinema with the room intended to celebrate the film festivals at Cabourg, Deauville and Honfleur. While the servery is found to starboard, to port a spacious children's area - Les Petits Mousses au Cinema - is located, containing both a soft adventure centre and a video area.

DESIGN

One advantage of the *Normandie's* design compared to the *Mont St Michel* is the raised deck head above the Le Derby Bar on Deck 9. While the *Mont St Michel* lacks this feature, it is an understandable sacrifice, for the loss of the extra height allows for an additional public space directly above on Deck 10. This houses Games Planet, which contains a vast array of diversions including table hockey, video games and a CD station. One feature notably missing on board however is an Internet cafe, which was listed among her attractions in early publicity but was later quietly dropped. Had Brittany Ferries been brave enough to proceed with this feature, then this light room would presumably have been a leading candidate to house it. With Internet stations appearing on vessels as diverse as Minoan Lines' *Europa Palace*, P&O's *Pride of Rotterdam* and Color Lines' *Color Viking*, it is to be regretted Brittany Ferries did not proceed with this useful amenity.

Of the *Mont St Michel's* 344 cabins, 223 are for passenger use offering a total of 808 berths. These are located aft of the reception hall on Deck 7 and forward of the Blue Note Bar on Deck 9, and consist of 173 4-berth cabins, 40 2-berth cabins and 2 cabins adapted for the disabled. In addition, 8 Commodore Class suites are available on Deck 9, which benefit from facilities such as DVD players, as well as the private Commodore lounge. All her passenger cabins boast innovative space-saving upper berths that fold into the ceiling. The remainder of the cabins are for crew, and are located on Deck 0. Her accommodation is completed with her spacious sun decks, which are spread over three levels, from Decks 8 to 10. Additionally, small side promenades can be found leading off the reception hall on Deck 7 and a helipad is located above the Games Planet on Deck 11. It is hoped that Brittany Ferries will provide deck furniture for passengers, which is sure to be in hot demand on summer crossings.

The vessel's technical specifications are listed in the adjoining table, but specifically noteworthy is her container loading system, located immediately forward of the Games Planet on Deck 10. Stores are loaded into trolleys and stored in the containers, which are then hoisted on board from the quayside by the ship's own mechanical spreader ready for easy dispersal onboard.

Overall, so much thought appears to have been invested in the *Mont St Michel*, that Brittany Ferries appear not just to be creating a ship, but a brand. How many other ferries can boast their own, specially designed logo? In addition to being used extensively in Brittany Ferries' publicity, the streamlined image features throughout the ship – on pens and napkins for instance.

The *Mont St Michel* does have flaws – as explained, in terms of layout, the division between the Blue Note Bar and Piano Bar does not work. Minor negative points include the fact that several cabins reportedly have their view obscured by lifeboats, while the black marble flooring in the atrium easily shows footmarks, meaning her crew will have their work cut out to keep it pristine. Perhaps in certain areas, the design element has been promoted above practicality? However, when considering the vessel as a whole, her positives do outweigh these criticisms. Her cosmopolitan interior displays detailed thought throughout – passenger flow is simple and efficient, few if any fittings are generic, she is brimming with artwork and her decor is fresh, bold and stylish. The *Mont St Michel* is a clear statement of Brittany Ferries' confidence in their future, and like the *Bretagne* and the *Normandie* before her, she deserves to be the benchmark against which others are judged.

Was she worth the wait? Undoubtedly!

Richard Seville

TECHNICAL SPECIFICATION

Passenger Capacity: 2140

Lane Metres: 2250m

Cars/Freight Vehicles: 800/130

Length: 173.95m

Width: 28.5m

Draft: 6.2m

Tonnage: 35,592

Engines: 4 x MaK 6M43 Diesels

Engine Power: 21,600 Kilowatts

Speed: 21.5 knots

Main Car Deck *(Brittany Ferries)*

Normandie *(Chris Randall)*

Pride of Kent *(Brian D. Smith)*

round **britain**
review 2002

EAST COAST

This year has seen considerable upheaval for many of the North Sea's established operators. The Harwich-based passenger fleet of DFDS Seaways has been entirely renewed with the loss of the old favourites *Dana Anglia* and the *Admiral of Scandinavia* and their replacement by tonnage both more recent and more suited to the present freight-orientated traffic - if not to the taste of traditional DFDS observers. First to depart was the *Dana Anglia*, which made her final sailing from Esbjerg on 28th September, thereafter assuming the new name of *Duke of Scandinavia* for DFDS' Copenhagen-Trelleborg-Gdansk service. Intermediate replacement at Esbjerg came in the form of the *Dana Gloria* (ex *Golfo dei Coralli*), the first of two Polish-built twins cancelled by Lloyd Sardegna and subsequently acquired by DFDS Seaways in July 2002. After commencing freight sailings in August, she took over the passenger service on 2nd October, but is due to be replaced in June 2003 by sister *Golfo dei Delfini*. As the new *Dana Sirena*, the second twin benefited from extensive rebuilding at Remontowa to increase both her public spaces and her cabin capacity.

The *Admiral of Scandinavia* closed the passenger operation to Cuxhaven on 13th November 2002, having been sold to Access Ferries of Greece in July. The freight-only *Nordo Link* maintained the Cuxhaven service during the winter, before passenger services were re-opened on 21st April by the new *Duchess of Scandinavia*. The latter is Fjord Line's 1993-built *Bergen*, which DFDS had secured on a 57-month charter. Although the loss of extensive passenger facilities on these routes is to be regretted, it is hoped the DFDS fleet will now be better placed to consolidate their position in the face of ever increasing competition - not least from budget airlines.

In contrast, DFDS Seaways activities at Newcastle have enjoyed a relatively quiet year with deployment unchanged. The Tyne-based *Princess of Scandinavia* hit national headlines however following an engine-room fire late on 17th May, and although there were no fatalities, the vessel was not able to re-enter service until 16th June. Fortunately, neither were any lives lost when P&O North Sea Ferries' *Norsea* was also disabled by fire in the early hours of 2nd September while en route to Zeebrugge. Happily, damage was limited and she was able to recommence service a week later.

The 37-year old brand North Sea Ferries disappeared during October as the operations were incorporated into the new P&O Ferries portfolio, and January 2003 saw the disappearance of the traditional 'Nor'- names with the *Norsun* and *Norsea* re-christened the *Pride of Bruges* and the *Pride of York* respectively – a move perhaps hastened due to the negative associations with the name *Norsea*.

Down at Felixtowe, the P&O name itself disappeared as the freight services to both Europort and Zeebrugge were axed. The Belgian route was terminated on 6th July and at the end of the month the Dutch services were handed over to Stena Line, reportedly part of a larger deal that saw Stena withdraw from the P&O Stena Line joint venture. Their £12 million purchase also included the *European Freeway, European Tideway* and the *Pride of Flanders*, which were initially renamed *Freeway, Ideway* and *Flanders*. The service was switched to Harwich on 15th September, and during their winter refits, the three ships became the *Stena Partner,* the *Stena Transfer* and the *Stena Transporter* respectively. Stena Line's original route from Harwich, the booming link to the Hook of Holland, was further boosted in April 2003 when the Korean-built *Stena Britannica* replaced the earlier Spanish-built vessel of the same name.

Further change appeared likely on the Tyne in November 2002, where the *Jupiter* came close to passing back to her former owners when Color Line launched a take-over bid for Fjord Line. Color Line initially acquired 59% of the shares in Fjord Line's owner, BNR, but both complex financial manoeuvring by rival shareholder FN and ultimate overruling by Norway's competition authorities prevented Color Line's ambitions. Color Line subsequently disposed of their interests in Fjord Line during December.

With the introduction of the *Duchess M* from Tilbury to Gravesend, the historic Thames link finally appears to have a secure future following an extremely turbulent patch. The service was suspended after the failure of the *Martin Chuzzlewit* in mid April 2002, but operator Lower Thames and Medway Passenger Boat Company were able to re-start crossings on 10th June.

EASTERN CHANNEL

The new *SeaFrance Rodin* has settled down well and the firm are seeing the results of their investment with substantially increased carryings – passengers and car figures for 2002 were 25% and 22% up on the previous year respectively. The redundant *SeaFrance Renoir* operated extra sailings throughout the summer, and looks set to remain part of the active fleet throughout 2003. The idea of converting the *SeaFrance Nord-Pas-de-Calais* has been shelved in favour of commissioning yet another newbuilding – although an order has yet to be confirmed, delivery is anticipated for 2005.

August saw the final links with the railway era swept away as P&O acquired Stena Line's 40% stake in their Dover-based joint venture. On 16th October, P&O's short-sea operations were then incorporated with those at Portsmouth and on the North Sea into the resurrected P&O Ferries brand, a move that also heralded the re-appearance of the P&O 'Pride of' nomenclature at Dover. Stena Line markings rapidly disappeared, but it was not until winter refits that the fleet appeared in the new, revised P&O Ferries livery.

As the *PO Canterbury*, the one-time Sealink British Ferries flagship *Fantasia* appeared uneasy just in P&O blue, but her operation by P&O Ferries was short-lived with the arrival of the new Darwin-project conversions displacing both her and the 1981-built *PO Kent*. The *European Highway* had closed the firm's Dover to Zeebrugge link on 15th December, after which she sailed to Bremerhaven to join the *European Pathway*. First to re-enter service in May 2003 was the former *European Pathway*, which became the second *Pride of Canterbury* following rebuilding by Lloyd Werft, while sister *European Highway* debuted in June as the *Pride of Kent*. The third Zeebrugge freighter, the *European Seaway*, was transferred permanently to the Calais station. It has been reported that Far Eastern yards are being considered to build two new sisters for 2006, to replace the *Pride of Provence* and the *Pride of Aquitaine*. The *Pride of Provence* hit the national press when she collided with the Dover breakwater on 18th April, but casualties were fortunately limited.

The main beneficiaries (and, to some extent, instigators) of the Zeebrugge closure continued to grow during 2002, both introducing new vessels. Norfolkline introduced a third ship in the form of the *Dawn Merchant* in September, initially still in Norse Merchant livery. Rumours that the fourth sister, *Brave Merchant*, would also appear on the Channel proved unfounded however, when the vessel was chartered to the MoD.

At Ramsgate, TransEuropa Ferries reported a 25% increase in traffic over 2001, and their thirst for new acquisitions still appears insatiable. Having finally commissioned the *Oleander* on 14th July, just five days later they took over the *European Endeavour* from P&O Irish Sea. While she was refitting as the *Gardenia*, prior to a debut in January 2003, October 2002 saw TransEuropa acquire sister *Regina 1*, the former *European Pathfinder*. TEF's other former Townsend Thoresen ship, the *Laburnum*, departed on charter to Comanav during January 2003, becoming their *Tadla* for service between Genoa and Tangier, while the *Roseanne* has also been chartered out. The Slovenian company is currently the leading candidate to acquire the displaced *PO Kent*. Ostend's other freight company, Ferryways, also continues to thrive with their routes to Killingholme and Ipswich.

Although freight services are booming, 2003 sees Ostend without a passenger link for the first time in 156 years. Hoverspeed announced the closure of their high-speed link to the Belgian resort in January 2003, which was operated in 2002 by the *Diamant*. Instead, they will concentrate on the core Dover to Calais route with three 74m InCats, including for the first time the 1992-built *SeaCat Scotland*. As rumours persist that SeaContainers are seeking to withdraw completely from UK ferry operations, Hoverspeed face increased competition from newcomer Speed Ferries. With Norfolkline handling Dover shore operations, Denmark's Mols- Linien will run from Dover to Boulogne from June 2003 using the Speed One, a 91 metre InCat that

Your first port of call

Take a short cut. Now everything you need to know about the Port of Dover is online, at the new-look official port website.

Use it to check the day's crossing conditions, news and ferry services.

So whatever you need to know about the Port of Dover, make www.doverport.co.uk your first port of call.

roll-on, roll-off in Oostende, it's fast, it's easy

The port of Oostende in Belgium offers you a long-established know-how in handling ro-ro freight. Its up-to-date infrastructure includes versatile berthing facilities and well-situated parking areas. Major terminus of European highways, inland waterways, railroads and an international airport make Oostende a true global cargo hub.

www.re-action.be

was formerly their *Mads Mols.*

The seasonal Hoverspeed service between Newhaven and Dieppe ran in 2002 with the *SuperSeaCat One*, which has survived the annual fleet reshuffle to operate the route again in 2003. Transmanche Ferries continue their year-round service, but with traffic levels seemingly poor, serious question marks must hang over the viability of this now marginal operation.

On the Solent, Red Funnel took delivery of the £2.6 million *Red Jet 4* in April, the craft having been transported by heavy lift ship from Tasmanian builders North West Bay Ships Pty Ltd. Plans have also been announced to add an extra car deck to the three Raptor class ferries, and the possibility of a fourth conventional ship has also been mooted. Rivals Wightlink's operations at Portsmouth have stabilised, with both the *St Clare* and the FastCats proving increasingly reliable, but the firm appears no closer to resolving the problem of finding replacements for the now 30-year old and increasingly troublesome C-Class at Lymington.

WESTERN CHANNEL

Brittany Ferries continue to dominate this sector with the arrival in December of their new £80 million *Mont St. Michel* from Van de Giessen de Noord. Originally due to enter service in July, her final outfitting was beset by severe delays which forced the Breton firm to deploy the *Quiberon* in her place when the *Duc de Normandie* switched to the Plymouth – Roscoff link as planned. Winter 2002 saw the latter 1978-built ship also introduce a new weekly link from Plymouth to Cherbourg, while the *Val de Loire* doubled up sailings between Portsmouth and St Malo thrice weekly until March 2003. Contruction of the replacement for the *Val de Loire*, named as the *Pont Aven*, meanwhile continues apace at German builders Meyer Werft. Due for delivery in Spring 2004, the £100 million, 27 knot vessel will slash crossing times and bring new standards of luxury to the Western Channel, with cabin balconies being just one of her amenities.

2002 saw the demise of the dedicated P&O Portsmouth operation, which was the third P&O division combined under the new P&O Ferries umbrella. Traffic figures for 2002 proved promising, with increases reported on all routes particularly Cherbourg. From September the division's fleet became composed solely of chartered tonnage with the disposal of the jumboised SuperViking twins *Pride of Cherbourg* and *Pride of Hampshire*, both sold to Egypt's El Salam Maritime. Their replacement, the former *Isle of Innisfree*, had entered service as the third *Pride of Cherbourg* on 12th September. P&O's fast craft, the 91 metre InCat *Catalonia* (marketed as the *Portsmouth Express*) had a difficult season in 2002 with continued breakdowns blighting her operation, particularly during the key month of July. The year has seen the charters of both the former Olau twins and the *Pride of Bilbao* extended for a further five years.

The Commodore Group was sold to a management buy-out for during August 2002 with ABN Amro financing the £150 million deal. The group enjoyed a trouble-free season on all fronts, and found success on their new venture providing a Sunday round trip from Portsmouth to Cherbourg during the peak season. Operated by the *Commodore Clipper*, this service specifically targeted caravans and will operate again in 2003. Condor Ferries continued their aggressive stance towards services between France and the Channel Islands, opening their direct link from Guernsey to St Malo using the *Condor 10* in March 2002. A price war with Emeraude Lines ensued, which resulted in the French operator terminating their services early on 8th October. Despite heavy opposite from Emeraude, who claim there is not enough traffic to justify two operators, Condor successfully lobbied the Jersey authorities for a license to run directly from St Helier to the French port for 2003. The license is runs from April to September, and as the *Condor 10* commenced services, Emeraude were launching legal action claiming their service agreement had been breached. Condor disposed of the redundant *Condor 9* in May 2002.

IRISH SEA

NorseMerchant Ferries moved their Belfast services to the new Twelve Quays terminal at Birkenhead in June 2002, followed by their Dublin-bound ferries in August, but this positive news was soon overshadowed. Speculation concerning parent company Cenargo's financial health was rife even before their failure to meet an £8.5 million interest payment in December 2002, and it was little surprise when they filed for Chapter 11 liquidation in the US on 14th January 2003. Although operations continued, threats of legal action from creditor Lombard prompted the operator to voluntarily go into administration in early February. Problems are believed to stem from the £175 million loans the firm took out in 1998 to finance the racehorse quartet of ro/paxes, and with freight rates driven down by increased competition on the Irish Sea, the firm's position became untenable. An indication of the situation is given by the fact that between October 2001 and June 2002, their revenue fell by £3.5 million. Visible evidence of their subsequent woes came in September 2002 with the charter of the *Dawn Merchant* to Maersk-subsidiary Norfolkline. After sister *Brave Merchant* was chartered to the MoD in February 2003, passenger services ceased on the Liverpool - Dublin route that was left in the hands of the *Norse Mersey* and the *Lindarosa*. Administrator Ernst & Young is currently running the firm as usual, with both Maersk and Irish Ferries just two rumoured purchasers for the beleaguered operator.

Speculation also continues concerning the long-term future of Sea Containers operations on the Irish Sea. Although all their routes operated in 2002, the Heysham to Belfast link was shut prematurely from 21st August after the *Rapide* was disabled an engine room fire. Predictions that the route would not re-open in 2003 proved true despite Sea Containers having previous announced a schedule commencing from 14th March. Their annual fleet rejig sees the *SuperSeaCat Two* taking sister *SuperSeaCat Three's* place on the Liverpool to Dublin service, whilst the freed-up *Rapide* will handle the Troon link after the transfer of the *SeaCat Scotland* to Dover. Rumours that SeaCo are seeking to divest themselves of all their UK ferry operations were re-ignited when the Isle of Man Steam Packet was put up for sale with a price tag of £150 million in March 2003.

The outlook appears more positive for P&O Irish Sea, who are set to continue independently outside the new P&O Ferries operation until at least 2004. In addition to introducing the brand new *European Highlander* at Cairnryan in July 2002, the firm successfully employed her half-sister *European Ambassador* on a weekly Dublin to Cherbourg crossing until November 2002. The route has been re-introduced for 2003 from March to November, and another seasonal route has been launched with the popular *SuperStar Express* running twice daily from Larne to Troon in between crossings to Cairnryan. The Liverpool - Larne service however ended in December 2002 upon the expiry of the *Northern Star's* charter. P&O disposals include the former Townsend Thoresen vessel *European Navigator* and sisters *European Endeavour* and *European Pathfinder*.

Harsher competition on the North Channel looms however with the announcement by Stena Line of a £70 million development plan for their services. The three-year project will see new terminals built at both sides, with the most significant news being the switch from Stranraer to Old House Point, closer to the mouth of Loch Ryan. When complete in 2005, Stena should be able to offer up to 18 sailings daily with crossing time slashed by up to 30%. The much-maligned company has bolstered its presence throughout the Irish Sea over the past season, with the *Stena Europe* settling down well at Rosslare despite losing power on 30th January whilst on passage to Fishguard. The new £65million, 1,500-passenger *Stena Adventurer* is due to join the Dublin - Holyhead route in June 2003, which will boost Stena's freight capacity by 70%. With new terminal facilities at Holyhead also being commissioned, her introduction should finally allow them to realistically rival Irish Ferries' *Ulysees*. Stena's business may be damaged however by the intermediate replacement of the departing *Stena Forwarder* by the freight-only *Stena Transporter*.

SCOTLAND

Following the Taygran Shipping debacle, CalMac introduced a permanent overnight freight sailing between Ullapool and Stornoway from 8th May 2002, which initially used the spare Northlink freighter *Hascosay*. However, with that ship required by her owners from 1st October, CalMac chartered the well-known *Belard* for the route, which was subsequently renamed *Muirneag*.

Political debate continues to rumble along concerning CalMac's Clyde services, which in the meantime saw the introduction of the chartered *Ali Cat* on 21st October to provide peak period passenger sailings. Despite media controversy when her gangway collapsed in January 2003, her charter was later extended until early 2004. Rivals Western Ferries meanwhile confirmed an order from Ferguson's of Port Glasgow for a sister to their flagship the *Sound of Scarba*. The new ferry is due to be delivered in September 2003. Elsewhere on the Clyde, the proposed river service from Clydefast has, unsurprisingly, failed to materialise. The firm promised links from central Glasgow to Dunoon and Rothesay using the two 119 pax craft from Belfast's failed Loughlink.

Caledonian MacBrayne themselves are expecting two new vessels for 2003, *the Loch Portain* from Mersey

Superstar Express *(John Hendy)*

Hrossey *(Miles Cowsill)*

builders McTay Marine for the Leverburgh to Berenay service across the Sound of Harris, while Devon yard Appledore will deliver the new Mallig to Armadale ferry *Coruisk*.

The transition from P&O Scottish Ferries to NorthLink looked likely to be troublesome with discontented Shetland hauliers being the leading force behind the establishment of a rival ro-ro service after disagreement concerning freight rates. Gulf Offshore and Cenargo are also involved with Norse Island Ferries, with Cenargo providing the *Merchant Venture* while Gulf Offshore acquired the *St. Rognvald*. Operations began on 3rd September 2002 using the redundant NorseMerchant vessel, but the ship was plagued with mechanical problems. Although intermediate replacement was found with a charter of the *European Mariner*, the service continues at present using just the *St. Rognvald*.

NorthLink meanwhile managed a smooth introduction of their overnight vessels the *Hjaltland* and the *Hrossey*, which use Kirkwall instead of Stromness as their Orcadian port of call. Both vessels were greeted with much favourable comment. The Pentland Firth vessel *Hamnavoe* had to wait until 21st April 2003 however for her debut, with Cal Mac's *Hebridean Isles* standing in until pier works were complete. All three P&O Scottish Ferries ships were subsequently sold for further service. Competitors Pentland Ferries sought to expand with the acquisition of the *Claymore* from Sea Containers, but the new Invergordon to St Margaret's Hope route, which she inaugurated on 11th November, lasted just three weeks. The firm now hopes to use her to double up sailings for 2003 on their original link to Gill's Bay, in support of their other CalMac exile, the *Pentalina B*. Shetland ained a third brand new vessel when Smyril Line's *Norrona* entered service in April 2003, with the incumbent *Norrona* retiring to Esbjerg to await sale. The SIC's new Whalsey vessel *Linga* has proved troublesome, with the £4 million Remontowa-built vessel suffering continued breakdowns after her introduction on 6th April 2002. The second Polish newbuild, ordered for the Skerries service, was launched as the *Filla* during December 2002. Due to enter service in April 2003, it remains to be seen whether she will be equally as trouble prone as the erstwhile *Linga*. It has been proposed that the previous *Filla*, which has been renamed the *Snolda*, should be used to provide a new ro-ro service to Papa Stour in a £3 million project.

Richard Seville

BRITISH ISLES
Scrabster
Stornoway
Ullapool
Aberdeen
Castlebay
Mallaig
Oban
Rosyth
Gourock
Largs
Troon
Cairnryan
Stranraer
Newcastle
Middlesbrough
Arranmore
Larne
Belfast
Douglas
Heysham
Portaferry
Fleetwood
Hull
Warrenpoint
Holyhead
Liverpool
Killingholme
Immingham
Mostyn
Dublin
Dun Laoghaire
Tarbert
Felixstowe
Castletownbere
Rosslare
Fishguard
Harwich
Passage East
Purfleet
Cork
Pembroke Dock
Sheerness
Dartford
Ramsgate
Southampton
Portsmouth
Dover
Weymouth
Newhaven
Poole
Fowey
Penzance
Dartmouth

Nordlandia *(Mike Louagie)*

Kronprins Frederik *(Mike Louagie)*

scandinavia & northern review

review 2002

2002 was another eventful year in northern waters - although perhaps the most eventful things were those which did not happen - the Color Line take-over of Fjord Line which failed and the Superfast Rostock - Södertälje service which did start but was abruptly terminated after three months. But there were some more positive events - Tallink's *Romantika*, the first Baltic cruise ferry of the new millennium, and a number of new routes to the Baltic states all point to continued growth and development in this area.

The following geographical review again takes the form of a voyage along the coast of The Netherlands and Germany, round the southern tip of Norway, down the Kattegat, through the Great Belt and into the Baltic (with a side journey to the Øresund) then up to the Gulf of Finland and Gulf of Bothnia.

In the Netherlands, Rederij Doeksen, who operate to the Frisian Islands of Terschelling and Vlieland, introduced a rather unusual craft, a *slow* speed catamaran. She is the *Noord-Nederland* and is designed to convey freight vehicles to the islands. The use of the catamaran layout enables a beam of 15 metres with a draft of only 1.8 metres – very useful in the shallow waters around the island.

German Frisian Island operator Reederei Norden-Frisia introduced a new car ferry, the *Frisia IV*, to replace the 1962 built *Frisia VIII*. She operates on the route from Norddeich to Norderney

In spring 2003 both Norwegian Hurtigruten operators introduced new ships - the *Finnmarken* of OVDS and the *Trollfjord* of TFDS. They were built to replace the 1960s generation *Lofoten* and *Harald Jarl* respectively although *Lofoten* – now regarded as a national monument – returned to service in the autumn to replace the *Nordkapp* which went down to Chile to operate a programme of cruises along the coast and to Antarctica. TFDS announced the order of a new ship to replace the 1982 built 'mid generation' *Midnatsol* – to bear the same names as the ship she replaces; she was delivered in April 2003. Plans to merge the two operators into a single company called Nord Norges Dampskipsselskap were dropped during the year due to problems in the two managements in agreeing a single policy for the future and fears of reduced subsidies.

Torghatten Trafikkselskap took over the newbuilding *Torghatten* from the Polish Szczecin ship repair yard Gryfia in the summer. She was started on Tyneside by Cammell Laird and had been completed after their bankruptcy in Szczecin.

The domestic activities of the Bergen based Norwegian ferry and land transport company Bergen Nordhordland Rutelag (BNR) were divided between two neighbouring companies - Hardanger Sunnhordlandske Dampskipsselskap in the Nordhordland area and Stavanger based Rogaland Trafikkselskap in the Boknafjorden Ferjeselskap area. This allowed BNR to concentrate on the international activities of their Fjord Line subsidiary. Towards the end of the year, Color Group had obtained a 56% share in BNR and announced their intention to launch a full take-over. However the intentions were frustrated in two ways. Firstly, a major debenture holder in the company converted their loan into shares which reduced the Oslo based company's holding to only 35% and secondly the Norwegian competition authorities ruled that the intended merger was anti-competitive. Color Group sold the bulk of their shares to Hurtigruten and local transport operator TFDS, and that company acquired shares from other sources, thus gaining control of Fjord Line. The take over battle held up plans to replace the *Bergen*, used on the increasingly busy Bergen - Egersund – Hanstholm route. Eventually it was announced that *Fjord Line* had acquired the Australian owned *Spirit of Tasmania*, formerly TT-Line's 1986 built *Peter Pan* and a sister of the *Val de Loire*, *Pride of Portsmouth* and *Pride of Le Havre*. Renamed the *Spir* for her delivery voyage, she was renamed the *Fjord Norway* on entry into service in spring 2003. The *Bergen* has been chartered to DFDS Seaways, to operate between Harwich and Cuxhaven as the *Duchess of Scandinavia*.

During 2003 little came of plans to launch a new service between Larvik and Lysekil in Sweden, other than a change of name from Larviklinjen to Lysekilslinjen, forced on them by Color Line who said that the former name was too close to Larvik Line, with which they merged a few years ago. The new company was linked with the *Blue Horizon* of Strintzis Line, the *Georg Ots* of ESCO and finally the former Color Line vessel *Sandefjord*, which was sold to South American interests but remained laid up in Norway. However, nothing has happened with regard to the building of essential shore facilities at either port and the project looks increasingly unlikely.

Apart from its abortive bid for Fjord Line, Color Line's year was fairly uneventful. The promised new service between Strömstad and Larvik – intended to see off the challenge of Larviklinjen/Lysekilslinjen – did not materialise and the former Fred. Olsen train ferry *Skagen* continues to operate as second ship on the Frederikshavn – Larvik route, primarily for freight but also conveying car and foot passengers at rather lower rates than the *Peter Wessel* due to her limited facilities. In the summer Color Line singed a letter of intent with Aker Finnyards to build a massive 74600 gt cruise ferry for their Oslo – Kiel route. The final ordering of this truly 'super' ferry was delayed until the end of the year as Color Line were waiting for the Norwegian Government to clarify the tax regime under which they would have to operate. In the event, whilst it was not as advantageous as they would have liked, and poorer than they enjoyed by many other Western European countries, it was not as bad as had been originally announced by the right-wing government pledged to slash state spending when they were elected in autumn 2001. So in December the order was confirmed and delivery is expected in time for Christmas 2004.

Stena Line's Gothenburg - Frederikshavn service operated much as before except that the two Kiel ships did not operate their customary round trip to Frederikshavn between their morning arrival at Gothenburg and evening departure during the summer. On the Oslo - Frederikshavn route, Stena Line announced plans to increase the passenger capacity from 1700 to 1900 on their *Stena Saga* through a major rebuild of the 1981 built ship. In the spring the rebuilt *Stena Nautica* entered service on the Grenaa – Varberg route. A major problem with this ship – and her sister, now *Color Viking* – had been that the upper vehicle deck could only take cars due to its low height. The solution was to remove the lower of the two passenger decks, allowing the height of the upper vehicle deck to be raised and concentring all passenger facilities on the upper deck. Since this deck was formerly partly mezzanine in character, this did not actually mean halving passenger accommodation. At the same time, separate vehicle access direct to the upper deck through the bow and stern was provided.

Mols-Linien continued to operate to the same pattern as before but interestingly, their longest route – the former Scandlines Kalundborg - Århus service - began to show real growth. The former Ebeltoft - Odden vessels *Maren Mols*, and *Mette Mols* seem to have proved the right vessel for this route flowing the failure of the too large *Peder Paars* (now *Color Viking*) and *Niels Klim* (now *Stena Nautica*) and the rather too basic *Ask* and *Urd* which replaced them in 1991. For many Danes, use of this route is a cheaper option than driving to the Great Belt Bridge when fuel costs and tolls are taken into account and proves once again that ferries can compete with a fixed link given the right circumstances. Traffic on the shorter Ebeltoft – Odden route declined however and Mols-Linien were reportedly considering replacing their two fast ferries with a single larger one; most of the time they only use one craft. Spare former CatLink ferry *Max Mols* spent the summer with Riga Sea Line between Riga and Nynäshamn.

The ships of Scandlines subsidiary *Scandlines Sydfyenske A/S* started to be painted in the Scandlines corporate livery of white with blue funnels. Previously they had been painted in the traditional Danish ship livery of black hulls, white superstructure with red-white-red striped funnels.

Scandlines' and HH Ferries' Helsingør – Helsingborg service also showed growth for the first time since the opening of the Øresundsbroen fixed link, but the Scandlines 'Flyvebadene' Copenhagen - Malmö fast ferry service was less fortunate and finished at the end of April. The service has been unable to compete with the twenty minute frequency train service, city centre to city centre. The three remaining high speed catamarans - the *Sælen*, *Sjöbjörnen* and *Svalen* - were sold to SNAV of Italy.

On the Gedser - Rostock route traffic continued to grow and Scandlines were reportedly considering replacing the now rather elderly *Dronning Margrethe II* with a larger ship; they are probably now regretting the sale of the *Kronprins Frederik* and *Prins Joachim's* sister *Dronning Ingrid*, now being converted to the hospital ship

Romantika *(Mike Louagie)*

Finnjet *(Mike Louagie)*

Stena Danica *(Mike Louagie)*

TT-Delphin *(Mike Louagie)*

Africa Mercy on Tyneside.

Traffic growth on Scandlines' Rødby – Puttgarden route grew to embarrassing proportions during the summer with long delays to traffic building up at peak times. The four highly specialised ships operating from specialised berths made supplementing the service with additional ships difficult. At one time is was considered building an additional two ships but later in the year the preferred solution was to add a vehicle deck to each of the ships. However, at time of going to press, nothing had been done so more delays this summer seem inevitable.

Routes between Germany and Sweden continued to be very busy, with four major players – TT-Line, Scandlines AG, Stena Line owned Scandlines AB of Sweden and Finnlines owned Nordö-Link – competing feverishly. The two Scandlines companies co-operate on the Rostock – Trelleborg and Sassnitz – Trelleborg routes but the Travemünde - Trelleborg route is a purely Scandlines AB service.

Nordö-Link was taken over by Finnlines during 2002 after a project take-over by Scandlines AG in 2001 was blocked by the competition authorities. The charter of Scandlines *Ask* was continued until the end of the year, when she was replaced by the *Finnarrow* which Finnlines transferred from their subsidiary FinnLink. Under Finnlines control, cars and their passengers were once more carried on the Travemünde - Malmö route, albeit only on some sailings, mainly the mid-morning departures from each port. The rail carrying facilities of the *Lübeck Link* and *Malmö Link* were again put to use during the year.

Scandlines AG decided to rebuilt their *Mecklenburg-Vorpommern* to increase lane metres for road traffic from the 2,500 to 3,100. This is being achieved by converting some of the passenger accommodation to vehicle accommodation as it had been found the balance between passengers and freight was increasingly out of kilter. She went to the Rementowa Shipyard at Gdansk at the end of the year and her place of the Rostock - Trelleborg route was taken by the *Ask*.

Scandlines AB continued to use the elderly ex train ferry *Götaland* and the chartered ro-pax *Svealand* on their Travemünde - Trelleborg route, although the latter vessel had to be withdrawn for major modifications in the autumn and her place was taken by the *Flanders*, formerly P&O's *Pride of Flanders*, which had been acquired by Stena Line earlier in the year when they took over the Felixstowe - Rotterdam route.

On the routes to the Danish holiday Island of Bornholm, the fast ferry service from Ystad continued to attract traffic at the expense of the conventional service from Copenhagen, leading to a cut-back in some of the day sailings. However, the Austal Ships fast ferry *Villum Clausen* did not have a problem-free year. In January she developed hull defects, thought to have been cause by the battering of the waves. Although these were repaired and a 3 metre wave height limit imposed (3.5m previously) there is a suspicion that these could develop again in certain weather conditions. It was thought likely that she would be laid up during the next winter and replaced by Mols-Linien's 91 metre InCat *Max Mols*, but this did not happen. In 2002 a ro-ro service was inaugurated between Køge and Rønne with two daily round trips. The vessel used was the former *Finnbeaver* of Finnlines, on charter from Oy Rettig Ab Bore of Finland. She was renamed the *Bore Mari*. This route is likely become the sole route from Sealand when the existing Copenhagen - Rønne route finishes at the end of this year. Ro-pax vessels with at least 300 passenger places and 1,800 lane meters will be used.

In 2001 BornholmsTrafikken and Scandlines AG agreed a joint service between Germany and Bornholm as 'Bornholm Direkt', with Scandlines' *Rügen* providing the Sassnitz - Rønne summer service and BornholmsTrafikken's two conventional vessels *Jens Kofoed* and *Povl Anker* operating in the winter. However, the EU commission have decreed that this is some way 'anti competitive' and the arrangement ceased at the end of 2002. Scandlines AG will continue to operate the *Rügen* in 2003 but there will no longer be a winter service and the long term future of the summer service is in doubt as years more as the *Rügen* will need a lot of work spent on her to bring her up to modern fire safety standards.

DFDS's Copenhagen – Gdynia service did not start as expected in the spring. The designated vessel, the *King of Scandinavia*, was instead sold to Reca Marmara Lines of Turkey becoming their *Cesme*. Start was deferred until early October, using the Harwich - Esbjerg vessel *Dana Anglia*, renamed the *Duke of Scandinavia*. The Polish destination was changed to Gdansk and a wayside call at Trelleborg was introduced. The Trelleborg - Gdansk portion of the route was in fact covered from the spring by DFDS Tor Line with the 12 passenger *Panevezys*, chartered from subsidiary company LISCO Baltic Service.

Stena Line also boosted their capacity on the Polish service between Karlskrona and Gdynia. The *Stena Europe* was swapped with the Fishguard - Rosslare vessel *Koningin Beatrix*, renamed the *Stena Baltica*. The *Stena Baltica* was originally built for the overnight Harwich - Hoek van Holland service and has more berths than the *Stena Europe*.

The growth in traffic between the Scandinavian countries and Poland was not something that the troubled company Polferries was able to benefit from, continuing to see their markets taken over by more efficient companies using bigger and better ships. The *Nieborow* was sold Montenegro Lines to operate between Italy and Montenegro as the *Sveti Stefan II*, leaving only three rather old and small ships to cover their routes from Poland to Denmark and Sweden.

Scandlines Amber Line chartered the Rederi AB Gotland owned 52 passenger *Gute* as second vessel on their growing Karlshamn (Sweden) - Liepaja (Latvia) route. The one time *Sally Sky* joined the 79 passenger *Kahleberg*. The port of Karlshamn now also sees the LISCO Baltic Services service to Klaipeda. The two vessels used were switched from Swedish ports of Stockholm and Åhus respectively during the year.

Superfast Ferries launched their much awaited Rostock - Södertälje service in January with *Superfast IX*, with the second ship, the *Superfast X* due to join her on 29th March. However, the service was dramatically withdrawn at the beginning of April and the two ships redeployed to the new Zeebrugge - Rosyth route. There were a number of factors which led to the sudden ending of this new route. Although passenger traffic was building up, freight loadings were poor. The company's *Superfast III* and *Superfast IV* had been sold to Australia and the *Superfast XI* and *Superfast XI*, under construction in Lübeck were running very late so there was a danger of the company not being able to operate all its profitable Mediterranean services. It was perhaps inevitable that freight traffic would take some time to develop as the route from Germany to central Sweden one which had not enjoyed a service for many years. There are a profusion of services from Germany to Southern Sweden and, with the competition comes low rates. It was obviously going to be difficult to persuade truckers and freight shippers to pay quite a bit more for a longer journey. Would the service have succeeded in time? Possibly - it certainly makes environmental sense to take goods for the Stockholm area

Pomerania *(John Hendy)*

as far as possible by sea - but alas we shall never know.

A Latvian company called Latlines started a new service from Lübeck and Riga. Initially operated by the Greek vessel *Sea Symphony*, she was soon replaced by the Turkish ro-pax *Kaptan Burhanettin Isim* of 199? - built initially to take trucks from Turkey to Italy bypassing the unstable Balkans and unfriendly Greece. In the autumn DFDS Tor Line launched a Kiel - Riga service, initially using a ro-ro but, at the end of the year with the ro-pax *Transparaden*. It was then announced that DFDS had taken over Latlines and that the *Kaptan Burhanettin Isim* was to be replaced the *Mermaid II* (formerly the *Finnmaid*) previously used by VV-Line. In the event the roles of the two ships was reversed but in 2003 all services operated from Lübeck.

Another new Latvian company, JSC Riga Sea Lines, was formed to try to re-launch the ill fated Riga - Stockholm route, last operated by Mono Line in 2001. A number of operators have tried to gain a foothold on this route in recent years and all have failed. The new venture, which was backed by the municipal authorities of Riga, was launched in April using the 91m InCat *Max Mols* chartered from Mols-Linien, operating to the coastal port of Nynäshamn. The journey initially took twelve hours and operated overnight on alternate days. From June, the company was able to run a day service and the crossing time was reduced to nine hours. The charter ended in September and there was then a gap until December when the service was re-launched as a conventional ship service, using the former Tallink vessel *Baltic Kristina*, a vessel which had operated on the route ten years ago as the *Illych* of Baltic Shipping Company. This time the service operated to Stockholm with a journey time of 17 hours 30 minutes.

VV-Line introduced sister vessel the *Fellow* (formerly the *Finnfellow)* between Nynäshamn (Sweden) and Ventspils (Latvia) during the summer. Their original vessel the *Mermaid II* (formerly the *Finnmaid*), operated between Vastervik (Sweden) and Paldiski (Estonia) - so both the 'Vs' in the company name were served but no longer linked. Following the transfer to the *Mermaid II* to Latlines, only the Vastervik - Paldiski service now operates.

A new service between St Petersburg and the Russian enclave of Kaliningrad started at the end of the year using the former Tallink vessel *Georg Ots*. Purchased from her owners ESCO by the Russian Government, the new service is designed to provide a direct link bypassing Lithuania, which is to join the EU in 2004 and will be required to impose visa restrictions on Russian citizens transiting their country. At the launch one service be per week was operated although it was hoped to raise this to two per week after the ice period.

Estonian domestic operator Saaremaa Laevakompanii (included in this book for the first time) added P&O Scottish Ferries Scrabster - Stromness vessel *St Ola* to their interesting fleet. Like their *Ofelia*, *Regula* and *Scania* she was formerly operated Scandinavian Ferry Lines on their Øresund services and like them entered service with the Estonian company without renaming. She is used on the Kuivastu – Virtsu route.

Tallink's new cruise ferry the *Romantika* - the first traditional Baltic cruise ferry to enter service for some years - entered service in May. Her delivery enabled the *Fantaasia* to be transferred to the Helsinki - Stockholm route. In September, Tallink replaced the *Vana Tallinn* with the *Meloodia* on day cruises from Helsinki to Tallinn in September and the *Vana Tallinn* replaced the smaller *Baltic Kristina* on the Paldiski - Kapellskär route. Tallink have ordered a sister ship from Aker Finnyards to be delivered in 2004. She is destined for the Tallinn - Stockholm route and her older sister might well join her if the ending of duty free sales on the Helsinki route when Estonia joins the EU in 2004 causes the popularity of 22 hour cruises from Helsinki to decline drastically. It is planned that the new ship will call at one of the ports in Åland in order to maintain duty free sales on the Stockholm route.

In similar vein, Viking Line announced that with effect from next September, the *Cinderella* would operate on 22 hour cruises from Stockholm with the smaller *Rosella* taking on the Helsinki - Tallinn route. Unlike the *Cinderella's* daily 'booze cruises' the *Rosella* will operate twice daily conventional ferry sailings. In anticipation of the move, the *Cinderella* would transfer to Swedish registry.

During 2002 Silja Line's parent company Silja Oyj Abp came completely under Sea Containers control when the UK based Bermudan company managed to purchase over 97% of the shares and applied to compulsorily purchase the rest and have the company delisted form the Helsinki Stock Exchange. Ferry operations of the company remained as the previous year but a new cruise programme from Helsinki was introduced with the *Silja Opera*, the former *Sally Albatross* which had been chartered out since her grounding when on passage

Polonia *(Dominic McCall)*

Peter Pan *(Mike Louagie)*

from Tallinn in 1994.

Silja Line subsidiary SeaWind Line's *Sky Wind* (the former 'DanLink' Helsingborg – Copenhagen train ferry *Öresund*) entered service on 1st October on the Stockholm – Turku route, enabling a full twice daily full passenger service to be operated. *Star Wind*, previously the former DB train ferry *Rostock*, operated with the passenger carrying *Sea Wind*, carrying rail wagons and accompanied freight with the ro-ro *Cupria* providing backup during the summer period, mainly for unaccompanied trailers. The *Star Wind* started a new Helsinki - Tallinn service on 15th October, undertaking two round trips per day and, for the first time for this ship under SeaWind Line ownership, carrying ordinary passengers on some sailings.

Finnlines subsidiary FinnLink started accepting passengers in cars on their morning sailings from Kapellskar (Sweden) and Naantali (Finland). The morning departure from Sweden was operated by the *Finneagle*, and the departure from Finland by the Indonesian built *Finnarrow* - to be replaced in 2003 by the *Finneagle's* sister, the *Finnclipper*.

Despite increases of 30 % respectively 45 % in passenger and freight traffic on their routes from Vaasa to Harnosand and Umeå for the first half-year 2002, in August Botnia Link were forced to seek temporary insolvency protection for three months from the regional court in Harnosand. Creditors include the port operators as well as Rederi AB Engship, who owned the chartered *Transparaden*. In November however, Botnia Link, went into liquidation and the chartered ro-pax *Transparaden* was returned to her owners and then chartered to DFDS Tor Line. Botnia Link failed to win the subsidy to operate the route from 2003 with an all year ro-pax and summer only fast ferry operated in conjunction with Nordic Jet Line but had continued to operate on a commercial basis. Financially supported operator RG-Line continued to operate between Vaasa and Umeå with the *Casino Express* (ex *Fennia*) with, as the name suggests, a heavy emphasis on gambling to compensate for the loss of duty free sales on this Gulf of Bothnia route.

Nick Widdows

Tallink AutoExpress 2 *(Mike Louagie)*

DURASTIC

Durastic Ltd is one of the world's leading suppliers and installers of marine deck covering systems offering a wide range of specifications.

From primary underlays; including Durastic's lightweight underlay, to weatherdecks, sound reduction and A60 Solas rated materials; all with associated finishes such as carpets, vinyls and epoxy resins.

A full specification service and experienced, supervised contract teams ensure the best deck coverings are installed to the highest standards. Durastic's products are covered by International Certifications and produced at its ISO 9002 Quality Assured manufacturing facility.

UNIT 47
CUTHBERT COURT
BEDE INDUSTRIAL ESTATE
JARROW
TYNE & WEAR
NE32 3HG
UNITED KINGDOM

T: +44(0)191 483 2299
F: +44(0)191 483 2295
E: john.english@rigblast.com
W: www.durastic-ltd.com

Branch Offices in Glasgow, Liverpool, Southampton & Jarrow.

Durastic is a member of the Rigblast Group

Bergen
NO
Stavanger
Sand
La
Egersund
Kristiansand
North
Sea
Hirt
Hanstholm
DEN
Kalundbo
Esbjerg
Spo
Ki
Cuxhaven
Norddeich
Harlingen
Emden
IJmuiden
Scheveningen
Hoek van Holland
NETH.
Vlissingen
Rotterdam
Harwich
Ramsgate
Dover
Ostend
Zeebrugge
Plymouth
Portsmouth
Newhaven
Calais
Dunkerque
English Channel
BELGIUM
GERM
Cherbourg
Dieppe
LUX.
Roscoff
Le Havre
Caen
U. K.
St Malo
FRANCE

FINLAND
Rauma
Naantali
Turku
Kotka
ÅLAND
Helsinki
Mariehamn
Långnäs
Hanko
Oslo
SWEDEN
Kapellskär
Tallinn
Paldiski
Moss
Stockholm
ESTONIA
Södertälje
Strömstad
Nynäshamn
othenburg
Västervik
Oskarshamn
Visby
Ventspils
Riga
havn
Varberg
GOTLAND
LATVIA
toft
ÖLAND
Liepaja
Helsingborg
singør
Karlskrona
Klaìpeda
Karlshamn
penhagen
Malmö
LITHUANIA
Ystad
Trelleborg
Rønne
Tars
BORNHOLM
Gedser
Gdynia
Sassnitz
Gdansk
en
Rostock
BYEL
avemünde
eck
Swinoujscie
POLAND
CZECH
UKR
SLOVAKIA

section ❙ *northern review*

gb & ireland

BRITTANY FERRIES

THE COMPANY *Brittany Ferries* is the trading name of *BAI SA*, a French private sector company and the operating arm of the *Brittany Ferries Group*. The UK operations are run by *BAI (UK) Ltd*, a UK private sector company, wholly owned by the *Brittany Ferries Group*.

MANAGEMENT Group Managing Director Michel Maraval, **Managing Director UK & Ireland** David Longden.

ADDRESS Millbay Docks, Plymouth, Devon PL1 3EW.

TELEPHONE Administration *Plymouth* +44 (0)8709 010500, *Portsmouth* +44 (0)8709 011300, **Reservations** *All Services* +44 (0)8705 360360.

FAX Administration & Reservations +44 (0)8709 011100.

INTERNET Website www.brittanyferries.com *(English, French, Spanish, German)*

ROUTES OPERATED Conventional Ferries *All year* Plymouth - Roscoff (6 hrs (day), 6 hrs - 7 hrs 30 mins (night); *(3,6)*; up to 3 per day (summer), 1 per day (winter)), Portsmouth - St Malo (8 hrs 45 mins (day), 10 hrs 30 mins - 11 hrs 30 mins (night); *(2 (summer), 2,6 (winter))*; 1/2 per day), Portsmouth - Caen (Ouistreham) (6 hrs (day), 6 hrs 15 mins - 8 hrs (night); *(4,5)*; 3 per day), Plymouth - Santander (Spain) (24 hrs; *(6)*; 2 per week (March - November)), Poole - Cherbourg (4 hrs 15 mins; *(1)*; up to 2 per day), **Summer only** Cork - Roscoff (14 hrs; *(6)*; 1 per week), **Winter only** Plymouth - St Malo (8 hrs; *(6)*; 1 per week, Plymouth - Cherbourg (10 hrs; *(3)*; 1 per week). **Fast Ferry** Poole - Cherbourg (2 hrs 15 mins; *(CONDOR VITESSE of Condor Ferries)*; 1 per day). Note The Poole - Cherbourg fast ferry service is operated from May to September by *Condor Ferries* jointly with *Brittany Ferries*.

1	BARFLEUR	20133t	92	19.3k	158.0m	1212P	590C	112T	BA	FR
2	BRETAGNE	24534t	89	21.0k	151.0m	1926P	580C	84T	BA	FR
3	DUC DE NORMANDIE	13505t	78	19.0k	131.0m	1500P	354C	38T	BA	FR
4	MONT ST MICHEL	35592t	02	21.5k	174.0m	2140P	880C	166T	BA2	FR
5	NORMANDIE	27541t	92	20.5k	161.0m	2120P	600C	126T	BA2	FR
6	VAL DE LOIRE	31788t	87	20.0k	162.0m	2140P	600C	104T	BA	FR

BARFLEUR Built at Helsinki for the *Truckline* Poole - Cherbourg service to replace two passenger vessels and to inaugurate a year round passenger service. In 1999 the *Truckline* branding was dropped for passenger services and she was repainted into full *Brittany Ferries* livery.

BRETAGNE Built at St Nazaire for the Plymouth - Santander and Cork - Roscoff services (with two sailings per week between Plymouth and Roscoff). In 1993 she was transferred to the Portsmouth - St Malo service.

DUC DE NORMANDIE Built at Heuseden, Netherlands as the PRINSES BEATRIX for *Stoomvaart Maatschappij Zeeland (Zeeland Steamship Company)* of The Netherlands for their Hoek van Holland - Harwich service. In September 1985 sold to *Brittany Ferries* and chartered back to *SMZ*, continuing to operate for them until the introduction of the KONINGIN BEATRIX (see STENA BALTICA) in May 1986. In June 1986 delivered to *Brittany Ferries* and inaugurated the Portsmouth - Caen service. From July 2002 she moved to the Plymouth - Roscoff route.

MONT ST MICHEL Built at Krimpen aan den IJssel, Rotterdam for *Brittany Ferries* to replace the DUC DE NORMANDIE on the Portsmouth - Caen route. The DUC DE NORMANDIE was transferred to

Only we sail direct to Brittany, Normandy & Spain

Brittany Ferries offer the widest choice of routes to Western France and Spain. Enjoy an unrivalled experience, from excellent shopping and on-board entertainment to fine cuisine. Choose from night or day crossings on classic cruise ferries, or a fast ferry option on our Poole to Cherbourg route.

Call 0870 411 1190 or visit **brittanyferries.com**

Brittany Ferries

Commodore Ferries' two all weather Ro-Ro vessels make more than 1200 cross-channel sailings every year. The **Commodore Goodwill** (introduced in 1996) and the **Commodore Clipper** (introduced in 1999) were designed and built specifically for the Channel Islands.

The twice daily Ro-Ro service from Portsmouth ensures that essential supplies reach both Guernsey and Jersey in time to meet the daily requirement of both Islands. On the return journey, Island produce and other exports destined for UK markets are loaded and carried the same day - avoiding any need for costly on-Island storage. Each vessel has capacity to carry over 1200 lane-metres of freight, and, while the majority of cargo is transported in vehicles and trailers in each direction, both vessels are adapted for 'out of gauge' traffic.

Services tailored to the needs of our customers

FREIGHT RESERVATIONS

Guernsey	**Tel: +44**	**(0)1481 728620**
Jersey	**Tel: +44**	**(0)1534 872509**
UK	**Tel: +44**	**(0)23 9266 4676**

TELEPHONE: 01481 728620

the Plymouth - Roscoff route, replacing the QUIBERON (11813t, 1975).

NORMANDIE Built at Turku, Finland for the Portsmouth - Caen route.

VAL DE LOIRE Built at Bremerhaven, Germany as the NILS HOLGERSSON for *TT-Line* of Sweden and Germany for their service between Travemünde and Trelleborg. In 1992 purchased by *Brittany Ferries* for entry into service in spring 1993. After a major rebuild, she was renamed the VAL DE LOIRE and introduced onto the Plymouth - Roscoff, Plymouth - Santander and Cork - Roscoff routes.

Under Construction

7	PONT-AVEN	39900t	04	27.0k	180.0m	2100P	650C	85L	BA	FR

PONT-AVEN Under construction at Papenburg, Germany. Will operate on the Plymouth - Roscoff, Plymouth - Santander and Cork - Roscoff routes.

COMMODORE FERRIES

THE COMPANY *Commodore Ferries (CI) Ltd* is a private sector company owned by the *Commodore Group*, Guernsey.

MANAGEMENT Managing Director Jeff Vidamour, **Commercial Manager** Len Le Page.

ADDRESS PO Box 10, New Jetty Offices, White Rock, St Peter Port, Guernsey GY1 3AF.

TELEPHONE Administration +44 (0)1481 728620, **Reservations (Passenger)** See *Condor Ferries*.

FAX Administration & Reservations +44 (0)1481 728521.

INTERNET Email jvidamour@comferries.com

ROUTE OPERATED *All year* Portsmouth - St Peter Port (Guernsey) (6 hrs 30 mins) - St Helier (Jersey) (10 hrs 30 mins) - Portsmouth (8 hrs 30 mins) (return Guernsey via Jersey, 12 hrs 30 mins); *(1)*; 6 per week, *Summer only* Portsmouth - Cherbourg (France) (5 hrs; *(1)*; 1 per week).

1	COMMODORE CLIPPER	14000t	99	18.25.0k	129.1m	500P	100C	92T	A	BS

COMMODORE CLIPPER Ro-pax vessel built at Krimpen aan den IJssel, Rotterdam to operate between Portsmouth and the Channel Islands. She replaced the ISLAND COMMODORE, a freight only vessel. Her passenger services are operated as part of the *Condor Ferries* network and she carries the logos of both companies. Her passenger capacity is normally restricted to 300 but is increased to 500 when the *Condor Ferries'* fast ferries are unable to operate.

CONDOR FERRIES

THE COMPANY *Condor Ferries Ltd* is a Channel Islands private sector company owned by the *Commodore Group*, Guernsey.

MANAGEMENT Managing Director Robert Provan, **General Manager, Sales & Marketing** Nicholas Dobbs.

ADDRESS Condor House, New Harbour Road South, Hamworthy, Poole, Dorset BH15 4AJ.

TELEPHONE Administration +44 (0)1202 207207, **Reservations** +44 (0)845 345 2000.

FAX Administration +44 (0)1202 685184, **Reservations** +44 (0)1305 760776.

INTERNET Email reservations@condorferries.co.uk **Website** www.condorferries.co.uk *(English)*

ROUTES OPERATED Fast Car Ferries *Winter Only* Weymouth - St Peter Port (Guernsey) (2 hrs) - St Helier (Jersey via Guernsey) (3 hrs 20 mins); *(2)*; twice weekly), *Spring and Autumn* Weymouth - St Peter Port (Guernsey) (2 hrs) - St Helier (Jersey via Guernsey) (3 hrs 20 mins); *(2)*; 1 per day, Poole - St Peter Port (Guernsey) (2 hrs 30 mins) - St Helier (Jersey via Guernsey) (3 hrs 50 mins); *(2)*; daily, *Summer* Weymouth - St Peter Port (Guernsey) (2 hrs) - St Helier (Jersey via Guernsey) (3 hrs 20 mins); *(2)*; 1 per day, Poole - St Peter Port (Guernsey) (2 hrs 30 mins) - St Helier (via

Guernsey 3 hrs 50 mins, direct 3 hrs) - St Malo (4 hrs 35 min) ; *(2,3)*; up to 2 per day to Jersey and Guernsey, 1 per day to St Malo (**Note** Poole - St Malo service operates via either Guernsey or Jersey), St Malo - St Peter Port (Guernsey) (2hrs 55 mins via Jersey, 1hr 45 mins direct; *(1)*; 2 per day), St Malo - St Helier (Jersey) (1 hr 10 mins; *(1)*; 1 per day - no cars conveyed on this service), Poole - Cherbourg (2 hrs 15 mins; *(3)*; 1 per day (service operated jointly with *Brittany Ferries*)). **Ro-pax Ferry** *All year* The car and passenger facilities on the ro-pax service between Portsmouth and The Channel Islands and Portsmouth and Cherbourg operated by *Commodore Ferries* (see above) are marketed by *Condor Ferries*.

1»	CONDOR 10	3241t	93	37.0k	74.3m	580P	80C	-	BA	SI
2»	CONDOR EXPRESS	5005t	96	39.0k	86.6m	774P	185C	-	A2	SI
3»	CONDOR VITESSE	5005t	97	39.0k	86.6m	774P	185C	-	A2	BS

CONDOR 10 InCat 74m catamaran. Built at Hobart, Australia for the *Holyman Group* for use by *Condor Ferries*. In summer 1995 she was chartered to *Viking Line* to operate between Helsinki and Tallinn under the name 'VIKING EXPRESS II' (although not officially renamed). In summer 1996 she was chartered to *Stena Line* to operate between Fishguard and Rosslare. During northern hemisphere winters she served for *TranzRail* of New Zealand for the service between Wellington (North Island) and Picton (South Island). In May 1997 she was transferred to *Holyman Sally Ferries* and inaugurated a new Ramsgate - Dunkerque (Est) service, replacing the Ramsgate - Dunkerque (Ouest) service of *Sally Ferries*. After further service in New Zealand during winter 1997/98, in summer 1998 she was due to operate between Weymouth, Guernsey and St Malo, but, in the event, the CONDOR VITESSE was chartered for that route and she was laid up in Australia. Refurbished during 2001, she returned to the UK in spring 2002 replacing the passenger-only CONDOR 9 between St Malo and Guernsey and Jersey.

CONDOR EXPRESS InCat 86m catamaran built at Hobart, Tasmania, Australia. She was delivered December 1996 and entered service in 1997.

CONDOR VITESSE InCat 86m catamaran built at Hobart. Built speculatively and launched as the INCAT 044. Moved to Europe in summer 1997 and spent time in the both the UK and Denmark but was not used. In 1998, she was chartered to *Condor Ferries* and renamed the CONDOR VITESSE. During winter 1999/2000 she was chartered to *TranzRail* of New Zealand. Returned to UK in spring 2000.

DFDS SEAWAYS

THE COMPANY *DFDS Seaways Group A/S* is the passenger division of the *DFDS Group*, a Danish private sector company. *DFDS Seaways Ltd* is a UK subsidiary.

MANAGEMENT Managing Director DFDS Seaways A/S Thor Johannesen, **Managing Director DFDS Seaways Ltd** John Crummie.

ADDRESS Scandinavia House, Parkeston, Harwich, Essex CO12 4QG.

TELEPHONE Administration +44 (0)1255 243456, **Reservations** *National* 08705 333000 (from UK only), *Harwich* +44 (0)1255 240240, *Newcastle* +44 (0)191-293 6283.

FAX Administration & Reservations *Harwich* +44 (0)1255 244370, *Newcastle* +44 (0)191-293 6245.

INTERNET Email john.crummie@dfds.co.uk **Website** www.dfdsseaways.co.uk *(English)*

www.dfdsseaways.com *(Danish, Dutch, German, Norwegian, Swedish)*

ROUTES OPERATED *All year* Harwich - Esbjerg (Denmark) (19 hrs; *(1)*; 3 per week (winter, spring, autumn), alternate days (summer)), Kristiansand (Norway) - Gothenburg (Sweden) (7 hrs (day), 13 hrs 30 min (night); *(4)* 1 per week (spring, summer and autumn), 3 per week (winter)), Harwich - Cuxhaven (Germany) (16 hrs; *(2)*; 3 per week (winter, spring, autumn), alternate days (summer), Newcastle (North Shields) - IJmuiden (near Amsterdam, Netherlands) (15 hrs; *(3,5)*; daily), **Spring, Summer and Autumn only** Newcastle - Kristiansand - Gothenburg (25 hrs; *(4)*; 2 per week).

Condor 10 (*Miles Cowsill*)

Queen of Scandinavia (*Mike Louagie*)

1	DANA SIRENA	c23000t	01	22.5k	199.4m	600P	316C	180T	A	DK
2	DUCHESS OF SCANDINAVIA	16794t	93	18.5k	134.4m	882P	160C	82T	BA	NO
3	PRINCE OF SCANDINAVIA	22528t	75	26.0k	182.3m	1692P	379C	35T	AS	DK
4	PRINCESS OF SCANDINAVIA	22528t	76	26.0k	182.3m	1572P	365C	34T	AS	DK
5	QUEEN OF SCANDINAVIA	33770t	81	21.0k	166.1m	1624P	360C	70T	BA	DK

DUCHESS OF SCANDINAVIA Built at Rissa, Norway as the BERGEN for *Rutelaget Askøy-Bergen* and used on the *Fjord Line* Bergen (Norway) - Egersund (Norway) - Hanstholm (Denmark) service. In 2003 chartered to *DFDS* and in April 2003, renamed the DUCHESS OF SCANDINAVIA and, after modifications, introduced onto the Harwich – Cuxhaven service.

DANA SIRENA Built in Szczecin, Poland for *Lloyd Sardegna* of Italy as the GOLFO DEI DELFINI for service between Italy and Sardinia. However, due to late delivery the order was cancelled. In 2002 purchased by *DFDS Seaways*, and, during winter 2002/3, passenger accommodation was enlarged and refitted, increasing passenger capacity from 308 to 600. In June 2003, renamed the DANA SIRENA, she replaced unmodified sister vessel, the DANA GLORIA (now with *Lisco Baltic Services* – see Section 6), on the Esbjerg – Harwich service.

PRINCE OF SCANDINAVIA Built at Lübeck, Germany as the TOR BRITANNIA for *Tor Line* of Sweden for their Amsterdam - Gothenburg and Felixstowe - Gothenburg services. She was acquired by *DFDS* in 1981 and subsequently re-registered in Denmark. From winter 1983/4 she also operated on the Harwich - Esbjerg service with the DANA ANGLIA. She has also operated Newcastle - Esbjerg and Amsterdam - Gothenburg. During winter 1989/90 she was used as an accommodation ship for refugees in Malmö. In 1991 renamed the PRINCE OF SCANDINAVIA following a major refurbishment. In summer 1994 and 1995 she operated on the IJmuiden (Netherlands) - Gothenburg (Sweden) and IJmuiden - Kristiansand (Norway) service and did not serve the UK. In 1996 she was chartered to *CoTuNav* of Tunisia for service between Tunisia and Italy. In March 1997 she was transferred to the Harwich - Hamburg route. During winter 1997/98 she covered for other ferries which were being refitted, including the Copenhagen - Oslo vessels, and had major modifications made at Gdansk. In

With an extensive network of routes to Scandinavia and Northern Europe, we can offer solutions to all of your travel needs. Whatever your destination, we are happy to book your requirements and provide you with the highest standards of service, quality and reliability.

Call 08705 333 666 for a brochure, call into your local travel agent or visit us at www.dfdsseaways.co.uk

Solidor 5 *(Miles Cowsill)*

Jonathan Swift *(Miles Cowsill)*

summer 1998 she operated every third trip from Hamburg to Newcastle instead of Harwich; this was repeated in 1999 but in summer 2000 she operated solely between Harwich and Hamburg. In 2001 she was transferred to the Newcastle - IJmuiden route.

PRINCESS OF SCANDINAVIA Built at Lübeck, Germany as the TOR SCANDINAVIA for *Tor Line* of Sweden for their Amsterdam - Gothenburg and Felixstowe - Gothenburg services. In 1979 she was used on a world trade cruise and was temporarily renamed the HOLLAND EXPO. Similar exercises were undertaken in 1980, 1982 and 1984, but on these occasions her temporary name was the WORLD WIDE EXPO. She was acquired by *DFDS* in 1981 and subsequently re-registered in Denmark. She has also operated on the Harwich - Esbjerg service. Between 1989 and 1993 she also operated Newcastle - Esbjerg and Amsterdam - Gothenburg services. In 1991, following a major refurbishment, she was renamed the PRINCESS OF SCANDINAVIA. Since 1994, she generally operated on the Harwich - Gothenburg and Newcastle - Gothenburg routes. During winter 1998/1999 she had major modifications made at Gdansk and during winter 1999/2000 she had a major engine rebuild. She now operates between Newcastle and Gothenburg via Kristiansand.

QUEEN OF SCANDINAVIA Built at Turku, Finland as the FINLANDIA for *EFFOA* of Sweden for *Silja Line* services between Helsinki and Stockholm. In 1990 she was sold to *DFDS*, renamed the QUEEN OF SCANDINAVIA and introduced onto the Copenhagen - Helsingborg - Oslo service. In 2001 transferred to the Newcastle - IJmuiden route.

EMERAUDE LINES

THE COMPANY *Emeraude Lines* is a French private sector company.

MANAGEMENT Managing Director (Channel Islands) Gordon Forrest, **Brittany and Normandy Office Manager** Jean-Luc Griffon.

ADDRESS Terminal Ferry du Naye, PO Box 16, 35401, St Malo Cedex, France.

TELEPHONE Administration & Reservations *St Malo* +33 (0)2 23 180 180, *Jersey* +44 (0)1534 766566.

FAX Administration & Reservations *St Malo* +33 (0) 2 23 181 500, *Jersey* +44 (0)1534 768741.

INTERNET Email sales@emeraude.co.uk **Website** www.emeraude.co.uk *(English)*

ROUTES OPERATED Fast Car Ferries St Malo (France) - St Helier (Jersey) (1 hr 10 mins; *(1,2)*; up to 4 per day), St Malo - St Peter Port (Guernsey) (1 hr 50 mins; *(1,2)*; up to 3 per day), St Helier - St Peter Port (1 hr; *(1,2)*; 1 per day).

1»	SOLIDOR 4	1064t	87	30.0k	49.5m	302P	36C	-	A	FR
2»	SOLIDOR 5	2300t	01	38.0k	60.0m	450P	60C	-	A	FR

SOLIDOR 4 Westamarin W5000CF catamaran, built at Mandal, Norway. Built for *Gods Trans* of Norway as the ANNE LISE, a high speed frozen fish carrier and used in the North Sea. In 1993 the fish hold was converted to a vehicle deck and additional passenger accommodation was provided. She was sold to *Brudey Frères* of Guadeloupe renamed the MADIKERA. In 1995 she was sold to *Elba Ferries* and renamed the ELBA EXPRESS; she operated a summer service between Piombino (Italy) and Portoferráio (Elba). In 1999 sold to *Emeraude Lines* and renamed the SOLIDOR 4. After refurbishment, entered service in spring 1999.

SOLIDOR 5 Fjellstrand JumboCat 60m catamaran, built at Omastrand, Norway for *Emeraude Lines* to replace the SOLIDOR 3. Entered service in January 2001.

FJORD LINE

THE COMPANY *Fjord Line* is a Norwegian company, 100% owned by *Bergen-Nordhordland Rutelag AS (BNR)*. It took over the Newcastle - Norway service from *Color Line* in December 1998.

MANAGEMENT Managing Director (UK) Dag Romslo, **Sales Director (UK)** Mike Wood.

ADDRESS Royal Quays, North Shields NE29 6EG.

TELEPHONE Administration +44 (0)191-296 1313, **Reservations** +44 (0)191-296 1313.

FAX Administration & Reservations +44 (0)191-296 1540, **Telex** 537275.

INTERNET Email fjordline.uk@fjordline.com **Website** www.fjordline.com *(English)*

ROUTES OPERATED Bergen (Norway) - Haugesund (Norway) - Stavanger (Norway) - Newcastle - Bergen (triangular route), Bergen - Haugesund - Stavanger - Newcastle (Bergen - Stavanger (via 6 hrs), Stavanger - Newcastle (direct 18 hrs 30 mins, via Bergen 29 hrs 30 mins), Bergen - Newcastle (21 hrs 15 mins); *(1)*; 3 sailings Norway - Newcastle per week).

Fjord Line also operates between Norway and Denmark; see Section 6.

1	JUPITER	20581t	75	21.0k	175.3m	1250P	285C	40T	BA	NO

JUPITER Built at Nantes, France as the WELLAMO for *EFFOA* of Finland for *Silja Line* services between Helsinki and Stockholm. In 1981 sold to *DFDS*, renamed the DANA GLORIA and placed onto the Gothenburg - Newcastle and Esbjerg - Newcastle services. In 1983 she was moved to the Copenhagen - Oslo service. In 1984 she was chartered to *Johnson Line* of Sweden for *Silja Line* service between Stockholm and Turku and renamed the SVEA CORONA - the name previously born by a sister vessel, which had been sold. This charter ended in 1985 and she returned to the Copenhagen - Oslo service and resumed the name DANA GLORIA. During winter 1988/89 she was lengthened in Papenburg, Germany and in early 1989 she was renamed the KING OF SCANDINAVIA. She returned to the Copenhagen - Oslo route; in 1990 a Helsingborg call was introduced. In 1994 she was sold to *Color Line* (as part of a deal which involved *DFDS* buying the VENUS from *Color Line*) and renamed the COLOR VIKING. In 1998 she was sold to *Fjord Line* and renamed the JUPITER.

IRISH FERRIES

THE COMPANY *Irish Ferries* is an Irish Republic private sector company, part of the *Irish Continental Group*. It was originally mainly owned by the state owned *Irish Shipping* and partly by *Lion Ferry AB* of Sweden. *Lion Ferry* participation ceased in 1977 and the company was sold into the private sector in 1987. Formerly state owned *B&I Line* was taken over in 1991 and from 1995 all operations were marketed as *Irish Ferries*.

MANAGEMENT Group Managing Director Eamon Rothwell, **Group Marketing Director** Tony Kelly.

ADDRESS 2 Merrion Row, Dublin 2, Republic of Ireland.

TELEPHONE Administration +353 (0)1 855 2222, **Reservations** *Dublin* +353 (0)1 638 3333, *Cork* +353 (0)21 455 1995, *Rosslare Harbour* +353 (0)53 33158, *Holyhead* 0990 329129 (from UK only), *Pembroke Dock* 0990 329543 (from UK only), *National* 08705 171717 (from UK only), *24 hour information* +353 (0)1 661 0715.

FAX Administration & Reservations *Dublin* +353 (0)1 661 0743, *Cork* +353 (0)21 450 4651, *Rosslare* +353 (0)53 33544.

INTERNET Email info@irishferries.com **Website** www.irishferries.com *(English)*

ROUTES OPERATED Conventional Ferries Dublin - Holyhead (3 hrs 15 mins; *(4)*; 2 per day), Rosslare - Pembroke Dock (3 hrs 45 mins; *(1)*; 2 per day), Rosslare - Cherbourg (France) (17 hrs 30 mins; *(3)*; 1 or 2 per week), Rosslare - Roscoff (France) (16 hrs; *(3)*; 1 or 2 per week) Note the Rosslare - Cherbourg/Roscoff service operates on a seasonal basis. **Fast Ferry** Dublin - Holyhead (1 hr 49 min; *(2)*; up to 4 per day). Marketed as 'DUBLIN*Swift*'.

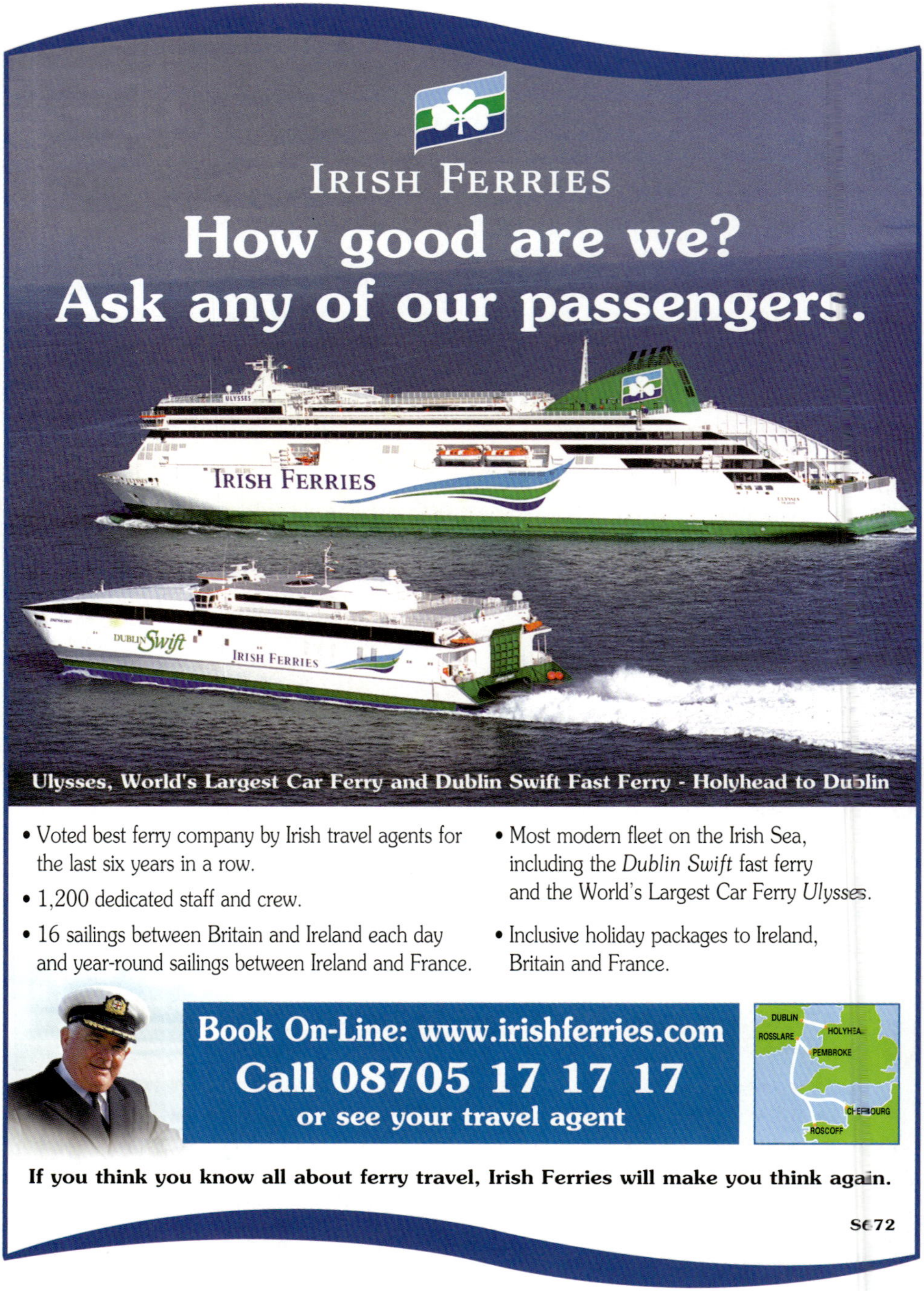
IRISH FERRIES
How good are we?
Ask any of our passengers.
IRISH FERRIES
DUBLIN Swift
IRISH FERRIES
Ulysses, World's Largest Car Ferry and Dublin Swift Fast Ferry - Holyhead to Dublin
• Voted best ferry company by Irish travel agents for the last six years in a row.
• 1,200 dedicated staff and crew.
• 16 sailings between Britain and Ireland each day and year-round sailings between Ireland and France.
• Most modern fleet on the Irish Sea, including the *Dublin Swift* fast ferry and the World's Largest Car Ferry *Ulysses*.
• Inclusive holiday packages to Ireland, Britain and France.
Book On-Line: www.irishferries.com
Call 08705 17 17 17
or see your travel agent
DUBLIN
ROSSLARE
PEMBROKE
ROSCOFF
If you think you know all about ferry travel, Irish Ferries will make you think again.

1	ISLE OF INISHMORE	34031t	97	21.5k	182.5m	2200P	802C	152T	BA2	IR
2»	JONATHAN SWIFT	5989t	99	39.5k	86.6m	800P	200C	-	BA	IR
3	NORMANDY	24872t	82	19.0k	149.0m	1526P	420C	62L	BA2	IR
4	ULYSSES	50938t	01	22.0k	209.0m	1875P	1342C	300T	BA2	IR

ISLE OF INISHMORE Built at Krimpen aan den IJssel, Rotterdam for *Irish Ferries* to operate on the Holyhead - Dublin service. In 2001 replaced by the ULYSSES and moved to the Rosslare - Pembroke Dock route. She also relives on the Dublin – Holyhead route when the ULYSSES receives her annual overhaul.

JONATHAN SWIFT Austal Auto-Express 86 catamaran built at Fremantle, Australia for *Irish Ferries* for the Dublin - Holyhead route.

NORMANDY Built at Gothenburg, Sweden. One of two vessels ordered by *Göteborg-Frederikshavn-Linjen* of Sweden (trading as *Sessan Linjen*) before the take over of their operations by *Stena Line AB* in 1981. Both were designed for the Gothenburg - Frederikshavn route (a journey of about three hours). However, *Stena Line* decided in 1982 to switch the first vessel, the KRONPRINSESSAN VICTORIA (now the STENA EUROPE of *Stena Line AB*), to their Gothenburg - Kiel (Germany) route since their own new tonnage for this route, being built in Poland, had been substantially delayed. She was modified to make her more suitable for this overnight route. Work on the second vessel - provisionally called the DROTTNING SILVIA - was suspended for a time but she was eventually delivered, as designed, in late 1982 and introduced onto the Gothenburg - Frederikshavn route on a temporary basis pending delivery of new *Stena Line* ordered vessels. She was named the PRINSESSAN BIRGITTA, the existing ex *Sessan Linjen* vessel of the same name being renamed the STENA SCANDINAVICA. In early 1983 she was substantially modified in a similar way to her sister. In June 1983 she was renamed the ST NICHOLAS, re-registered in Great Britain and entered service on five year charter to *Sealink UK* on the Harwich - Hoek van Holland route. In 1988 she was purchased and re-registered in The Bahamas. In 1989 she was sold to *Rederi AB Gotland* of Sweden and then chartered back. In 1991 she was renamed the STENA NORMANDY and inaugurated a new service between Southampton and Cherbourg. She was withdrawn in December 1996, returned to *Rederi AB Gotland* and renamed the NORMANDY. In 1997 she was chartered to *Tallink* and operated between Helsinki and Tallinn; this charter ended at the end of the year. In 1998 she was chartered to *Irish Ferries*. She briefly operated between Rosslare and Pembroke Dock before switching to the their French services. In 1999 she was purchased by *Irish Ferries*. She also operates between Rosslare and Pembroke Dock when the regular vessel is away on overhaul.

ULYSSES Built at Rauma, Finland for *Irish Ferries* for the Dublin - Holyhead service.

NORFOLKLINE

THE COMPANY *Norfolkline* (before 1st January 1999 *Norfolk Line*) is a Dutch private sector company owned by *A P Møller Finance* of Denmark.

MANAGEMENT Managing Director D G Sloan, **Deputy Managing Director** J Al-Erhayen, **Corporate Manager Ferry Division** Kell Robdrup, **Manager Dover - Dunkerque** Wayne Bullen, **Manager Scheveningen – Felixstowe** Marc Lagrand.

ADDRESS *Netherlands* Kranenburgweg 180, 2583 ER Scheveningen, Netherlands. *UK* Norfolk House, The Dock, Felixstowe, Suffolk IP11 8UY, *Dover* Export Freight Plaza, Eastern Docks, Dover, Kent CT16 1JA.

TELEPHONE Administration *Netherlands* +31 (0)70 352 74 00, *UK* +44 (0)1394 673676, **Reservations** +44 (0)1304 225151.

FAX Administration & Reservations *Netherlands* +31 (0)70 352 74 35, *Felixstowe* +44 (0)1394 603673, *Dover* +44 (0)1304 208517.

INTERNET Email info@norfolkline.com   dover@norfolkline.com   dunkerque@norfolkline.com **Website** www.norfolkline.com *(English)*

ROUTE OPERATED Dover - Dunkerque (France) (2 hrs; *(1,2,3)*; up to 10 per day).

Midnight Merchant *(John May)*

Pride of Portsmouth *(Brian D. Smith)*

1	DAWN MERCHANT	22152t	98	22.5k	180.0m	250P	-	144T	BA	UK
2	MIDNIGHT MERCHANT	22152t	00	22.5k	180.0m	300P	-	144T	BA2	UK
3	NORTHERN MERCHANT	22152t	00	22.5k	180.0m	250P	-	144T	BA2	UK

DAWN MERCHANT Built at Seville, Spain for parent company *Cenargo* and chartered to *Merchant Ferries*. On delivery in autumn 1998, chartered to *UND RoRo Isletmeri* of Turkey to operate between Istanbul and Trieste. Returned to *Merchant Ferries* in late 1998 and in February 1999, inaugurated a new service between Liverpool and Dublin. In 2002 chartered to *Norfolkine*.

MIDNIGHT MERCHANT Built at Seville, Spain for *Cenargo* (owners of *NorseMerchant Ferries*). On delivery, chartered to *Norfolkline* to operate as second vessel on the Dover - Dunkerque (Ouest) service. In 2002 modified to allow two deck loading.

NORTHERN MERCHANT Built at Seville, Spain for *Cenargo* (owners of *NorseMerchant Ferries*). On delivery, chartered to *Norfolkline* to inaugurate a Dover - Dunkerque (Ouest) service in March 2000. In 2002 modified to allow two deck loading.

NORSEMERCHANT FERRIES

THE COMPANY *NorseMerchant Ferries* is a British private sector company, owned by *Cenargo*. In 1999 the operations of *Belfast Freight Ferries* were integrated into *Merchant Ferries plc* and *Norse Irish Ferries Ltd* was acquired. In January 2001 *Merchant Ferries plc* and *Norse Irish Ferries Ltd* started trading as *NorseMerchant Ferries*.

MANAGEMENT Managing Director Philip Shepherd, **Commercial Director** Richard Harrison, **Freight Sales Director** Declan Cleary.

ADDRESS Twelve Quays Terminal, BIRKENHEAD, Merseyside.

TELEPHONE *Administration* +44 (0)151 906 2700, *Reservations UK* 08706 004321, *Irish Republic* +353 (0)1 819 2999.

FAX Administration +44 (0)28 9078 1599.

INTERNET Email enquiries@norsemerchant.com **Website** www.norsemerchant.com *(English)*

ROUTES OPERATED Port of Liverpool (Twelve Quays River Terminal, Birkenhead) - Belfast (8 hrs; *(2,3)*; 1 per day (Sun, Mon), 2 per day (Tue-Sat)). *NorseMerchant Ferries* also operate a freight-only services between Heysham and Dublin and Heysham and Belfast; see Section 3. The Port of Liverpool - Dublin service is now freight-only and the vessels used are now shown in Section 3.

1	BRAVE MERCHANT	22046t	98	22.5k	180.0m	250P	-	144T	BA	UK
2	LAGAN VIKING	21856t	97	24.0k	186.0m	340P	100C	170T	A	UK
3	MERSEY VIKING	21856t	97	24.0k	186.0m	340P	100C	170T	A	UK

BRAVE MERCHANT Built at Seville, Spain for parent company *Cenargo* and chartered to *Merchant Ferries*. In February 1999 she inaugurated a new service between Liverpool and Dublin. In 2003 chartered to the *British MoD* to convey equipment to the Persian Gulf.

LAGAN VIKING, MERSEY VIKING Built at Donada, Italy for *Levantina Trasporti* of Italy and chartered to *Norse Irish Ferries*, operating between Liverpool and Belfast. to In 1999 charter was taken over by *Merchant Ferries*. Purchased by *NorseMerchant Ferries* in 2001. In 2002 service transferred to Twelve Quays River Terminal, Birkenhead.

P&O FERRIES

THE COMPANY *P&O Ferries Ltd* is a private sector company, a subsidiary of the *Peninsular and Oriental Steam Navigation Company* of Great Britain. In autumn 2002 *P&O North Sea Ferries*, *P&O Portsmouth* and *P&O Stena Line* (*Stena Line* involvement having ceased) were merged into a single operation.

MANAGEMENT Managing Director Russ Peters, **Commercial Director Tourist Services** John Govett, **Communications Director** Chris Laming, **Commercial Director Freight Services** Brian Cork.

ADDRESSES *Head Office and Dover Services* Channel House, Channel View Road, Dover, Kent CT17 9TJ, *Portsmouth* Peninsular House, Wharf Road, Portsmouth PO2 8TA, *Hull* King George Dock, Hedon Road, Hull HU9 5QA, *Rotterdam* Beneluxhaven, Rotterdam (Europoort), Postbus 1123, 3180 Rozenburg ZH, Netherlands, *Zeebrugge* Leopold II Dam 13, Havendam, B-8380 Zeebrugge, Belgium.

TELEPHONE Administration *UK* +44 (0)1304 863000, **Reservations** *Passenger* UK 08705 202020, *France* +33 (0)1 55 69 82 28, *Belgium* +32 (0)2 710 7444, *Netherlands* +31 (0)20 20 13333, *Freight (Dover)* +44 (0)1304 863344.

FAX *UK Passenger* +44 (0)1304 863223, **Telex** 965104, *Freight (Dover)* +44 (0)1304 863399, **Telex** 96316. *Netherlands* +31 (0)181 255215, *Belgium* +32 (0)50 54 71 12.

INTERNET Email customer.services@poferries.com **Website** www.poferries.com *(English)*

ROUTES OPERATED Dover - Calais (1 hr 15 mins - 1 hr 30 mins; *(4,7,8,9,11,13,16)*; up to 35 per day), Hull - Zeebrugge (Belgium) (12 hrs 30 mins - 14 hrs 30 mins); *(6,18)*; 1 per day), Hull - Rotterdam (Beneluxhaven, Europoort) (Netherlands) (10 hrs - 12 hrs; *(12,17)*; 1 per day), Portsmouth - Cherbourg (4 hrs 30 mins (day), (longer at night; *(5,10, (5 once weekly))*; 2 per day), Portsmouth - Le Havre (5 hrs 30 mins (day), 7 hrs 30 mins - 8 hrs (night); *(14,15)*; 2 day crossings, one night crossing per day), Portsmouth - Bilbao (Santurzi) (35 hrs (UK - Spain), 30 hrs (Spain - UK); *(5)*; 2 per week). **Fast Ferry** *Summer only* Portsmouth - Cherbourg (2 hrs 45 mins; *(1)*; 2 per day).

1»	CATALONIA	5902t	98	41.0k	91.3m	920P	225C	-	A	SP
2•	PO CANTERBURY	25122t	80	19.0k	163.5m	1800P	550C	85L	BA2	UK
3•	PO KENT	20446t	80	21.0k	163.4m	1825P	460C	64L	BA2	UK
4	PRIDE OF AQUITAINE	28833t	91	21.0k	163.6m	2000P	600C	100L	BA2	UK
5	PRIDE OF BILBAO	37583t	86	22.0k	177.0m	2553P	600C	77T	BA	UK
6	PRIDE OF BRUGES	31598t	87	18.5k	179.0m	1000P	850C	166T	A	NL
7	PRIDE OF BURGUNDY	28138t	93	21.0k	179.7m	1420P	600C	120L	BA2	UK
8	PRIDE OF CALAIS	26433t	87	22.0k	169.6m	2290P	650C	100L	BA2	UK
9	PRIDE OF CANTERBURY	c30000t	92	21.0k	179.7m	2000P	650C	120L	BA2	UK
10	PRIDE OF CHERBOURG	22365t	95	22.0k	181.6m	1650P	600C	130T	BA	UK
11	PRIDE OF DOVER	26433t	87	22.0k	163.5m	2290P	650C	100L	BA2	UK
12	PRIDE OF HULL	59925t	01	22.0k	215.1m	1360P	250C	240T	AS	UK
13	PRIDE OF KENT	c30000t	92	21.0k	179.7m	2000P	650C	120L	BA2	UK
14	PRIDE OF LE HAVRE	33336t	89	21.0k	161.2m	1600P	575C	91T	BA	UK
15	PRIDE OF PORTSMOUTH	33336t	90	21.0k	161.2m	1600P	575C	91T	BA	UK
16	PRIDE OF PROVENCE	28559t	83	19.0k	154.9m	2036P	550C	85L	BA2	UK
17	PRIDE OF ROTTERDAM	59925t	01	22.0k	215.1m	1360P	250C	240T	AS	NL
18	PRIDE OF YORK	31785t	87	18.5k	179.0m	1000P	850C	166T	A	UK

CATALONIA InCat 91m catamaran. Built at Hobart, Australia for *Buquebus* of Argentina as the CATALONIA 1 and used by *Buquebus España* on their service between Barcelona (Spain) and Mallorca. In April 2000 chartered to *P&O Portsmouth* and renamed the PORTSMOUTH EXPRESS. During winter 2000/2001 she operated for *Buquebus* between Buenos Aires (Argentina) and Piriapolis (Uruguay) and was renamed the CATALONIA. Returned to *P&O Portsmouth* in spring 2001

Pride of Calais and **Pride of Aquitaine** *(Brian D. Smith)*

Pride of Burgundy *(Miles Cowsill)*

and was renamed the PORTSMOUTH EXPRESS. Returned to *Buquebus* in autumn 2001 and then returned to *P&O Portsmouth* in spring 2002. Laid up in Europe during winter 2002/3 and renamed the CATALONIA. She returned to *P&O Ferries* in spring 2003, not being renamed but operating under the marketing name 'Express'.

PO CANTERBURY Built at Malmö, Sweden as the SCANDINAVIA for *Rederi AB Nordö* of Sweden. After service in the Mediterranean for *UMEF*, she was, in 1981, sold to *SOMAT* of Bulgaria, renamed the TZAREVETZ and used on *Medlink* services between Bulgaria and the Middle East and later on other routes. In 1986 she was chartered to *Callitzis* of Greece for a service between Italy and Greece. In 1988 she was sold to *Sealink*, re-registered in the Bahamas and renamed the FIESTA. She was then chartered to *OT Africa Line*. During autumn 1989 she was rebuilt at Bremerhaven to convert her for passenger use and in March 1990 she was renamed the FANTASIA and placed on the Dover - Calais service. Later in 1990 she was renamed the STENA FANTASIA. In 1998, transferred to *P&O Stena Line*. In 1999 she was renamed the P&OSL CANTERBURY. In 2002 renamed the PO CANTERBURY. Replaced in the spring 2003 by the PRIDE OF CANTERBURY and laid up Dunkerque for sale.

PO KENT Built at Bremerhaven, Germany for *European Ferries (Townsend Thoresen)* as the SPIRIT OF FREE ENTERPRISE for the Dover - Calais service, also operating on the Dover - Zeebrugge service during the winter. She was renamed the PRIDE OF KENT in 1987. Sister vessel of the PRIDE OF BRUGES. During winter 1991/92 she was lengthened in Palermo, Italy to give her similar capacity to the PRIDE OF CALAIS and the PRIDE OF DOVER. Now operates Dover - Calais only. In 1998, transferred to *P&O Stena Line*. Later in 1998 renamed the P&OSL KENT. In 2002 renamed the PO KENT. Due to be laid up for sale or charter when the PRIDE OF KENT entered service in spring 2003.

PRIDE OF AQUITAINE Built at Temse, Belgium as the PRINS FILIP for *Regie voor Maritiem Transport (RMT)* of Belgium for the Ostend - Dover service. Although completed in 1991, she did not enter service until May 1992. In 1994 the British port became Ramsgate. Withdrawn in 1997 and laid up for sale. In 1998 she was sold to *Stena RoRo* and renamed the STENA ROYAL. In November 1998 she was chartered to *P&O Stena Line* to operate as a freight only vessel on the Dover - Zeebrugge route. In spring 1999 it was decided to charter the vessel on a long term basis and she was repainted into *P&O Stena Line* colours and renamed the P&OSL AQUITAINE. In autumn 1999 she was modified to make her suitable to operate between Dover and Calais and was transferred to that route, becoming a passenger vessel again. In 2002 renamed the PO AQUITAINE and in 2003 the PRIDE OF AQUITAINE.

PRIDE OF BILBAO Built at Turku, Finland as the OLYMPIA for *Rederi AB Slite* of Sweden for *Viking Line* service between Stockholm and Helsinki. In 1993 she was chartered to *P&O European Ferries* to inaugurate a new service between Portsmouth and Bilbao. During the summer period she also operates, at weekends, a round trip between Portsmouth and Cherbourg. In 1994 she was purchased by the *Irish Continental Group* and re-registered in the Bahamas. *P&O* have since entered her into the British bareboat register. In 2002 her charter was extended for a further five years.

PRIDE OF BRUGES Built as the NORSUN at Tsurumi, Japan for the Hull - Rotterdam service of *North Sea Ferries*. She was owned by *Nedlloyd* and was sold to *P&O* in 1996 but retains Dutch crew and registry. In May 2001 replaced by the PRIDE OF ROTTERDAM and in July 2001, after a major refurbishment, she was transferred to the Hull - Zeebrugge service, replacing the NORSTAR (26919t, 1974). In 2003 renamed the PRIDE OF BRUGES.

PRIDE OF BURGUNDY Built at Bremerhaven, Germany for *P&O European Ferries* for the Dover - Calais service. When construction started she was due to be a sister vessel to the EUROPEAN HIGHWAY, EUROPEAN PATHWAY and EUROPEAN SEAWAY (see Section 3) called the EUROPEAN CAUSEWAY and operate on the Zeebrugge freight route. However, it was decided that she should be completed as a passenger/freight vessel (the design allowed for conversion) and she was launched as the PRIDE OF BURGUNDY. In 1998, transferred to *P&O Stena Line*. In 1998 renamed the P&OSL BURGUNDY. In 2002 renamed the PO BURGUNDY and in 2003 renamed the PRIDE OF BURGUNDY.

PRIDE OF CALAIS Built at Bremerhaven, Germany for *European Ferries* as the PRIDE OF CALAIS for the Dover - Calais service. In 1998, transferred to *P&O Stena Line*. In 1999 renamed the P&OSL

CALAIS. In 2003 renamed PO CALAIS and in 2003 renamed the PRIDE OF CALAIS.

PRIDE OF CANTERBURY Built at Bremerhaven, Germany for *P&O European Ferries* as the EUROPEAN PATHWAY for the Dover - Zeebrugge freight service. (Sister vessel EUROPEAN SEAWAY is shown in Section 3). In 1998 transferred to *P&O Stena Line*. In 2001 car/foot passengers were again conveyed on the route. In 2002/3 rebuilt as a full passenger vessel and renamed the PRIDE OF CANTERBURY; now operates between Dover and Calais.

PRIDE OF CHERBOURG Built at Krimpen aan den IJssel, Rotterdam as the ISLE OF INNISFREE for *Irish Ferries* to operate on the Holyhead - Dublin service. In 1997 transferred to the Rosslare - Pembroke Dock service; for a short period, before modifications at Pembroke Dock were completed, she operated between Rosslare and Fishguard. In spring 2001 she was replaced by the ISLE OF INISHMORE and laid up. In July 2002 she was chartered to *P&O Portsmouth* for 5 years and renamed the PRIDE OF CHERBOURG. Entered service in October 2002.

PRIDE OF DOVER Built at Bremerhaven, Germany for *European Ferries* as the PRIDE OF DOVER for the Dover - Calais service. In 1998, transferred to *P&O Stena Line*. In 1999 renamed the P&OSL DOVER. In 1999 renamed the P&OSL CALAIS. In 2002 renamed PO DOVER and in 2003 renamed the PRIDE OF DOVER.

PRIDE OF HULL Built at Venice, Italy for *P&O North Sea Ferries* to replace (with the PRIDE OF ROTTERDAM) the NORSEA and NORSUN plus the freight vessels NORBAY and NORBANK on the Hull - Rotterdam service. She can accommodate 125 x 12 metre double stacked containers.

PRIDE OF KENT Built at Bremerhaven, Germany for *P&O European Ferries* as the EUROPEAN HIGHWAY for the Dover - Zeebrugge freight service. In 1998 transferred to *P&O Stena Line*. In summer 1999 she operated full time between Dover and Calais. She returned to the Dover - Zeebrugge route in the autumn when the P&OSL AQUITAINE was transferred to the Dover - Calais service. In 2001 car/foot passengers were again conveyed on the route. In 2002/3 rebuilt as a full passenger vessel and renamed the PRIDE OF KENT; now operates between Dover and Calais.

PRIDE OF LE HAVRE Built at Bremerhaven, Germany as the OLAU HOLLANDIA for *TT-Line* of Germany, to operate for associated company *Olau Line*. In 1994 she was chartered to *P&O European Ferries*, re-registered in the UK and renamed the PRIDE OF LE HAVRE. After a brief period on the Portsmouth - Cherbourg service she became a regular vessel on the Portsmouth - Le Havre service from June 1994.

PRIDE OF PORTSMOUTH Built at Bremerhaven, Germany as the OLAU BRITANNIA for *TT-Line* of Germany, to operate for associated company *Olau Line*. In 1994 she was chartered to *P&O European Ferries*, re-registered in the UK and renamed the PRIDE OF PORTSMOUTH. After a brief period on the Portsmouth - Cherbourg service she became a regular vessel on the Portsmouth - Le Havre service from June 1994.

PRIDE OF PROVENCE Built at Dunkerque, France as the STENA JUTLANDICA for *Stena Line* for the Gothenburg - Frederikshavn service. In 1996 she was transferred to the Dover - Calais route and renamed the STENA EMPEREUR. In 1998, transferred to *P&O Stena Line*. Later in 1998 renamed the P&OSL PROVENCE. In 2002 renamed the PO PROVENCE and in 2003 renamed the PRIDE OF PROVENCE.

PRIDE OF ROTTERDAM Built at Venice, Italy. Keel laid as the PRIDE OF HULL but launched as the PRIDE OF ROTTERDAM. Further details as the PRIDE OF HULL.

PRIDE OF YORK Built as the NORSEA at Glasgow, UK for the Hull - Rotterdam service of *North Sea Ferries* (jointly owned by *P&O* and *The Royal Nedlloyd Group* of The Netherlands until 1996). In December 2001, she was replaced by the new PRIDE OF HULL and, after a two month refurbishment, in 2002 transferred to the Hull - Zeebrugge service, replacing the NORLAND (26290t, 1974). In 2003 renamed the PRIDE OF YORK.

Norsea (In 2003 renamed **Pride of York)** *(Rob de Visser)*

European Ambassador *(Miles Cowsill)*

We've Got It Covered

With 7 Routes to Britain and France

Larne - Cairnryan
Larne - Troon
Larne - Fleetwood
Dublin - Liverpool
Dublin - Mostyn
Dublin - Cherbourg
Rosslare - Cherbourg

For more information

see your travel agent

phone **0870 24 24 777**

or log on to our website.

P&O
Irish Sea

www.poirishsea.com

P&O IRISH SEA

THE COMPANY *P&O Irish Sea* is the trading name of *P&O European Ferries (Irish Sea) Ltd*, a British private sector company and a subsidiary of the *Peninsular and Oriental Steam Navigation Company.* It was formed in 1998 by the merger of the shipping activities *Pandoro Ltd* and the Cairnryan - Larne services of *P&O European Ferries (Felixstowe) Ltd.*

MANAGEMENT Chairman Russ Peters, **Managing Director** J H Kearsley, **Passenger Services – Sales and Marketing Manager** James Essler.

ADDRESS Compass House, Dock Street, Fleetwood, Lancashire FY7 6HP.

TELEPHONE Administration +44 (0)1253 615700, **Reservations** *UK* 08702 424777, *Irish Republic* 1 800 409 049.

FAX Administration & Reservations +44 (0)1253 615740.

INTERNET Email **Website** www.poirishsea.com *(English)*

ROUTES OPERATED Conventional Ferries Cairnryan - Larne (1 hr 45 min; *(2,4)*; 7 per day), Mostyn - Dublin (5 - 6 hrs, *(1,3)*; Mostyn to Dublin - 1 per day (Sun, Tue-Sat), Dublin to Mostyn, 2 per day (Tue-Sat) (5-6 hrs) (note the EUROPEAN ENVOY does not convey ordinary passengers on night crossings except on Sunday nights when she operates Mostyn - Dublin (in the summer the Sunday Dublin - Mostyn service is operated by the NORBAY (See Section 3) which then runs to Liverpool), **Summer only** Dublin - Cherbourg (18 hrs; *(1)*; 1 per week). **Fast Ferry (April - September)** Cairnryan - Larne (1 hr; *(5)*; 2 per day), Troon – Larne (1 hr 49 min; *(5)*; 2 per day). Note: some private cars and their passengers are conveyed on some (mainly daytime) sailings on the Fleetwood - Larne and all sailings on the Rosslare - Cherbourg and Liverpool - Dublin routes. However, as these are primarily freight services, the vessels are shown in Section 3. Passengers are not conveyed on the Liverpool - Larne and Troon – Larne freight services.

1	EUROPEAN AMBASSADOR	24500t	01	25.0k	169.8m	405P	375C	122T	BA2	BS
2	EUROPEAN CAUSEWAY	20800t	00	23.0k	159.5m	410P	375C	107T	BA2	BS
3	EUROPEAN ENVOY	18653t	79	18.2k	150.0m	107P	-	142T	A	BD
4	EUROPEAN HIGHLANDER	20800t	02	23.0k	159.5m	410P	375C	107T	BA2	BS
5»	SUPERSTAR EXPRESS	5517t	97	36.0k	82.3m	900P	175C	-	A	BB

EUROPEAN AMBASSADOR Built at Shimonoeki, Japan for *P&O Irish Sea* for the Liverpool - Dublin service. Service transferred to Mostyn in November 2001.

EUROPEAN CAUSEWAY Built at Shimonoeki, Japan for *P&O Irish Sea* for the Cairnryan - Larne service.

EUROPEAN ENVOY Built at Tamano, Japan as the IBEX for *P&O* for *Pandoro* Irish sea services. In 1980 chartered to *North Sea Ferries*, renamed the NORSEA and used on the Ipswich - Rotterdam service. In 1986 she was renamed the NORSKY. In 1995 she returned to *Pandoro* and was re-registered in Bermuda. Later in 1995 she resumed her original name of IBEX. An additional deck was added in 1996. In late 1997 she was renamed the EUROPEAN ENVOY. Operates on the Mostyn - Dublin service.

EUROPEAN HIGHLANDER Built at Shimonoeki, Japan for *P&O Irish Sea* for the Cairnryan - Larne service.

SUPERSTAR EXPRESS Austal Ships 82 catamaran, built at Fremantle, Australia for *Star Cruises* of Malaysia for their service between Butterworth and Langkawi. Built as the SUPERSTAR EXPRESS, she was renamed the SUPERSTAR EXPRESS LANGKAWI later in 1997. She was due, in 1998, to circumnavigate the world and to seek to take the Hales Trophy from HOVERSPEED GREAT BRITAIN. However, these plans did not materialise and instead she was chartered to *P&O European Ferries (Portsmouth)* and placed on the Portsmouth - Cherbourg route. She resumed the name SUPERSTAR EXPRESS. In April 2000 she was transferred to *P&O Irish Sea*. She is chartered during the summer period. In 2003 began a Larne – Troon service.

SuperSeaCat One (John Hendy)

Ben-my-Chree (Miles Cowsill)

SEA CONTAINERS FERRIES

THE COMPANY *Sea Containers Ferries Ltd* is a British private sector company, part of the *Sea Containers Group.*

MANAGEMENT Senior Vice President, Passenger Transport David Benson.

ADDRESS Sea Containers House, 20 Upper Ground, London SE1 9PF.

TELEPHONE Administration +44 (0)20 7805 5000.

FAX Administration +44 (0)20 7805 5900.

INTERNET Email info@seacontainers.com **Website** www.seacontainers.com *(English)*

Ferry services in the UK are operated through three subsidiaries - *Hoverspeed Ltd, Sea Containers Ferries Scotland Ltd* (trading as *SeaCat*) and the *Isle of Man Steam Packet Company* (trading as *Steam Packet*). See also *Silja Line* in Section 6. Because of interchange of fast ferries between companies, they are shown in one section at the end. *IOMSP Co* and *Sea Containers Ferries Scotland* routes are now integrated and are also shown together.

HOVERSPEED

THE COMPANY *Hoverspeed Ltd* is a British private sector company. It was formed in October 1981 by the merger of *Seaspeed*, a wholly owned subsidiary of the *British Railways Board*, operating between Dover and Calais and Dover and Boulogne and *Hoverlloyd*, a subsidiary of *Broström AB* of Sweden, operating between Ramsgate (Pegwell Bay) and Calais. The Ramsgate - Calais service ceased after summer 1982. In early 1984 the company was sold by its joint owners to a management consortium. In 1986 the company was acquired by *Sea Containers*. It was retained by *Sea Containers* in 1990 following the sale of most of *Sealink British Ferries* to *Stena Line*.

MANAGEMENT Managing Director Geoffrey Ede.

ADDRESS The International Hoverport, Marine Parade, DOVER, Kent CT17 9TG.

TELEPHONE Administration +44 (0)1304 865000, **Reservations** 08705 240241 (from UK only).

FAX Administration +44 (0)1304 865087, **Reservations** +44 (0)1304 240088.

INTERNET Email info@hoverspeed.co.uk **Website** www.hoverspeed.co.uk *(English)*

ROUTES OPERATED *All year* Dover - Calais (55 mins; *(3,6,9)*; up to 15 per day), *Summer only* Newhaven - Dieppe (2 hrs; *(10)*; up to 3 per day).

ISLE OF MAN STEAM PACKET COMPANY

THE COMPANY The *Isle of Man Steam Packet Company Limited*, trading as *Steam Packet Company*, is an Isle of Man registered company owned by *Sea Containers Ferries Ltd*. The company is currently for sale.

MANAGEMENT Managing Director Hamish Ross, **Chief Operating Manager** Mark Woodward.

ADDRESS Imperial Buildings, Douglas, Isle of Man IM1 2BY.

TELEPHONE Administration +44 (0)1624 645645, **Reservations** *From UK* 08705 523523, *From elsewhere* +44 (0)1624 661661.

FAX Administration +44 (0)1624 645609.

INTERNET Email spc@steam-packet.com **Website** www.steam-packet.com *(English)*

ROUTES OPERATED Conventional Ferries Douglas (Isle of Man) - Heysham (3 hrs 30 mins; *(1,4 (during TT races only))*; up to 2 per day), Douglas - Liverpool (4 hrs; *(4)*; winter), **SeaCats** Listed with *Sea Containers Ferries Scotland* services below.

SEA CONTAINERS FERRIES SCOTLAND

THE COMPANY *Sea Containers Ferries Scotland Ltd* is a subsidiary of *Sea Containers Ferries Ltd.*

MANAGEMENT Managing Director Hamish Ross, **General Manager, Sales and Marketing, Belfast** Diane Poole, **Chief Operating Manager** John Burrows.

ADDRESS SeaCat Terminal, Troon Harbour, Troon, Ayrshire KA10 6DX.

TELEPHONE Administration +44 (0)1292 319103, **Reservations** *From UK* 08705 523523, *From elsewhere* +44 (0)28 9031 3543.

FAX Administration +44 (0)1292 319108.

INTERNET Email spc@steam-packet.com **Website** www.seacat.co.uk *(English)*

ROUTES OPERATED - SEA CONTAINERS' IRISH SEA FAST FERRIES SERVICES - IOMSP & SEA CONTAINERS FERRIES, SCOTLAND Douglas - Liverpool (2 hrs 30 mins; *(8,11)* up to 3 per day), Douglas - Belfast (2 hrs 45 mins; *(8)*; up to 3 per week), Douglas - Dublin (2 hrs 45 mins; *(8)*; up to 3 per week), Douglas - Heysham (2 hrs; *(8)*; occasional), Troon - Belfast (2 hrs 30 mins; *(5)*; 3 per day), Liverpool - Dublin; (3 hrs 45 mins; *(11)*; 1/2 per day).

1	BEN-MY-CHREE	12504t	98	19.0k	124.9m	500P	-	90T	A	IM
2»•	DIAMANT	3454t	96	37.0k	81.1m	654P	140C	-	A	LX
3»	HOVERSPEED GREAT BRITAIN									
		3000t	90	37.0k	74.3m	577P	80C	-	BA	UK
4	LADY OF MANN	4482t	76	21.0k	104.5m	800P	130C	0T	S	IM
5»	RAPIDE	4112t	96	37.0k	81.1m	654P	140C	-	A	LX
6»	SEACAT DANMARK	3003t	91	37.0k	74.3m	432P	80C	-	BA	UK
7»•	SEACAT FRANCE	3012t	90	35.0k	74.3m	350P	80C	-	BA	UY
8»	SEACAT ISLE OF MAN	3003t	91	37.0k	74.3m	500P	80C	-	BA	UK
9»	SEACAT SCOTLAND	3003t	91	37.0k	74.3m	450P	80C	-	BA	UK
10»	SUPERSEACAT ONE	4462t	97	38.0k	100.0m	782P	175C	-	A	LX
11»	SUPERSEACAT TWO	4462t	97	38.0k	100.0m	782P	175C	-	A	UK
12»•THE PRINCESS ANNE		-	69	50.0k	56.4m	360P	55C	-	BA	UK
13»•THE PRINCESS MARGARET		-	68	50.0k	56.4m	360P	55C	-	BA	UK

BEN-MY-CHREE Built at Krimpen aan den IJssel, Rotterdam for the *IOMSP Co* and operates between Douglas and Heysham and Christmas period Douglas - Dublin sailings.

DIAMANT InCat 81m catamaran built at Hobart, Tasmania, Australia. Ordered by *Del Bene SA* of Argentina. In 1996, before completion, purchased by the *Holyman Group* of Australia and named the HOLYMAN EXPRESS. In 1997 she was renamed the HOLYMAN DIAMANT, transferred to *Holyman Sally Ferries* and in March was introduced onto the Ramsgate - Ostend route. In March 1998 transferred to the Dover - Ostend route, operating for the *Hoverspeed - Holyman (UK)* joint venture, and renamed the DIAMANT. In 1999 this became a 100% *Hoverspeed* operation and in 2000 *Sea Containers* purchased her. During winter 1999/2000 she also operated between Dover and Calais at times. During summer 2001 she operated between Newhaven and Dieppe; in summer 2002 she operated between Dover and Ostend and Dover and Calais. Deployment in 2003 is not decided.

HOVERSPEED GREAT BRITAIN InCat 74m catamaran built at Hobart, Tasmania. Launched as the CHRISTOPHER COLUMBUS but renamed before entering service. During delivery voyage from Australia, she won the Hales Trophy for the 'Blue Riband' of the Atlantic. She inaugurated a car and passenger service between Portsmouth and Cherbourg, operated by *Hoverspeed*. This service was suspended in early 1991 and later that year she was, after modification, switched to a new service between Dover (Eastern Docks) and Boulogne/Calais, replacing hovercraft. In 1992 operated on Channel routes, including services from Folkestone. During winter 1992/3 she was chartered to *Ferry Lineas* of Argentina, operating between Buenos Aires (Argentina) and Montevideo (Uruguay). In summer 1993 she was used to provide additional sailings on the Belfast – Stranraer route, transferring back to the channel later that year. Following the ending of the Folkestone - Boulogne service in autumn 2000, she was transferred to the Dover - Calais route. In summer 2001 she

PROUD OF OUR ROUTES.

BELFAST TROON
ISLE OF MAN LIVERPOOL
ISLE OF MAN BELFAST
ISLE OF MAN HEYSHAM
ISLE OF MAN DUBLIN
LIVERPOOL DUBLIN

To book call
+44 1624 661 661,
visit
www.steam-packet.com
or contact your
travel agent.

Lady of Mann *(Miles Cowsill)*

Diamant *(Mike Louagie)*

operated between Heysham and Belfast; in summer 2002 she operated between Dover and Calais and this will be repeated in 2003.

LADY OF MANN Built at Troon, UK for the *IOMSP Co.* Cars and small vans are side loaded but no ro-ro freight is conveyed. In 1994 replaced by the SEACAT ISLE OF MAN and laid up for sale. She was used in 1995 during the period of the 'TT' motor cycle races between 26th May to 12th June. Later in 1995 she was chartered to *Porto Santo Line* of Madeira for a service from Funchal to Porto Santo. In 1996 she operated throughout the summer, as no SeaCat was chartered. In 1997, she operated for the TT races and then inaugurated a new Liverpool - Dublin service in June, with a weekly Fleetwood - Douglas service until replaced by the SUPERSEACAT TWO in March 1998. In summer 1998, 2000 and 2002 she operated during the TT race period, plus a number of special cruises and was then chartered to *Acor Line* for service in the Azores. In 2001 the TT was cancelled, as were her extra sailings and cruises, but the charter went ahead. During winter 1998/99 she provided back-up to the fast ferries on the Liverpool - Dublin and Douglas - Liverpool routes. Between November 2000 and February 2001 she operated on the Liverpool – Douglas route and this was repeated between and the same periods 2001/2 and 2002/3. In summer 2002 she was again chartered to *Acor Line* and this will be repeated in 2003.

RAPIDE InCat 81m catamaran built at Hobart, Tasmania, Australia. Built for the *Holyman Group* as the CONDOR 12. In summer 1996 operated by *Condor Ferries* (at that time part owned by the *Holyman Group*). In 1997 she was renamed the HOLYMAN RAPIDE, transferred to *Holyman Sally Ferries* and in March was introduced onto the Ramsgate - Ostend route. In March 1998 transferred to the Dover - Ostend route, operating for the *Hoverspeed - Holyman (UK)* joint venture, and renamed the RAPIDE. In 1999 this became a 100% *Hoverspeed* operation and in 2000 *Sea Containers* purchased her. During winter 1999/2000 she also operated between Dover and Calais at times. In summer 2001, she operated between Liverpool and Dublin and Liverpool and Douglas; in summer 2002 she operated between Heysham and Belfast. In 2003 she will operate between Troon and Belfast.

SEACAT DANMARK InCat 74m catamaran built at Hobart, Tasmania, Australia. Christened in 1991 as the HOVERSPEED BELGIUM and renamed HOVERSPEED BOULOGNE before leaving the builders yard. She was the third SeaCat, introduced in 1992 to enable a three vessel service to be operated by *Hoverspeed* across the Channel, including a new SeaCat route between Folkestone and Boulogne (replacing the *Sealink Stena Line* ferry service which ceased at the end of 1991). With the HOVERSPEED FRANCE (now SEACAT ISLE OF MAN) and the HOVERSPEED GREAT BRITAIN she operated on all three Channel routes (Dover - Calais, Dover - Boulogne and Folkestone - Boulogne). In 1993 she was transferred to *SeaCat AB* and renamed the SEACATAMARAN DANMARK and inaugurated a new high-speed service between Gothenburg and Frederikshavn. For legal reasons it was not possible to call her the SEACAT DANMARK as intended but in 1995 these problems were resolved and she was renamed the SEACAT DANMARK. From January 1996 transferred to the new joint venture company *ColorSeaCat KS*, jointly with *Color Line* of Norway. During winter 1996/97 she operated on the Dover - Calais route. *ColorSeaCat* did not operate in 1997 and she again operated for *SeaCat AB*. In autumn 1997 she replaced the SEACAT SCOTLAND on the Stranraer - Belfast route. During summer 1998, she operated for the *IOMSP Co.* In 1999 operated for *Sea Containers Ferries Scotland* between Belfast and Heysham and Belfast and Douglas. In 2000 she was transferred to *SeaCat AB* to operate between Gothenburg, Frederikshavn and Langesund under the *Silja Line SeaCat* branding. In August 2000 moved to the Dover - Calais service.

SEACAT FRANCE Built at Hobart, Tasmania as the SEACAT TASMANIA for *Sea Containers* subsidiary *Tasmanian Ferry Services* of Australia to operate between George Town (Tasmania) and Port Welshpool (Victoria). In 1992 chartered to *Hoverspeed* to operate Dover - Calais and Folkestone - Boulogne services. Returned to Australia after the 1992 summer season but returned to Britain in summer 1993 to operate Dover - Calais and Folkestone - Boulogne services during the summer. She was repainted into *Hoverspeed* livery and renamed the SEACAT CALAIS. In 1994 chartered for five years (with a purchase option) to *Navegacion Atlantida* for *Ferry Linas Argentinas AS* of Uruguay service between Montevideo (Uruguay) - Buenos Aires (Argentina) service and renamed the ATLANTIC II. The purchase option was not taken up and in 1999 she was returned to *Sea Containers* and operated for Hoverspeed between Dover and Calais. In 2000 she was chartered to *SNAV Aliscafi* of Italy to operate between Ancona (Italy) and Split (Croatia) in a joint venture with *Sea Containers* and renamed the CROATIA JET. This operation was repeated in 2001. In 2002 renamed the SEACAT FRANCE and transferred to operate between Dover and Calais. At the end of the 2002 summer period laid up for sale or charter in Birkenhead.

SEACAT ISLE OF MAN InCat 74m catamaran built at Hobart, Tasmania, Australia. Built as the HOVERSPEED FRANCE, the second SeaCat. She inaugurated Dover - Calais/Boulogne service in 1991. In 1992 she was chartered to *Sardinia Express* of Italy and renamed the SARDEGNA EXPRESS; she did not operate on the Channel that year. This charter was terminated at the end of 1992 and in 1993 she was renamed the SEACAT BOULOGNE and operated on the Dover - Calais and Folkestone - Boulogne services. In 1994 she was chartered to *IOMSP Co*, renamed the SEACAT ISLE OF MAN and replaced the LADY OF MANN on services between Douglas (Isle of Man) and Britain and Ireland. During winter 1994/5 operated for *SeaCat Scotland* between Stranraer and Belfast. She returned to *IOMSP Co* in June 1995. During spring 1995 she was chartered to *Condor Ferries*; she then was chartered again to *IOMSP Co* and returned to *Sea Containers* in the autumn. In 1996 she was chartered to *ColorSeaCat KS*, renamed the SEACAT NORGE and inaugurated a new service between Langesund (Norway) and Frederikshavn (Denmark). During winter 1996/97 she operated between Dover and Calais. In early 1997 she was again renamed the SEACAT ISLE OF MAN. During summer 1997 she operated for *IOMSP Co*, serving on Liverpool, Dublin and Belfast seasonal services to Douglas (May to September) plus a weekly Liverpool - Dublin service when the LADY OF MANN operated from Fleetwood. In late 1997 she was transferred to the *Hoverspeed* Dover - Calais route and operated on this route throughout 1998. In 1999 she operated between Douglas and Liverpool and Douglas and Dublin for *IOMSP Co*. In 2000, 2001 and 2002 she also operated between Douglas and Belfast and Douglas and Heysham (plus provide some additional sailings between Liverpool and Dublin in 2002). In early 2003 she replaced the SEACAT SCOTLAND on the Belfast – Troon service. Returned to Isle of Man services in March 2003.

SEACAT SCOTLAND InCat 74m catamaran built at Hobart, Tasmania, Australia, the fifth SeaCat to be constructed. In 1992 she inaugurated a new high-speed car and passenger service for *SeaCat Scotland* on the Stranraer - Belfast route. In autumn 1994 she was chartered to *Q-Ships* of Qatar for services between Doha (Qatar) and Bahrain and Dubai and renamed the Q-SHIP EXPRESS. In spring 1995 she returned to the Stranraer - Belfast service and resumed the name SEACAT SCOTLAND. In autumn 1997 chartered to *Navegacion Atlantida SA* of Uruguay for service between Colonia (Uruguay) and Buenos Aires (Argentina). She returned to the UK in spring 1998 and operated on to the Stranraer - Belfast route. In 1999 and 2000 she operated for *Sea Containers Ferries Scotland* between Stranraer and Belfast (service now ended) and Troon and Belfast. This was repeated in 2001 and 2002. In 2003 to operate between Dover and Calais.

SUPERSEACAT ONE Fincantieri MDV1200 monohull vessel built at La Spézia, Italy. Built for *Sea Containers*. Between 1997 and 1999 operated for *SeaCat AB* on the Gothenburg - Frederikshavn route. In 2000 transferred to *Hoverspeed* to operate on the Newhaven - Dieppe service. In summer 2001 she operated between Dover and Ostend and Dover and Calais. In 2002 she again operated between Newhaven and Dieppe and this will be repeated in 2003.

SUPERSEACAT TWO Fincantieri MDV1200 monohull vessel built at Riva Trigoso, Italy. Built for *Sea Containers*. In 1997 operated on the *Hoverspeed* Dover - Calais route. She was withdrawn from this route at the end of 1997 and in March 1998, she inaugurated a Liverpool - Dublin fast ferry service, operated by *IOMSP Co*. In summer 1999 she operated for *Hoverspeed* between Newhaven and Dieppe. In 2000 she returned to the Irish Sea, operating on the Belfast - Heysham service. In summer 2001 she operated between Dover and Calais and Dover and Ostend. In 2001 she was laid up for sale or charter. In 2003 she will operate between Liverpool and Douglas and Liverpool and Dublin.

THE PRINCESS ANNE, THE PRINCESS MARGARET British Hovercraft Corporation SRN4 type hovercraft built at Cowes, UK for *Seaspeed*. Built at to Mark I specification. In 1978/1979 respectively lengthened to Mark III specification. They underwent complete refurbishment at the beginning of 1999. Withdrawn 2000 and laid up at the Hovercraft Museum at Lee on Solent.

SeaFrance Rodin (*Mike Louagie*)

SeaFrance Manet (*John Hendy*)

SeaFrance Nord Pas-de-Calais and **European Seaway** *(John Hendy)*

SEAFRANCE

THE COMPANY *SeaFrance SA* (previously *SNAT (Société Nouvelle Armement Transmanche)*) is a French state owned company. It is jointly owned by *Société Nationale des Chemins de fer Français (French Railways)* and *Compagnie Générale Maritime Français (French National Shipping Company)*. *SNAT* was established in 1990 to take over the services of *SNCF Armement Naval*, a wholly owned division of *SNCF*. At the same time a similarly constituted body called *Société Proprietaire Navires (SPN)* was established to take over ownership of the vessels; *Sealink British Ferries* (and later *Stena Line Ltd*) also had involvement in this company. Joint operation of services with *Stena Line* ceased at the end of 1995 and *SeaFrance SA* was formed. *Stena Line* involvement in *SPN* ended in 1999.

MANAGEMENT President du Directoire Eudes Riblier, **Directeur Sealink Calais** M Jachet, **Managing Director (UK)** Robin Wilkins.

ADDRESS *France* 3 rue Ambroise Paré, 75475, Paris Cedex 10, France, *UK* Whitfield Court, Honeywood Close, Whitfield, Dover, Kent CT16 3PX.

TELEPHONE Administration *France* +33 1 55 31 58 92, *UK* +44 (0)1304 828300, **Reservations** *France* +33 3 21 46 80 79, *UK (Passenger)* 08705 711711 (from UK only), *UK (Freight)* +44 (0)1304 203030.

FAX Administration & Reservations *France* +33 1 48 74 62 37, *UK* +44 (0)1304 828384.

INTERNET Email sfadmin@seafrance.com **Website** www.seafrance.com *(English, French)*

ROUTE OPERATED Calais - Dover (1 hr 10 mins - 1 h 30 mins; *(1,2,3,4)*; up to 20 per day).

1	SEAFRANCE CEZANNE	25122t	80	19.5k	163.5m	1800P	600C	66L	BA2	FR
2	SEAFRANCE MANET	15093t	84	18.0k	130.0m	1800P	330C	43L	BA2	FR
3	SEAFRANCE RENOIR	15612t	81	18.0k	130.0m	1600P	330C	43L	BA2	FR
4	SEAFRANCE RODIN	34000t	01	25.0k	185.0m	1900P	700C	133L	BA2	FR

SEAFRANCE CEZANNE Built at Malmö, Sweden as the ARIADNE for *Rederi AB Nordö* of Sweden. Renamed the SOCA before entering service on *UMEF* freight services (but with capacity for 175 drivers) in the Mediterranean. In 1981 she was sold to *SO Mejdunaroden Automobilen Transport (SOMAT)* of Bulgaria and renamed the TRAPEZITZA. She operated on *Medlink* services between Bulgaria and the Middle East. In 1988 she was acquired by *Sealink British Ferries*, re-registered in the Bahamas and in 1989 renamed the FANTASIA. Later in 1989 she was modified in Bremerhaven, renamed the CHANNEL SEAWAY and, in May, she inaugurated a new freight-only service between Dover (Eastern Docks) and Calais. During winter 1989/90 she was modified in Bremerhaven to convert her for passenger service. In spring 1990 she was renamed the FIESTA, transferred to *SNAT*, re-registered in France and replaced the CHAMPS ELYSEES (now the SEAFRANCE MANET) on the Dover - Calais service. In 1996 she was renamed the SEAFRANCE CEZANNE.

SEAFRANCE MANET Built at Nantes, France for *SNCF* as the CHAMPS ELYSEES to operate Calais - Dover and Boulogne - Dover services, later operating Calais - Dover only. In 1990 transferred to the Dieppe - Newhaven service. Chartered to *Stena Sealink Line* in June 1992 when they took over the operation of the service. She was renamed the STENA PARISIEN and carried a French crew. In 1997 the charter was terminated; she returned to *SeaFrance* and was renamed the SEAFRANCE MANET.

SEAFRANCE RENOIR Built at Le Havre, France for *SNCF* as the COTE D'AZUR for the Dover - Calais service. She also operated Boulogne - Dover in 1985. In 1996 she was renamed the SEAFRANCE RENOIR. Following the delivery of the SEAFRANCE RODIN she became the reserve vessel. During summer 2002 she operated her own roster at peak periods with reduced passenger facilities. During summer 2003 she will operate a full roster to enable 20 passenger sailings per day to operate.

SEAFRANCE RODIN Built at Rauma, Finland for *SeaFrance*.

SMYRIL LINE

THE COMPANY *Smyril Line* is a Faroe Islands registered company.

MANAGEMENT Managing Director Óli Hammer, **Financial Manager** Joannes A Vali.

ADDRESS Jonas Bronksgöta 37, PO Box 370, FO-100 Tórshavn, Faroe Islands.

TELEPHONE Administration +298-345900, **Reservations** Faroe Islands +298-345900, *UK* +44 (0)1595 690845 (Smyril Line Shetland).

FAX Administration & Reservations +298-343950.

INTERNET Email office@smyril-line.fo **Website** www.smyril-line.com *(English, Danish, German, Faroese, Icelandic, Norwegian)*

ROUTES OPERATED Tórshavn (Faroes) - Hanstholm (Denmark) (31 hrs; *(1)*; 1 per week), Tórshavn - Lerwick (Shetland) (14 hrs; *(1)*; 1 per week) - Bergen (Norway) (via Lerwick) (24 hrs - 27 hrs 30 mins; *(1)*; 1 per week), Tórshavn - Seydisfjordur (Iceland) (15 hrs - 18 hrs; *(1)*; 1 per week). Note: Lerwick sailings ceased after the 1992 season but resumed in 1998. The service now operates all year round except that Seydisfjordur is not served in the winter.

1	NORRÖNA	36000t	03	21.0k	164.0m	1482P	800C	134T	BA	FA
2•	NORRÖNA 1	11999t	73	19.0k	129.0m	1050P	300C	40L	BA2	FA

NORRÖNA Built at Lübeck, Germany for *Smyril Line*, to replace the existing NORRÖNA. Originally due to enter service in summer 2002, start of building was delayed by financing difficulties. Originally to have been built at Flensburg, Germany but delays led to change of shipyard.

NORRÖNA 1 Built at Rendsburg, Germany as the GUSTAV VASA for *Lion Ferry AB* of Sweden, a sister vessel of the NILS DACKE (which became the recently sold QUIBERON of *Brittany Ferries*). In 1982 the Travemünde - Malmö service ceased and in 1983 she was sold to *Smyril Line* and renamed the NORRÖNA. She was rebuilt at Flensburg, Germany, to increase passenger capacity and in the summer took over services from the SMYRIL of *Strandfaraskip Landsins*. In 1993 Esbjerg replaced Hanstholm as the Danish port and calls at Lerwick (Shetland) ceased. Because the service only operated in the summer period, she has, since purchase, undertaken a number of charters and cruises during the winter months. During autumn 1994 she initially served on the short-lived service between Wismar (Germany) and Newcastle for *North Sea Baltic Ferries*. During the early part of 1996 she was chartered to *Stena Line* to operate between Stranraer and Belfast. In 1998 the Danish port became Hanstholm again and Lerwick sailings resumed. Since winter 1999/2000 a winter service has been operated and operated for *Smyril Line* all year round. Now laid up for sale.

SPEEDFERRIES

THE COMPANY *SpeedFerries Ltd* is a UK company wholly owned by *Mols-Linien A/S* of Denmark. Operations started in Summer 2003.

MANAGEMENT President Curt Stavis, **Project Manager, SpeedFerries Limited** Marianne Illum.

ADDRESS Not Known .

TELEPHONE Administration Not Known, **Reservations** +44 (0)8700 603900

FAX Administration Not Known, **Reservations** +44 (0)8700 603900

INTERNET Email mail@speedferries.com **Website** www.speedferries.com *(English)*

ROUTE OPERATED Dover – Boulogne (50 mins; *(1)*; 5 per day).

1»	SPEED ONE	5619t	98	43.0k	91.3m	800P	220C	-	A	DK

SPEED ONE InCat 91 metre catamaran, built speculatively at Hobart, Tasmania, Australia. In spring 1998, following *InCat's* acquisition of a 50% share in *Scandlines Cat-Link A/S*, she was chartered to that company, operating between Århus and Kalundborg and named the CAT-LINK V. She is the current holder of the Hales Trophy for fastest crossing of the Atlantic during her delivery voyage between the USA and Falmouth, UK. In 1999 the charter was transferred to *Mols-Linien*, she was renamed the MADS MOLS and operated between Århus and Odden. In 2003 transferred to *SpeedFerries* and renamed the SPEED ONE.

STENA LINE

THE COMPANY *Stena Line Limited* is incorporated in Great Britain and registered in England and Wales. *Stena Line* bv is a Dutch company. The ultimate parent undertaking is *Stena AB* of Sweden.

MANAGEMENT Route Director - Hoek van Holland - Harwich Pim de Lange, **Route Director - Fishguard - Rosslare** Mary Gallagher, **Route Director - Holyhead - Dun Laoghaire/Dublin** Vic Goodwin, **Route Director - Stranraer - Belfast** Alan Gordon.

ADDRESS *UK* Charter House, Park Street, Ashford, Kent TN24 8EX, *Netherlands* PO Box 2, 3150 AA, Hoek van Holland, Netherlands.

TELEPHONE Administration *UK* +44 (0)1233 647022, *Netherlands* +31 (0)174 389333, **Reservations** *UK* 08075 707070 (from UK only), *Netherlands* +31 (0)174 315811.

FAX Administration & Reservations *UK* +44 (0)1233 202349, *Netherlands* +31 (0)174 387045, **Telex** 31272.

INTERNET Email info@stenaline.com **Website** www.stenaline.com *(English, Swedish)*

ROUTES OPERATED Conventional Ferries Stranraer - Belfast (3 hrs 15 mins; *(3)*; 2 per day), Holyhead - Dublin (3 hrs 45 mins; *(1)*; 2 per day), Fishguard - Rosslare (3 hrs 30 mins; *(5)*; 2 per day), **Ro-pax Ferries** Harwich - Hoek van Holland (Netherlands) (7 hrs 30 mins; *(2,7)*; 2 per day) (car passengers only conveyed - no foot passengers). **Fast Ferries** Stranraer - Belfast (1 hr 45 mins; *(9)*; up to 5 per day), Holyhead - Dun Laoghaire (1 hr 39 mins; *(6)*; up to 4 per day), Fishguard - Rosslare (Summer Only) (1 hr 39 mins; *(8)*; up to 4 per day), Harwich - Hoek van Holland - (3 hrs 40 mins; *(4)*; 2 per day.

THE INTERNET IS NOT THE ONLY NETWORK OFFERING FAST, MODERN COMMUNICATIONS.

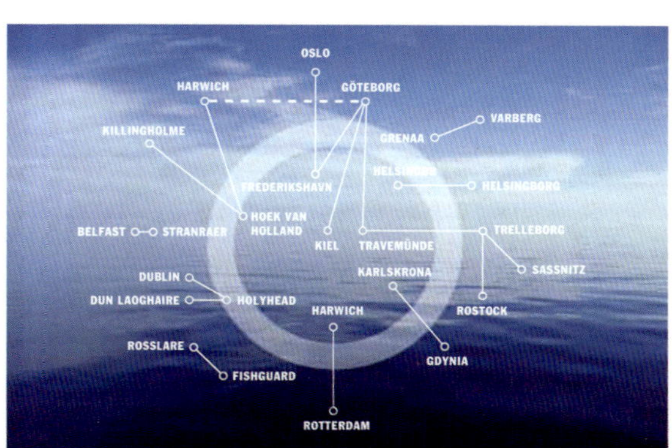

Stena Line is one of the world's largest ferry companies with a comprehensive route network throughout northern Europe.

We offer freight customers and holiday-makers rapid and efficient transportation. Our modern fleet comprises 36 ship – fast ferries, multi-purpose ferries and freight ships – operating 17 strategically located routes.

Our passenger ships provide an un-rivalled onboard experience in terms of food, shopping, conferences, business trips and general service.

No other ferry company can currently offer so many travel options or routes as Stena Line. If you would like to find out more about our services, visit our website at **www.stenaline.com**

Stena Hollandica *(Philippe Holthof)*

Stena Voyager *(John Hendy)*

1	STENA ADVENTURER	44000t	03	22.0k	210.8m	1500P	-	250T	BA2	UK
2	STENA BRITANNICA	44000t	02	22.0k	210.8m	900P	-	250T	BA2	UK
3	STENA CALEDONIA	12619t	81	19.5k	129.6m	1000P	280C	56L	BA2	UK
4»	STENA DISCOVERY	19638t	97	40.0k	126.6m	1500P	375C	50L	A	NL
5	STENA EUROPE	24828t	81	19.0k	149.0m	2076P	456C	60T	BA2	UK
6»	STENA EXPLORER	19638t	96	40.0k	126.6m	1500P	375C	50L	A	UK
7	STENA HOLLANDICA	33796t	01	22.0k	188.3m	380P	-	216T	BA	NL
8»	STENA LYNX III	4113t	96	35.0k	81.1m	620P	181C	-	A	UK
9»	STENA VOYAGER	19638t	96	40.0k	126.6m	1500P	375C	50L	A	UK

STENA ADVENTURER Ro-pax vessel built at Ulsan, South Korea, for *Stena RoRo* and chartered to *Stena Line* to operate between Holyhead and Dublin, replacing the STENA FORWARDER.

STENA BRITANNICA Ro-pax vessel built at Ulsan, South Korea, for *Stena RoRo*. Launched and delivered as the STENA BRITANNICA II. Chartered to *Stena Line* for use on the Hoek van Holland - Harwich service, replacing the 2000 built STENA BRITANNICA, now the FINNFELLOW of *Finnlines*. In 2003 renamed the STENA BRITANNICA.

STENA CALEDONIA Built at Belfast, UK as the ST DAVID for the Holyhead - Dun Laoghaire and Fishguard - Rosslare services. It was originally planned that she would replace the chartered STENA NORMANDICA (5607t, 1975) but it was subsequently decided that an additional large vessel was required for the Irish Sea routes. Until 1985 her normal use was, therefore, to substitute for other Irish Sea vessels as necessary (including the Stranraer - Larne route) and also to operate additional summer services on the Holyhead - Dun Laoghaire route. During the spring of 1983 she operated on the Dover - Calais service. From March 1985 she operated between Dover and Ostend, a service which ceased in December 1985 with the decision of *RMT* to link up with *Townsend Thoresen*. During the early part of 1986 she operated between Dover and Calais and then moved to the Stranraer - Larne route (later Stranraer – Belfast) where she became a regular vessel. In 1990 she was renamed the STENA CALEDONIA. In September 1996 she became mainly a freight-only vessel but passengers were carried on certain sailings and when the STENA VOYAGER was unavailable; cars and passengers are now conveyed on all sailings.

STENA DISCOVERY Finnyards HSS1500 ('High-speed Sea Service') built at Rauma, Finland for *Stena Line* to replace two vessels on the Harwich - Hoek van Holland service.

STENA EUROPE Built at Gothenburg, Sweden as the KRONPRINSESSAN VICTORIA for *Göteborg-Frederikshavn-Linjen* of Sweden (trading as *Sessan Linjen*) for their Gothenburg - Frederikshavn service. Shortly after delivery, the company was taken over by *Stena Line* and services were marketed as *Stena-Sessan Line* for a period. In 1982 she was converted to an overnight ferry by the conversion of one vehicle deck to two additional decks of cabins and she was switched to the Gothenburg - Kiel route (with, during the summer, daytime runs from Gothenburg to Frederikshavn and Kiel to Korsør (Denmark)). In 1989 she was transferred to the Oslo - Frederikshavn route and renamed the STENA SAGA. In 1994, transferred to *Stena Line bv*, renamed the STENA EUROPE and operated between Hoek van Holland and Harwich. She was withdrawn in June 1997, transferred to the *Lion Ferry* (a *Stena Line* subsidiary) Karlskrona - Gdynia service and renamed the LION EUROPE. In 1998 she was transferred back to *Stena Line* (remaining on the same route) and renamed the STENA EUROPE. In early 2002 the cabins installed in 1982 were removed and other modifications made and she was transferred to the Fishguard - Rosslare route.

STENA EXPLORER Finnyards HSS1500 built at Rauma, Finland for *Stena RoRo* and chartered to *Stena Line*. Operates on the Holyhead - Dun Laoghaire route.

STENA HOLLANDICA Ro-pax ferry built at Cadiz, Spain for *Stena RoRo* and chartered to *Stena Line bv* to operate between Hoek van Holland and Harwich.

STENA LYNX III InCat 81m catamaran built at Hobart, Tasmania, Australia. Chartered new by *American Fast Ferries* of Argentina to *Stena Line* in June 1996 and named the STENA LYNX III. Initially used on the Dover - Calais service. From summer 1997 until autumn 1998 she operated between Newhaven and Dieppe. In March 1998 she was transferred to *P&O Stena Line* and renamed the ELITE. She was then renamed the P&O STENA ELITE (although only carrying the name ELITE on the bow). In late 1998 she was transferred back to *Stena Line* and renamed the STENA LYNX III. In 1999 she was placed on the Fishguard - Rosslare service, replacing the STENA LYNX (3231t, 1993). The charter ended in autumn 2000 but was immediately renewed as a summer only operation (with winter lay up).

STENA VOYAGER Finnyards HSS1500 built at Rauma, Finland for *Stena RoRo* and chartered to *Stena Line*. Operates on the Stranraer - Belfast route.

SUPERFAST FERRIES

THE COMPANY *SuperFast Ferries* is a Greek company, owned by *Attica Enterprises*.

MANAGEMENT Managing Director Alexander P Panagopulos, **Corporate Marketing Director** Yannis B Criticos, **Manager Superfast Ferries Scotland** Denise Holmes.

ADDRESS *Greece* 157 Alkyonidon Avenue, Voula, GR-16673 Athens, Greece, *UK* Superfast Ferries, The Terminal Building, Port of Rosyth, Fife KY11 2XP, *Belgium* Superfast Ferries, Terminal A, Port of Zeebrugge, Doverlaan 7, Box 14, 8380 Zeebrugge, Belgium.

TELEPHONE Administration *Greece & Scotland* +30 (0)210 8919500, *Belgium* +32 (0)50 252211, **Reservations** *UK* 0870 234 0870, *Belgium* +32 (0)50 252252.

FAX Administration *Greece & Scotland* +30 (0)210 8919509.

INTERNET Email criticos@superfast.com **Website** www.superfast.com *(English, German, Dutch, French)*

ROUTES OPERATED Rosyth (Scotland) - Zeebrugge (Belgium) (17 hrs 30 mins; *(1,2)*; 1 per day). Service started in May 2002.

1	SUPERFAST IX	30285t	01	29.2k	203.3m	626P	661C	140T	BA2	GR
2	SUPERFAST X	30285t	02	29.2k	203.3m	626P	661C	140T	BA2	GR

SUPERFAST IX and SUPERFAST X Built at Kiel, Germany for *Attica Enterprises* for use by *SuperFast Ferries* SUPERFAST IX operated between Rostock and Södertälje from January until April 2002. In May 2002 both began operating between Rosyth and Zeebrugge.

SWANSEA CORK FERRIES

THE COMPANY *Swansea Cork Ferries* is a company established in 1987 to re-open the Swansea - Cork service abandoned by *B&I Line* in 1979. It was originally jointly owned by *West Glamorgan County Council, Cork Corporation, Cork County Council* and *Kerry County Council*. The service did not operate in 1989 but resumed in 1990. In 1993 the company was acquired by *Strintzis Lines* of Greece. In 1999 it was purchased from *Strintzis Lines* by a consortium of Irish businessmen.

MANAGEMENT Managing Director Thomas Hunter McGowan, **Sales Manager** *IR* Simone Collins, *UK* John Doonican.

ADDRESS *IR* 52 South Mall, Cork, Republic of Ireland, *UK* Kings Docks, Swansea SA1 1SF.

TELEPHONE Administration *Head Office* +353 (0)21 427 6000, *Cork Ferry Port* +353 (0)21 437 8036, **Reservations** *IR* +353 (0)21 427 1166, *UK* +44 (0)1792 456116.

FAX Administration *IR* +353 (0)21 427 5814, *UK* +44 (0)1792 644356, **Reservations** *IR* +353 (0)21 427 5061, *UK* +44 (0)1792 644356.

INTERNET Email scf@iol.ie **Website** www.swansea-cork.ie *(English)*

ROUTE OPERATED *March - January* Cork - Swansea (10 hrs; *(1)*; 1 per day or alternate days, according to season. Due to tidal restrictions at Swansea, the service operates to Pembroke Dock on a few days each year.

1	SUPERFERRY	15127t	72	21.0k	137.8m	1100P	300C	45L	BA2	SV

SUPERFERRY Built at Hashihama, Japan as the CASSIOPEIA for *Ocean Ferry KK* of Japan. In 1976 the company became *Ocean Tokyu Ferry KK* and she was renamed the IZU NO 3. She was used on the service between Tokyo (Honshu) - Tokushima (Shikoko) - Kokura (Kyshu). In 1991 she was sold to *Strintzis Lines* and briefly renamed the IONIAN EXPRESS. Following major rebuilding, she was renamed the SUPERFERRY and used on their services between Greece and the Greek islands. In 1993 time chartered to *Swansea Cork Ferries*. The charter continued following the sale of *SCF* by *Strintzis Lines*. In winter she used to return to *Strintzis Lines* in Greece for refit and also operated for them on Mediterranean routes. The charter was not renewed for 2001 and she remained in the Mediterranean, operating for *Strintzis Lines* under the *Blue Ferries* name (following the reorganisation of the company after its acquisition by *Attica Enterprises*). She was renamed the BLUE AEGEAN. In 2002 she was sold to *Swansea Cork Ferries* and renamed the SUPERFERRY.

TRANSMANCHE FERRIES

THE COMPANY *Transmanche Ferries* is a French company, controlled by the *Syndicat Mixte de L'Activité Transmanche*. *Hoverspeed* act as booking agents in the UK.

ADDRESS Transmanche Ferries, Quai Gaston Lalitte, 76200 Dieppe, France.

TELEPHONE Administration +33 02 32 14 52 03, **Reservations** 0800 9171201 *(Hoverspeed)*, 0800 650100.

FAX Administration +33 02 32 14 52 00.

INTERNET Website www.transmancheferries.com *(English, French)*

ROUTE OPERATED Newhaven - Dieppe (4 hrs; *(1,2)*; 4 per day).

1	DIEPPE	17672t	81	19.0k	145.9m	250P	-	140T	BA	FR
2	SARDINIA VERA	11637t	75	18.5k	120.8m	700P	479C	58T	BA	IT

DIEPPE Built at Kalmar, Sweden as the SAGA STAR for *TT-Saga-Line* and, from 1982, used on freight services between Travemünde and Trelleborg/Malmö. In 1989 sold to *Cie Meridonale* of France, renamed the GIROLATA and used on *SNCM* (later *CMR*) services in the Mediterranean. In 1993 she was chartered back to *TT-Line*, resumed her original name and was used on the Travemünde - Trelleborg service. Following delivery of the ROBIN HOOD and the NILS DACKE in 1995, she was transferred to the Rostock - Trelleborg route. In July 1997 she was purchased by *TT-Line* and in 1998 passenger facilities were completely renovated to full ro-pax format; following the delivery of the TOM SAWYER she was transferred back to the Travemünde - Trelleborg route, operating additional freight sailings. Briefly transferred back to Rostock - Trelleborg when the charter of the TT-TRAVELLER ended. Withdrawn in 2002, sold to *Transmanche Ferries* and renamed the DIEPPE.

SARDINIA VERA Built at Bremerhaven, Germany for *Stena Line AB* of Sweden. Laid down as the STENA ATLANTICA but launched as the MARINE ATLANTICA. On delivery, chartered to *CN Marine* (from 1986 *Marine Atlantic*) of Canada for service between North Sydney (Nova Scotia) and Port-aux-Basques (Newfoundland). In 1986 she was sold to *Tourship Co AS* of Italy (parent company of *Corsica Ferries*) and renamed the CORSICA VERA. In 1987 renamed the SARDINIA VERA. Used on services between Italy and France and Corsica and Sardinia. In 2001 chartered to the *Transmanche Ferries*.

SARDINIA VERA
OLBIA
TRANSM

Sardinia Vera *(John Hendy)*

section **2** domestic services

gb & ireland

ARGYLL AND BUTE COUNCIL

THE COMPANY *Argyll and Bute Council* is a British local government authority.

MANAGEMENT Director of Transportation and Property Alistair Gow.

ADDRESS Manse Brae, Lochgilphead, Argyll PA31 8RD.

TELEPHONE Administration +44 (0)1546 604657.

FAX Administration +44 (0)1546 606618.

INTERNET Email alistair.gow@argyll-bute.gov.uk **Website** www.argyll-bute.gov.uk *(English)*

ROUTES OPERATED Vehicle ferries Seil - Luing (5 mins; *(1)*; approx half hourly), Port Askaig (Islay) - Feolin (Jura) (5 mins; *(3)*; approx hourly). **Passenger only ferries** Port Appin – Lismore (10 mins; *(4)*; approx half hourly), Ellenabeich – Easdale (5 mins; *(2)*; as required).

1	BELNAHUA	35t	72	8.0k	17.1m	40P	5C	1L	BA	UK
2p	EASDALE	-	93	6.5k	6.4m	11P	0C	0L	-	UK
3	EILEAN DHIURA	86t	98	9.0k	25.6m	50P	13C	1L	BA	UK
4p	LISMORE	12t	88	8.0k	9.7m	20P	0C	0L	-	UK

BELNAHUA Built at Campbeltown, UK for *Argyll County Council* for the Seil - Luing service. In 1975, following local government reorganisation, transferred to *Strathclyde Regional Council*. In 1996, transferred to *Argyll and Bute Council*.

EASDALE Built for *Strathclyde Regional Council* for the Ellenabeich - Easdale passenger only service. In 1996, following local government reorganisation, transferred to *Argyll and Bute Council*.

EILEAN DHIURA Built at Bromborough, Birkenhead, UK for *Argyll and Bute County Council* to replace the *Western Ferries (Argyll)* SOUND OF GIGHA on the Islay - Jura route. *Serco-Denholm Ltd* manage and operate this vessel on behalf of the *Argyll and Bute Council*.

LISMORE Built for *Strathclyde Regional Council* for the Port Appin – Lismore passenger only service. In 1996, following local government reorganisation, transferred to *Argyll and Bute Council*.

ARRANMORE ISLAND FERRY SERVICES

THE COMPANY *Arranmore Island Ferry Services* is an Irish Republic company, supported by *Údarás na Gaeltachta (The Gaeltacht Authority)*, a semi-state owned body responsible for tourism and development in the Irish speaking areas of The Irish Republic. The operation is also known as *Maoin-Na-Farraige* (literally 'sea treasure' or 'sea wealth').

MANAGEMENT Managing Director Cornelius Bonner.

ADDRESS Bridge House, Leabgarrow, Arranmore, County Donegal, Republic of Ireland.

TELEPHONE Administration & Reservations +353 (0)75 20532.

FAX Administration & Reservations + 353 (0)75 20750.

ROUTE OPERATED Burtonport (County Donegal) - Leabgarrow (Arranmore Island) (20 mins; *(1,2,3)*; up to 8 per day (summer), 5 per day (winter)) (Note only one vessel is generally in use at any one time).

Eilean Dhiura *(Miles Cowsill)*

Isle of Arran *(Miles Cowsill)*

SECTION 2 – DOMESTIC SERVICES

1	ÁRAINN MHÓR	64t	72	8.0k	23.8m	138P	6C	-	B	IR
2	COLL	69t	74	8.0k	25.3m	152P	6C	-	B	IR
3	RHUM	69t	73	8.0k	25.3m	164P	6C	-	B	IR

ÁRAINN MHÓR Built at Port Glasgow, UK as the KILBRANNAN for *Caledonian MacBrayne*. Used on a variety of routes until 1977, she was then transferred to the Scalpay (Harris) - Kyles Scalpay service. In 1990 she was replaced by the CANNA and, in turn, replaced the CANNA in her reserve/relief role. In 1992 sold to *Arranmore Island Ferry Services* and renamed the ÁRAINN MHÓR. She was subsequently sold to *Údarás na Gaeltachta* and leased back to *Arranmore Island Ferry Services*.

COLL Built at Port Glasgow, UK for *Caledonian MacBrayne*. For several years she was employed mainly in a relief capacity. In 1986 she took over the Tobermory (Mull) - Kilchoan service from a passenger only vessel; the conveyance of vehicles was not inaugurated until 1991. In 1996 she was transferred to the Oban - Lismore route. In 1998 she was sold to *Arranmore Island Ferry Services*.

RHUM Built at Port Glasgow, UK for *Caledonian MacBrayne*. Until 1987, she was used primarily on the Claonaig - Lochranza (Arran) service. After that time she served on various routes. In 1994 she inaugurated a new service between Tarbert (Loch Fyne) and Portavadie. In 1997 operated between Kyles Scalpay and Scalpay until the opening of the new bridge on 16th December 1997. In 1998 she was sold to *Arranmore Island Ferry Services*.

BERE ISLAND FERRIES

THE COMPANY *Bere Island Ferries Ltd* is an Irish Republic private sector company.

MANAGEMENT Operator Colm Harrington.

ADDRESS Ferry Lodge, West End, Bere Island, County Cork, Republic of Ireland.

TELEPHONE Administration +353 (0)27 75009, **Reservations** Not applicable.

INTERNET Email biferry@eircom.net **Website** www.bereisland.net *(English)*

ROUTE OPERATED Castletownbere (County Cork) - Bere Island (10 mins; *(2,3)*; up to 10 per day).

1•	F.B.D. DUNBRODY	139t	60	8.0k	39.6m	107P	18C	-	BA	IR
2	MISNEACH	30t	78	7.0k	18.9m	80P	4C	-	B	IR
3	MORVERN	64t	73	8.0k	23.8m	138P	6C	-	B	IR

F.B.D. DUNBRODY Built at Hamburg, Germany as the BERNE-FARGE for the service between Berne and Farge, across the River Weser in Germany. Subsequently she was sold to *Elbe Clearing* of Germany, renamed the ELBE CLEARING 12 and used as a floating platform for construction works in the Elbe. In 1979 she was sold to *Passage East Ferry Company* and renamed the F.B.D. DUNBRODY. Withdrawn in January 1998 and became a spare vessel. Later in 1998 she was sold to *Bere Island Ferries* and replaced the MISNEACH as main vessel. In 2000 badly damaged when she broke loose during gales and laid up. She is currently for sale, and will be used as a work platform or similar; she is no longer usable as a ferry.

MISNEACH Built at New Ross, Irish Republic for *Arranmore Island Ferry Services* of the Irish Republic and used on the Burtonport - Arranmore service. In 1992 sold to *Bere Island Ferries*. In 1993 inaugurated a car ferry service between Castletownbere and Bere Island. Became reserve vessel when F.B.D. DUNBRODY entered service but resumed full service when that vessel was withdrawn. Now reserve again following delivery of the MORVERN.

MORVERN Built at Port Glasgow, UK for *Caledonian MacBrayne*. After service on a number of routes she was, after 1979, the main vessel on the Fionnphort (Mull) - Iona service. In 1992 replaced by the LOCH BUIE and became a spare vessel. In 1995 sold to *Arranmore Island Ferry Services*. In 2001 sold to *Bere Island Ferries*.

CALEDONIAN MACBRAYNE

THE COMPANY *Caledonian MacBrayne Limited* is a British state owned company, the responsibility of the First Minister of Scotland. Until 1990 it was part of the state owned *Scottish Transport Group* (formed in 1969). *Caledonian MacBrayne Limited* as such was formed in 1973 by the merger of the *Caledonian Steam Packet Company Ltd* (which had been formed in 1889) and *David MacBrayne Ltd* (whose origins go back to 1851). The company has more vessels sailing under the British flag than any other.

MANAGEMENT Managing Director Lawrie Sinclair, **Head of Marketing** Hugh D MacLennan.

ADDRESS The Ferry Terminal, Gourock PA19 1QP.

TELEPHONE Administration +44 (0)1475 650100, **Vehicle Reservations** 08705 650000 (from UK only).

FAX Administration +44 (0)1475 637607, **Vehicle Reservations** +44 (0)1475 635235.

INTERNET Email hugh.maclennan@calmac.co.uk **Website** www.calmac.co.uk *(English)*

ROUTES OPERATED All year vehicle ferries (frequencies are for summer) Ardrossan - Brodick (Arran) (55 mins; *(3)*; up to 6 per day), Largs - Cumbrae Slip (Cumbrae) (10 mins; *(16,24)*; every 30 or 15 mins), Wemyss Bay - Rothesay (Bute) (35 mins; *(14,15,31)*; up to 18 per day), Colintraive - Rhubodach (Bute) (5 mins; *(19)*; frequent service), Tarbert (Loch Fyne) - Portavadie (20 mins; *(11)*; up to 12 per day), Gourock - Dunoon (20 mins; *(14,15,31)*; hourly service), Kennacraig - Port Ellen (Islay) (2 hrs 15 mins; *(8)*; 1 or 2 per day), Kennacraig - Port Askaig (Islay) (2 hrs; *(8,10)*; 1 or 2 per day), Tayinloan - Gigha (20 mins; *(23)*; up to 10 per day), Oban - Lismore (50 mins; *(7)*; up to 4 per day), Oban - Colonsay (2 hrs 10 mins; *(5,8,28)*; 5 per week), Oban - Craignure (Mull) (40 mins; *(13)*; up to 7 per day), Oban - Coll (2 hrs 45 mins (direct), 4 hrs 50 mins (via Tiree); *(5,28)*; up to 6 per week), Oban - Tiree (3 hrs 30 mins (direct), 4 hrs 15 mins (via Coll); *(13* (summer), *5,28)*; up to 7 per week), Oban - Castlebay (Barra) (5 hrs (direct); *(5,28)* up to 5 per week), Oban - Lochboisdale (South Uist) (5 hrs (direct), 7 hrs (via Barra); *(5,28)*; up to 56 per week), Bernaray - Leverburgh (Harris) (1 hr 10 mins; *(22)*; 3-4 per day), Lochaline - Fishnish (Mull) (15 mins; *(20)*; up to 16 per day), Tobermory (Mull) - Kilchoan (35 mins; *(21)*; up to 11 per day), Ceann a Gharaidh (Eriskay) - Aird Mhor (Barra) (40 mins; *(17)*; up to 5 per day), Mallaig - Armadale (Skye) (30 mins; *(5* (summer), *27* (winter)); up to 7 per day (2 in winter)), Sconser (Skye) - Raasay (15 mins; *(25)*; up to 10 per day), Uig (Skye) - Tarbert (Harris) (1 hr 45 mins; *(9)*; 1 or 2 per day), Uig (Skye) - Lochmaddy (North Uist) (1 hr 45 mins; *(9)*; 1 or 2 per day), Ullapool - Stornoway (Lewis) (2 hrs 40 mins; *(12)*; up to 3 per day). **All year passenger and restricted vehicle ferries** (frequencies are for summer) Fionnphort (Mull) - Iona (5 mins; *(18)*; frequent), Ballycastle (Northern Ireland) - Rathlin Island (40 mins; *(4)*; 2 per day), Mallaig - Eigg - Muck - Rum - Canna - Mallaig (round trip 7 hrs (all islands); *(27)*; at least 1 sailing per day - most islands visited daily). Note although these services are operated by vehicle ferries, special permission is required to take a vehicle and tourist vehicles are not normally conveyed. **Summer only vehicle ferries** Claonaig - Lochranza (Arran) (30 mins; *(26)*; up to 9 per day), Kennacraig - Port Askaig - Colonsay - Oban (3 hrs 35 mins; *(8)*; 1 per week). **Winter only vehicle ferry** Tarbert (Loch Fyne) - Lochranza (Arran) (1 hr; *(varies)*; 1 per day). All year passenger only ferries (frequencies are for summer) Gourock - Dunoon (20 mins; *(1)*; 3 per day).

1p	ALI CAT	74t	99	-	19.8m	250P	0C	0L	-	UK
2	BRUERNISH	69t	73	8.0k	22.5m	121P	6C	-	B	UK
3	CALEDONIAN ISLES	52211t	93	15.0k	93.5m	1000P	120C	10L	BA	UK
4	CANNA	69t	73	8.0k	22.5m	140P	6C	-	B	UK
5	CLANSMAN	5400t	98	16.5k	99.0m	638P	90C	6L	BA	UK
6	CORUISK	c1100t	03	14.0k	60.0m	250P	40C	-	BA	UK
7	EIGG	69t	75	8.0k	22.5m	75P	6C	-	B	UK
8	HEBRIDEAN ISLES	3040t	85	15.0k	85.1m	494P	68C	10L	BAS	UK
9	HEBRIDES	5299t	00	16.5k	99.0m	612P	110C	6L	BA	UK
10	ISLE OF ARRAN	3269t	84	15.0k	85.0m	446P	68C	8L	BA	UK

Lord of the Isles *(Miles Cowsill)*

Loch Striven *(Miles Cowsill)*

11	ISLE OF CUMBRAE	201t	77	8.5k	32.0m	139P	18C	-	BA	UK
12	ISLE OF LEWIS	6753t	95	18.0k	101.2m	680P	123C	10L	BA	UK
13	ISLE OF MULL	4719t	88	15.0k	90.1m	962P	80C	20L	BA	UK
14	JUNO	854t	74	12.0k	69.0m	381P	40C	-	AS	UK
15	JUPITER	848t	74	12.0k	69.0m	381P	40C	-	AS	UK
16	LOCH ALAINN	396t	98	10.0k	41.0m	150P	24C	-	BA	UK
17	LOCH BHRUSDA	246t	96	8.0k	30.0m	150P	18C	-	BA	UK
18	LOCH BUIE	295t	92	9.0k	30.2m	250P	9C	-	BA	UK
19	LOCH DUNVEGAN	549t	91	9.0k	54.2m	200P	36C	-	BA	UK
20	LOCH FYNE	549t	91	9.0k	54.2m	200P	36C	-	BA	UK
21	LOCH LINNHE	206t	86	9.0k	30.2m	199P	12C	-	BA	UK
22	LOCH PORTAIN	c800t	03	11.0k	50.0m	200P	32C	-	BA	UK
23	LOCH RANZA	206t	86	9.0k	30.2m	199P	12C	-	BA	UK
24	LOCH RIDDON	206t	86	9.0k	30.2m	199P	12C	-	BA	UK
25	LOCH STRIVEN	206t	86	9.0k	30.2m	199P	12C	-	BA	UK
26	LOCH TARBERT	211t	92	9.0k	30.2m	149P	18C	-	BA	UK
27	LOCHNEVIS	941t	00	9.0k	49.1m	190P	14C	-	A	UK
28	LORD OF THE ISLES	3504t	89	16.0k	84.6m	506P	56C	16L	BAS	UK
29	PIONEER	1071t	74	16.0k	67.4m	218P	33C	-	AS	UK
30	RAASAY	69t	76	8.0k	22.5m	75P	6C	-	B	UK
31	SATURN	851t	78	12.0k	69.0m	381P	40C	-	AS	UK

ALI CAT Catamaran built for *Solent & White Line Cruises* of Ryde, Isle of Wight. Operated a passenger service between Cowes to Hamble and Warsash and cruises from Cowes. At times chartered to *Wightlink* to cover for the fast catamarans when there were only two in their fleet. In 2002 chartered to *Red Funnel Ferries* who had contracted with *Caledonian MacBrayne* to operate passenger only services between Gourock and Dunoon in the morning and evening peaks. In April 2003 this contract was extended by another year.

BRUERNISH Built at Port Glasgow, UK. Until 1980 she served on a variety of routes. In 1980 she inaugurated ro-ro working between Tayinloan and the island of Gigha and served this route until June 1992 when she was replaced by the LOCH RANZA and became a relief vessel. In summer 1994 she operated as secondary vessel on the Tobermory (Mull) - Kilchoan service for one season only. In December 1996 she started a vehicle ferry service between Ballycastle (on the North West coast of Northern Ireland) and Rathlin Island under charter; the route became a *Caledonian MacBrayne* operation in April 1997 - see the CANNA. In 1997 she operated on the Tarbert - Portavadie service and in 1998 on the Oban - Lismore service. Since 1999 she has been a spare vessel.

CALEDONIAN ISLES Built at Lowestoft, UK for the Ardrossan - Brodick (Arran) service.

CANNA Built at Port Glasgow, UK. She was the regular vessel on the Lochaline - Fishnish (Mull) service. In 1986 she was replaced by the ISLE OF CUMBRAE and until 1990 she served in a relief capacity in the north, often assisting on the Iona service. In 1990 she replaced the KILBRANNAN (see the ÁRAINN MHÓR, *Arranmore Island Ferry Services*) on the Kyles Scalpay (Harris) - Scalpay service (replaced by a bridge in autumn 1997). In spring 1997 she was transferred to the Ballycastle - Rathlin Island route.

CLANSMAN Built at Appledore, UK to replace the LORD OF THE ISLES on the Oban - Coll and Tiree and Oban - Castlebay and Lochboisdale service in the summer. She also serves as winter relief vessel on the Stornoway, Tarbert, Lochmaddy, Mull, Islay and Brodick routes.

CORUISK Built at Appledore, UK to replace the LORD OF THE ISLES on the Mallaig - Armadale route during the summer. She will operate on the Clyde during the winter.

EIGG Built at Port Glasgow, UK. Since 1976 she was employed mainly on the Oban - Lismore service. In 1996 she was transferred to the Tobermory (Mull) - Kilchoan route, very occasionally making special sailings to the Small Isles (Canna, Eigg, Muck and Rum) for special cargoes. In 1999 her wheelhouse was raised to make it easier to see over taller lorries and she returned to the Oban - Lismore route.

HEBRIDEAN ISLES Built at Selby UK for the Uig - Tarbert/Lochmaddy service. She was used initially on the Ullapool - Stornoway and Oban - Craignure/Colonsay services pending installation of link-span facilities at Uig, Tarbert and Lochmaddy. She took up her regular role in May 1986. Since May 1996 she no longer operated direct services between Tarbert and Lochmaddy, this role being taken on by the new Harris - North Uist services of the LOCH BHRUSDA. In 2001 replaced by the HEBRIDES and transferred to the Islay service. In autumn 2002 she operated between Scrabster and Stromness for *NorthLink Orkney and Shetland Ferries* before port modifications at Scrabster enabled the HAMNAVOE to enter service in spring 2003. She then returned to the Islay service.

HEBRIDES Built at Port Glasgow, UK for the Uig - Tarbert and Uig - Lochmaddy services.

ISLE OF ARRAN Built at Port Glasgow, UK for the Ardrossan - Brodick service. In 1993 transferred to the Kennacraig - Port Ellen/Port Askaig service, also undertaking the weekly Port Askaig - Colonsay - Oban summer service. Until 1997/98 she also relieved on the Brodick, Coll/Tiree, Castlebay/Lochboisdale, Craignure and Tarbert/Lochmaddy routes in winter. In 2001 replaced by the HEBRIDEAN ISLES and is now reserve for the larger vessels. She will also operate on the Islay service in summer 2003.

ISLE OF CUMBRAE Built at Troon, UK for the Largs - Cumbrae Slip (Cumbrae) service. In 1986 she was replaced by the LOCH LINNHE and the LOCH STRIVEN and transferred to the Lochaline - Fishnish (Mull) service. She used to spend most of the winter as secondary vessel on the Kyle of Lochalsh - Kyleakin service; however this ceased following the opening of the Skye Bridge in 1995. In 1997 she was transferred to the Colintraive - Rhubodach service. In summer 1999 she was transferred to the Tarbert - Portavadie service.

ISLE OF LEWIS Built at Port Glasgow, UK for the Ullapool - Stornoway service.

ISLE OF MULL Built at Port Glasgow, UK for the Oban - Craignure (Mull) service. She also operates the Oban - Colonsay service and until 1997/98 was the usual winter relief vessel on the Ullapool - Stornoway service. She has also deputised on the Oban - Castlebay/Lochboisdale and Oban - Coll/Tiree routes.

JUNO, JUPITER, SATURN Built at Port Glasgow, UK for the Gourock - Dunoon, Gourock - Kilcreggan and Wemyss Bay - Rothesay services. The JUPITER has been upgraded to Class III standard for the Ardrossan - Brodick service. Before 1986, the JUNO and JUPITER operated mainly on the Gourock - Dunoon and Gourock - Kilcreggan (now withdrawn) services and the SATURN on the Wemyss Bay - Rothesay service. Since 1986 they have usually rotated on a three weekly basis on the three services; until 2000 this, in summer, included Clyde cruising but this was not repeated in 2001

LOCH ALAINN Built at Buckie, UK for the Lochaline - Fishnish service. Launched as the LOCH ALINE but renamed the LOCH ALAINN before entering service. After a brief period on the service she was built for, she was transferred to the Colintraive - Rhubodach route. In summer 1998 she was transferred to the Largs - Cumbrae Slip service.

LOCH BHRUSDA Built at Bromborough, Birkenhead, UK to inaugurate a new Otternish (North Uist) - Berneray - Leverburgh (Harris) service. In 2001 the service became Berneray - Leverburgh In 2003 moved to the Eriskay - Barra service, previously operated by *Comhairle Nan Eilean Siar* vessels. Note 'Bhrusda' is pronounced "Vroosta".

LOCH BUIE Built at St Monans, UK for the Fionnphort (Mull) - Iona service to replace the MORVERN (see *Arranmore Island Ferry Services*) and obviate the need for a relief vessel in the summer. Due to height restrictions, loading arrangements for vehicles taller than private cars are bow only. Only islanders' cars and service vehicles (eg mail vans, police) are carried; no tourist vehicles are conveyed.

LOCH DUNVEGAN Built at Port Glasgow, UK for the Kyle of Lochalsh - Kyleakin service. On the opening of the Skye Bridge in October 1995 she was withdrawn from service and put up for sale. In autumn 1997, returned to service on the Lochaline - Fishnish route. In 1998 she was due to be transferred to the Colintraive - Rhubodach route but this was delayed due to problems in providing terminal facilities. She operated on the Clyde and between Mallaig and Armadale during the early summer and was taken laid up. In 1999 she was transferred to the Colintraive - Rhubodach route.

Clansman *(Miles Cowsill)*

LOCH FYNE Built at Port Glasgow UK for the Kyle of Lochalsh - Kyleakin service (see the LOCH DUNVEGAN). In autumn 1997, she also served on the Lochaline - Fishnish route and was transferred to this route as regular vessel in 1998.

LOCH LINNHE Built at Hessle, UK. Until 1997 she was used mainly on the Largs - Cumbrae Slip (Cumbrae) service and until winter 1994/95 she was usually used on the Lochaline - Fishnish service during the winter. Since then she had relieved on various routes in winter. In summer 1998 she operated mainly on the Tarbert - Portavadie route. In 1999 she was transferred to the summer only Tobermory - Kilchoan service. In 2003 she launched the new Sound of Barra before delivery of the LOCH PORTAIN allowed the LOCH BHRUSDA to be moved to that route.

LOCH PORTAIN Built at Bromborough, Birkenhead, UK (hull constructed in Poland) to replace the LOCH BHRUSDA on the Berneray - Leverburgh service. The LOCH BHRUSDA has been moved to the Eriskay - Barra route, replacing the *Comhairle Nan Eilean Siar* vessels previously used.

LOCH RANZA Built at Hessle, UK for the Claonaig - Lochranza (Arran) seasonal service and used a relief vessel in the winter. In 1992 she was replaced by the LOCH TARBERT and transferred to the Tayinloan - Gigha service.

LOCH RIDDON Built at Hessle, UK. Until 1997 she was used almost exclusively on the Colintraive - Rhubodach service. In 1997, she was transferred to the Largs - Cumbrae Slip service.

LOCH STRIVEN Built at Hessle, UK. Used mainly on the Largs - Cumbrae Slip service until 1997. In winter 1995/6 and 1996/67 she was used on the Tarbert - Portavadie and Claonaig - Lochranza routes. In 1997 she took over the Sconser - Raasay service.

LOCH TARBERT Built at St Monans, UK for the Claonaig - Lochranza service. She has been the regular winter vessel on the Largs - Cumbrae Slip route since winter 1994/5 and is also the winter relief vessel for the Otternish - Leverburgh route.

LOCHNEVIS Built at Troon, UK to replace the LOCHMOR on the Mallaig - Small Isles service and the winter Mallaig - Armadale service. Although a vehicle ferry, cars are not normally carried to the Small Isles; the ro-ro facility is used for the carriage of agricultural machinery and livestock and it is possible to convey a vehicle on the ferry from which goods can be unloaded directly onto local transport rather than transhipping at Mallaig. Ramps are being provided at each island and, when complete, the practice of tendering at Eigg, Muck and Rum will cease, the LAIG BAY being disposed of.

LORD OF THE ISLES Built at Port Glasgow, UK to replace the CLAYMORE on the Oban - Castlebay and Lochboisdale services and also the COLUMBA (1420t, 1964) on the Oban - Coll and Tiree service. She took over Mallaig - Armadale and Mallaig - Outer Isles service in July 1998 but returned to her previous routes during the winter period. In spring 2003 the Mallaig – Armadale service was taken over by the CORUISK and she will operate services from Oban to South Uist and Barra.

PIONEER Built at Leith, UK to operate on the West Loch Tarbert - Port Ellen service (see the PENTALINA B, *Pentland Ferries*). When the IONA was at last able to operate this service in 1978 (following the move to Kennacraig) the PIONEER was transferred to the Mallaig - Armadale service, operating as a relief vessel in the winter on Upper Clyde and Small Isles routes. In 1989 she was replaced at Mallaig by the IONA and became the company's spare vessel, replacing the GLEN SANNOX (1269t, 1957). Since summer 1995 she has undertaken Wemyss Bay - Rothesay and Rothesay - Largs - Brodick sailings. She serves as a Clyde and Small Isles relief vessel in the winter replacing the JUNO, JUPITER, SATURN and LOCHNEVIS for annual overhaul. In 1998 she opened the Mallaig - Armadale/Outer Isles service and temporarily operated between Oban and Craignure before returning to the Clyde in July. In summer 2000 she operated on the Wemyss Bay - Rothesay route. Her role as reserve for the larger vessels has ceased following the delivery of the HEBRIDES but she continued to operate on the Wemyss Bay - Rothesay route in 2001 and this was repeated in 2002. In 2003 operated on the Mallaig - Armadale service until the delivery of the CORUISK.

RAASAY Built at Port Glasgow, UK for and used primarily on the Sconser (Skye) - Raasay service. In 1997 she was replaced by the LOCH STRIVEN and became a spare/relief vessel.

SATURN Built at Troon, UK. As the JUNO and JUPITER. In earlier days operated mainly on the

Wemyss Bay - Rothesay service.

Caledonian MacBrayne also operates the LAIG BAY, an 8k, 10.5m motor vessel built in 2000 and carrying up to 28 passengers. She tenders to the LOCHNEVIS at Eigg. She will be withdrawn and sold when a ramp is built on the island later in 2003.

CROMARTY FERRY COMPANY

THE COMPANY The *Cromarty Ferry Company* operate under contract to *The Highland Council*

MANAGEMENT Managing Director Mr John Henderson.

ADDRESS Udale Farm, Poyntzfield, BY DINGWALL, IV7 8LY.

TELEPHONE +44 (0)1381 610269, Mobile +44 (0)7768 653674.

FAX +44 (0)1381 610408.

INTERNET Email john@udalefarm.com **Website** www.cromarty-ferry.co.uk *(English)*

ROUTE OPERATED *Summer only* Cromarty - Nigg (Ross-shire) (10 mins; *(1)*; half hourly - 0800 to 1800 ex Cromarty (19.00 in July and August)).

1	CROMARTY ROSE	28t	87	8.0k	14.0m	50P	2C	-	B	UK

CROMARTY ROSE Built at Ardrossan, UK for *Seaboard Marine (Nigg) Ltd* who operated the service until 2001. In 2001 *The Highland Council* decided to financially support the service and, after a tendering process, the contract was awarded in 2002 to the *Cromarty Ferry Company*. The new company purchased the CROMARY ROSE from *Seaboard Marine (Nigg) Ltd*.

CROSS RIVER FERRIES

THE COMPANY *Cross River Ferries Ltd* is an Irish Republic company, jointly owned by *Marine Transport Services Ltd* of Cobh and *Arklow Shipping Ltd* of Arklow, County Wicklow.

MANAGEMENT Operations Manager Eoin O'Sullivan.

ADDRESS Westlands House, Rushbrooke, Cobh, County Cork, Republic of Ireland.

TELEPHONE Administration +353 (0)21 481 1223, **Reservations** Not applicable.

FAX Administration +353 (0)21 481 2645, **Reservations** Not applicable.

ROUTE OPERATED Carrigaloe (near Cobh, on Great Island) - Glenbrook (Co Cork) (4 mins; *(1,2)*; frequent service 07.00 - 00.15 (one or two vessels used according to demand)).

1	CARRIGALOE	‡225t	70	8.0k	49.1m	200P	27C	-	BA	IR
2	GLENBROOK	‡225t	71	8.0k	49.1m	200P	27C	-	BA	IR

CARRIGALOE Built at Newport (Gwent) UK as the KYLEAKIN for *Caledonian Steam Packet Company* (later *Caledonian MacBrayne*) for the Kyle of Lochalsh - Kyleakin service. In 1991 sold to *Marine Transport Services Ltd* and renamed them the CARRIGALOE. She entered service in March 1993. In summer 2002 chartered to the *Lough Foyle Ferry Company*, returning in spring 2003.

GLENBROOK Built at Newport (Gwent) UK as the LOCHALSH for *Caledonian Steam Packet Company* (later *Caledonian MacBrayne*) for the Kyle of Lochalsh - Kyleakin service. In 1991 sold to *Marine Transport Services Ltd* and renamed the GLENBROOK. She entered service in March 1993.

Glenachulish *(Ross Settles)*

Maid of Glencoul *(Andrew Cooke)*

GLENELG - KYLERHEA FERRY

THE COMPANY The *Glenelg - Kylerhea Ferry* is privately operated.

MANAGEMENT Ferry Master R MacLeod.

ADDRESS Corriehallie, Inverinate, Kyle IV40 8HD.

TELEPHONE Administration & Reservations +44 (0)1599 511302.

FAX Administration & Reservations +44 (0)1599 511477.

INTERNET Email roddy@skyeferry.co.uk **Website** www.skyeferry.co.uk *(English)*

ROUTE OPERATED *Easter - October only* Glenelg - Kylerhea (Skye) (10 mins; *(1)*; frequent service).

1	GLENACHULISH		44t	69	9.0k	20.0m	12P	6C	-	BSt	UK

GLENACHULISH Built at Troon, UK for the *Ballachulish Ferry Company* for the service between North Ballachulish and South Ballachulish, across the mouth of Loch Leven. In 1975 the ferry was replaced by a bridge and she was sold to *Highland Regional Council* and used on a relief basis on the North Kessock - South Kessock and Kylesku - Kylestrome routes. In 1984 she was sold to the operator of the Glenelg - Kylerhea service. She is the last turntable ferry in operation.

THE HIGHLAND COUNCIL

THE COMPANY *The Highland Council* (previously *Highland Regional Council*) is a British local government authority.

MANAGEMENT Area Road & Transport Manager James C Tolmie, **Ferry Manager** J McAuslane.

ADDRESS *Area Office* Lochybridge Depot, Carr's Corner Industrial Estate, Fort William PH33 6TQ, *Ferry Office* Ferry Cottage, Ardgour, Fort William.

TELEPHONE Administration *Area Office* +44 (0)1397 703701, *Corran* +44 (0)1855 841243, *Camusnagaul* +44 (0)1397 772483, **Reservations** Not applicable.

FAX Administration *Area Office* +44 (0)1397 705735, *Corran* +44 (0)1855 841243, **Reservations** Not applicable.

ROUTES OPERATED Conventional Ferries Corran - Ardgour (5 mins; *(2,3)*; half hourly), **Passenger Only Ferry** Fort William - Camusnagaul (10 mins; *(1)*; Frequent).

1p	CAILIN AN AISEAG	-	80	7.5k	9.8m	26P	0C	0L	-	UK
2	CORRAN	351t	01	10.0k	42.0m	150P	30C	2L	BA	UK
3	MAID OF GLENCOUL	‡166t	75	8.0k	32.0m	116P	16C	1L	BA	UK

CAILIN AN AISEAG Built at Buckie, UK for *Highland Regional Council* and used on the Fort William - Camusnagaul service.

CORRAN Built at Hull, UK for *The Highland Council* to replace the MAID OF GLENCOUL as main vessel.

MAID OF GLENCOUL Built at Ardrossan, UK for *Highland Regional Council* for the service between Kylesku and Kylestrome. In 1984 the ferry service was replaced by a bridge and she was transferred to the Corran - Ardgour service. In April 1996, ownership transferred to *The Highland Council*. In 2001 became the reserve vessel.

ISLES OF SCILLY STEAMSHIP COMPANY

THE COMPANY *Isles of Scilly Steamship Company* is a British private sector company.

MANAGEMENT Chief Executive J Marston, **Marketing Manager** L Ramzan.

ADDRESS *Scilly* PO Box 10, Hugh Town, St Mary's, Isles of Scilly TR21 0LJ, *Penzance* Steamship House, Quay Street, Penzance, Cornwall, TR18 4BZ.

TELEPHONE Administration & Reservations *Scilly* +44 (0)1720 424220, *Penzance* +44 (0)1736 334220.

FAX Administration & Reservations *Scilly* +44 (0)1720 422192, *Penzance* +44 (0)1736 351223.

INTERNET Email sales@islesofscilly-travel.co.uk **Website** www.ios-travel.co.uk *(English)*

ROUTES OPERATED *Passenger service* Penzance - St Mary's (Isles of Scilly) (2 hrs 40 mins; *(1,3)*; 1 per day), *Freight services* St Mary's - Tresco/St Martin's/St Agnes/Bryher; *(2)*; irregular).

1	GRY MARITHA	590t	81	10.5k	57.2m	12P	5C	1L	C	UK
2F	LYONESSE LADY	50t	91	9.0k	-	12P	1C	0L	A	UK
3	SCILLONIAN III	1256t	77	15.5k	67.7m	600P	-	-	C	UK

GRY MARITHA Built at Kolvereid, Norway for *Gjofor* of Norway. In design she is a coaster rather than a ferry. In 1990 sold to *Isles of Scilly Steamship Company*. She operates a freight and passenger service all year (conveying all goods to and from the islands - tourist cars are not conveyed). During the winter she provides the only sea service to the islands, the SCILLONIAN III being laid up.

LYONESSE LADY Built at Fort William UK, for inter-island ferry work. Does not normally convey passengers.

SCILLONIAN III Built at Appledore, UK for the Penzance - St Mary's service. She operates from Easter to late autumn and is laid up in the winter. Last major conventional passenger/cargo ferry built for UK waters and probably Western Europe. Extensively refurbished during winter 1998/99. The SCILLONIAN III can carry cars in her hold as cargo; however, since the purchase of the GRY MARITHA most cars conveyed to and from the island have been carried on that vessel and she has functioned as a passenger vessel.

KERRERA FERRY

THE COMPANY The *Kerrera Ferry* is privately operated.

MANAGEMENT Ferry Master Duncan MacEachen.

ADDRESS The Ferry, Isle of Kerrera, By Oban PA34 4SX.

TELEPHONE Administration +44 (0)1631 563665.

ROUTE OPERATED Gallanach (Argyll) - Kerrera (5 mins; *(1)*; on demand 10.30 - 12.30 and 14.00 - 18.00, Easter - October, other times by arrangement).

1	GYLEN LADY	9t	99	8.0k	10.0m	12P	1C	-	B	UK

GYLEN LADY Built at Corpach, UK to inaugurate a vehicle ferry service to the Isle of Kerrera, replacing open passenger boat.

Hamnavoe *(Miles Cowsill)*

Graemsey *(Miles Cowsill)*

SECTION 2 – DOMESTIC SERVICES

LOUGH FOYLE FERRY COMPANY

THE COMPANY *Lough Foyle Ferry Company Ltd* is an Irish Republic Company.

MANAGEMENT Managing Director: Jim McClenaghan.

ADDRESS The Pier, Greencastle, Co Donegal, Republic of Ireland.

TELEPHONE Administration +353 (0)74 93 81901.

FAX Administration: +353 (0)74 93 81903.

INTERNET Email: info@loughfoyleferry.com **Website:** www.loughfoyleferry.com *(English)*

ROUTES OPERATED *Lough Foyle Service* Greencastle (Inishowen, Co Donegal, Republic of Ireland) - Magilligan (Co Londonderry, Northern Ireland) (10 mins; *(1 or 2)*; about every 20 mins), *Lough Swilly Service (1st April – 30th September)* Buncrana (Inishowen, Co Donegal) - Rathmullen (Co Donegal) (20 mins; *(1 or 2)*; hourly) Note: This service may start in September 2003 or April 2004 depending on delivery of vessel.

1	FOYLE RAMBLER	190t	72	10.0k	35.0m	100P	20C	-	BA	IR
2	FOYLE VENTURE	360t	78	10.0k	47.9m	300P	44C	-	BA	IR

FOYLE VENTURE Built at Bowling, Dumbarton, UK as the SHANNON WILLOW for *Shannon Ferry Ltd.* In 2000 replaced by the SHANNON BREEZE and laid up for sale. In 2003 sold to *Lough Foyle Ferry Company Ltd* and renamed the FOYLE VENTURE.

FOYLE RAMBLER Built in Germany as the STEDINGEN for *Fähren Bremen-Stedingen GmbH* to operate across the River Weser. In 2003 to be purchased by *Lough Foyle Ferry Company Ltd* and renamed the FOYLE RAMBLER. Delivery expected in September 2003 when her current service is replaced by a tunnel.

MURPHY'S FERRY SERVICE

THE COMPANY *Murphy's Ferry Service* is privately operated.

MANAGEMENT Operator Patrick Murphy.

ADDRESS Anchorage, Lawrence Cove, Bere Island, Co Cork, Republic of Ireland.

TELEPHONE Administration +353 (0)27 75014 **Mobile** +353 (0)87 2386095.

FAX Administration +353 (0)27 75014.

INTERNET Email info@murphysferry.com **Website** www.murphysferry.com *(English)*

ROUTE OPERATED Castletownbere (Pontoon - 3 miles to east of town centre) - Bere Island (Lawrence Cove, near Rerrin) (20 mins ; *(1)*; up to 8 per day).

1	IKOM K	55t	99	10.0k	16.0m	60P	4C	1L	B	IR

IKOM K Built at Arklow, Irish Republic for *Murphy's Ferry Service.*

NORTHLINK FERRIES

THE COMPANY *NorthLink Orkney and Shetland Ferries Ltd* is a Scottish company jointly owned by *Caledonian MacBrayne* and *The Royal Bank of Scotland*. It took over the service from Scotland to Orkney and Shetland from *P&O Scottish Ferries* in October 2002.

MANAGEMENT Chief Executive Bill Davidson, **Commercial Director** Gareth Crichton.

ADDRESS Ferry Terminal, Stromness, Orkney KW16 3BH.

TELEPHONE Administration +44 (0)1856 851144, **Reservations** +44 (0)845 6000 449.

FAX Administration +44 (0)1856 851155.

INTERNET Email info@northlinkferries.co.uk **Website** www.northlinkferries.co.uk *(English)*

ROUTES OPERATED Scrabster - Stromness (Orkney) (1 hr 30 min; *(1)*; up to 3 per day), Aberdeen - Lerwick (Shetland) (direct) (12 hrs; *(2,3)*; 3 northbound/4 southbound), Aberdeen - Kirkwall, Hatston New Pier (Orkney) (5 hrs 45 mins) - Lerwick (14 hrs) (*(2,3)*; 4 northbound/3 southbound per week).

1	HAMNAVOE	8600t	02	19.0k	112.0m	600P	95C	20L	BA	UK
2	HJALTLAND	12000t	02	24.0k	125.0m	600P	150C	30L	BA	UK
3	HROSSEY	12000t	02	24.0k	125.0m	600P	150C	30L	BA	UK

HAMNAVOE Built at Rauma, Finland for *NorthLink Orkney and Shetland Ferries Ltd* to operate on the Scrabster - Stromness route. Did not enter service until spring 2003 due to late completion of work at Scrabster to accommodate the ship. *Caledonian MacBrayne's* HEBRIDEAN ISLES covered between October 2002 and spring 2003.

HJALTLAND, HROSSEY Built at in Rauma, Finland for *NorthLink Orkney and Shetland Ferries Ltd* to operate on the Aberdeen - Kirkwall - Lerwick route when services started in 2002.

ORKNEY FERRIES

THE COMPANY *Orkney Ferries Ltd* (previously the *Orkney Islands Shipping Company*) is a British company, owned by *The Orkney Islands Council*.

MANAGEMENT Operations Director N H Mills, **Ferry Services Manager** A Henderson.

ADDRESS Shore Street, Kirkwall, Orkney KW15 1LG.

TELEPHONE Administration +44 (0)1856 872044, **Reservations** +44 (0)1856 872044.

FAX Administration & Reservations +44 (0)1856 872921, **Telex** 75475.

INTERNET Email info@orkneyferries.co.uk **Website** www.orkneyferries.co.uk *(English)*

ROUTES OPERATED Kirkwall (Mainland) to Eday (1 hr, 15 mins), Westray (1 hr 25 mins), Sanday (1 hr 25 mins), Stronsay (1 hr 35 mins), Papa Westray (1 hr 50 mins), North Ronaldsay (2 hrs 30 mins) ('North Isles service') (timings are direct from Kirkwall - sailings via other islands take longer; *(1,2,9)*; 1 per day except Papa Westray which is twice weekly and North Ronaldsay which is weekly), Pierowall (Westray) - Papa Westray (25 mins; *(4)*; up to six per day (passenger only)), Kirkwall - Shapinsay (25 mins; *(7)*; 6 per day), Houton (Mainland) to Lyness (Hoy) (35 mins; *(6)*; 5 per day), and Flotta (35 mins; *(6)*; 4 per day) ('South Isles service') (timings are direct from Houton - sailings via other islands take longer), Tingwall (Mainland) to Rousay (20 mins; *(3)*; 6 per day), Egilsay (30 mins; *(3)*; 5 per day) and Wyre (20 mins; *(3)*; 5 per day) (timings are direct from Tingwall - sailings via other islands take longer), Stromness (Mainland) to Moaness (Hoy) (25 mins; *(5)*; 2/3 per day) and Graemsay (25 mins; *(5)*; 2/3 per day) (passenger/cargo service - cars not normally conveyed).

1	EARL SIGURD	771t	90	12.0k	45.4m	190P	26C	-	BA	UK
2	EARL THORFINN	771t	90	12.0k	45.4m	190P	26C	-	BA	UK
3	EYNHALLOW	79t	87	9.5k	26.2m	95P	8C	-	BA	UK
4p	GOLDEN MARIANA	33t	73	9.5k	16.2m	40P	0C	-	-	UK
5	GRAEMSAY	82t	96	10.0k	17.1m	73P	1C	-	C	UK
6	HOY HEAD	358t	94	9.8k	39.6m	125P	18C	-	BA	UK
7	SHAPINSAY	199t	89	9.5k	30.2m	91P	12C	-	BA	UK
8	THORSVOE	400t	91	10.5k	35.1m	96P	16C	-	BA	UK
9	VARAGEN	950t	89	12.0k	50.0m	144P	33C	5L	BA	UK

EARL SIGURD, EARL THORFINN Built at Bromborough, Birkenhead, UK to inaugurate ro-ro working on the 'North Isles' service (see above).

EYNHALLOW Built at Bristol, UK to inaugurate ro-ro services from Tingwall (Mainland) to Rousay, Egilsay and Wyre. In 1991 she was lengthened by 5 metres, to increase car capacity.

Hoy Head *(Miles Cowsill)*

Pentalina B *(Miles Cowsill)*

GOLDEN MARIANA Built at Bideford, UK. Passenger only vessel. Generally operates feeder service between Pierowall (Westray) and Papa Westray.

GRAEMSAY Built at Troon UK to operate between Stromness (Mainland), Moaness (Hoy) and Graemsay. Designed to offer an all year round service to these islands, primarily for passengers and cargo.

HOY HEAD Built at Bideford, UK to replace the THORSVOE on the 'South Isles' service (see above).

SHAPINSAY Built at Hull, UK for the service from Kirkwall (Mainland) to Shapinsay.

THORSVOE Built at Campbeltown, UK for the 'South Isles' service (see above). In 1994 replaced by new HOY HEAD and became the main reserve vessel for the fleet.

VARAGEN Built at Selby, UK for *Orkney Ferries*, a private company established to start a new route between Gills Bay (Caithness, Scotland) and Burwick (South Ronaldsay, Orkney). However, due to problems with the terminals it was not possible to maintain regular services. In 1991, the company was taken over by *OISC* and the VARAGEN became part of their fleet, sharing 'North Isles' services with the EARL SIGURD and the EARL THORFINN and replacing the freight vessel ISLANDER (494t, 1969).

PASSAGE EAST FERRY

THE COMPANY *Passage East Ferry Company Ltd* is an Irish Republic private sector company.

MANAGEMENT Managing Director Derek Donnelly. **Operations Manager** Conor Gilligan.

ADDRESS Barrack Street, Passage East, Co Waterford, Republic of Ireland.

TELEPHONE Administration +353 (0)51 382480, **Reservations** Not applicable.

FAX Administration +353 (0)51 382598, **Reservations** Not applicable.

INTERNET Email passageferry@eircom.net **Website** www.passageferry.com *(English)*

ROUTE OPERATED Passage East (County Waterford) - Ballyhack (County Wexford) (7 mins; *(1)*; frequent service).

1	EDMUND D	300t	68	9.0k	45.1m	143P	30C	-	BA	IR

EDMUND D Built at Dartmouth UK as the SHANNON HEATHER for *Shannon Ferry Ltd* and used on their service between Killimer (County Clare) and Tarbert (County Kerry). Withdrawn from regular service in 1996 and, in 1997, sold to *Passage East Ferry* and renamed the EDMUND D. She entered service in January 1998.

PENTLAND FERRIES

THE COMPANY *Pentland Ferries* is a UK private sector company.

Managing Director Andrew Banks, **Marketing Manager** Linda Knott.

ADDRESS Pier Road, St Margaret's Hope, South Ronaldsay, Orkney KW172SW.

TELEPHONE Administration & Reservations +44 (0)1856 831226.

FAX Administration & Reservations +44 (0)1856 831614.

INTERNET Email sales@pentlandferries.co.uk **Website** www.pentlandferries.com *(English)*

ROUTE OPERATED Gills Bay (Scotland) - St Margaret's Hope (South Ronaldsay, Orkney) (1 hr; *(1,2)*; 3 per day).

1	CLAYMORE	1871t	78	14.0k	77.2m	300P	50C	8T	AS	UK
2	PENTALINA B	1908t	70	16.0k	74.3m	250P	46C	7L	BAS	UK

CLAYMORE Built at Leith, UK for *Caledonian MacBrayne* for the Oban - Castlebay/Lochboisdale service, also serving Coll and Tiree between October and May, replacing the IONA (see the

PENTALINA B, *Pentland Ferries*). In 1989 she was transferred to the Kennacraig - Port Ellen/Port Askaig (Islay) route, again replacing the IONA. In summer she also operated a weekly service from Port Askaig (Islay) to Colonsay and Oban. She relieved on the Ardrossan - Brodick service during winter 1990. In autumn 1993 she was replaced by the ISLE OF ARRAN and became a spare vessel. Her summer duties in 1994, 1995 and 1996 included Saturday sailings from Ardrossan to Douglas (Isle of Man), returning on Sundays plus standby duties and charter to the *Isle of Man Steam Packet Company* to provide extra sailings between Heysham and Douglas during the TT Season. During the winter she was general relief vessel, spending several months on Islay sailings. In 1997 she was sold to *Sea Containers* to operate for *Sea Containers Ferries Scotland Ltd* (trading as the *Argyll and Antrim Steam Packet Company*) between Campbeltown (Scotland) and Ballycastle (Northern Ireland) (summer only). During the winter she has been chartered back to *Caledonian MacBrayne* to cover during the refit period. The Campbeltown - Ballycastle service did not resume in 2000 and during the summer she was chartered to *Strandfaraskip Landsins* of the Faroe Islands and used on the Tórshavn - Suderoy service. She was then laid up for sale. In 2002 she was sold to *Pentland Ferries* and inaugurated a new Invergordon - St Margaret's Hope service. This service was withdrawn after a short period and she was laid up until the summer period when it was planned she would operate along-side the PENTALINA B.

PENTALINA B Built at Troon, UK as the IONA for *David MacBrayne*. She was built to operate the Islay service. However, shortly after the order was placed, plans to build a new pier at Redhouse, near the mouth of West Loch Tarbert, were abandoned, so she was not able to operate on this route until *Caledonian MacBrayne* acquired the *Western Ferries'* pier in deeper water at Kennacraig in 1978. She operated on the Gourock - Dunoon service in 1970 and 1971, between Mallaig and Kyle of Lochalsh and Stornoway in 1972 and between Oban and Craignure in 1973. From 1974 until 1978 she operated mainly on the Oban to Castlebay/Lochboisdale service and in addition the winter Oban - Coll/Tiree route. From 1978 until 1989 she operated mainly on the Islay service. In 1989 she was replaced by the CLAYMORE and then replaced the PIONEER as the summer Mallaig - Armadale vessel. Full ro-ro working was introduced on the route in 1994 and she also operated a twice weekly sailing between Mallaig, Lochboisdale and Castlebay and, in 1997, a weekly Mallaig - Coll and Tiree sailing. She was withdrawn in October 1997 and sold to *Pentland Ferries*. In 1998 she was renamed the PENTALINA B. In spring 1998 she was chartered back to *Caledonian MacBrayne* to operate between Oban and Craignure following the breakdown of the ISLE OF MULL. Pentland Ferries services started in summer 2001.

RED FUNNEL FERRIES

THE COMPANY *Red Funnel Ferries* is the trading name of the *Southampton, Isle of Wight and South of England Royal Mail Steam Packet Public Limited Company*, a British private sector company. The company was acquired by *JP Morgan International Capital Corporation* in 2000.

MANAGEMENT Managing Director A M Whyte, **Marketing Director** Ms O H Glass.

ADDRESS 12 Bugle Street, Southampton SO14 2JY.

TELEPHONE Administration +44 (0)870 444 8889, **Reservations** +44 (0)870 444 8898.

FAX Administration & Reservations +44 (0)870 444 8897.

INTERNET Email post@redfunnel.co.uk **Website** www.redfunnel.co.uk *(English)*

ROUTES OPERATED Conventional Ferries Southampton - East Cowes (55 mins; *(1,2,7)*; hourly). **Fast Passenger Ferries** Southampton - Cowes (22 mins; *(3,4,5,6)*; every half hour).

1	RED EAGLE	3028t	96	13.0k	83.6m	895P	140C	16L	BA	UK
2	RED FALCON	2881t	94	13.0k	83.6m	895P	140C	16L	BA	UK
3»p	RED JET 1	168t	91	34.0k	31.5m	138P	0C	0L	-	UK
4»p	RED JET 2	168t	91	34.0k	31.5m	138P	0C	0L	-	UK
5»p	RED JET 3	213t	98	34.0k	32.9m	190P	0C	0L	-	UK
6»p	RED JET 4	345t	03	35.0k	39.0m	277P	0C	0L	-	UK

7	RED OSPREY	2881t	94	13.0k	83.6m	895P	140C	16L	BA	UK

RED EAGLE, RED FALCON, RED OSPREY Built at Port Glasgow, UK for the Southampton - East Cowes service.

RED JET 1, RED JET 2, RED JET 3 FBM Marine catamarans built at Cowes, UK for the Southampton - Cowes service.

RED JET 4 North West Bay Ships Pty Ltd catamaran built in Hobart, Tasmania, Australia for the Southampton - Cowes service. Due to enter service in June.

SHANNON FERRY LTD

THE COMPANY *Shannon Ferry Ltd* is an Irish Republic private company owned by six families on both sides of the Shannon Estuary.

MANAGEMENT Managing Director J J Meehan.

ADDRESS Ferry Terminal, Killimer, County Clare, Republic of Ireland.

TELEPHONE Administration +353 (0)65 9053124, **Reservations** Not applicable.

FAX Administration +353 (0)65 9053125, **Reservations** Not applicable.

INTERNET Email enquiries@shannonferries.com **Website** www.shannonferries.com *(English, German, French, Italian)*

ROUTE OPERATED Killimer (County Clare) - Tarbert (County Kerry) (20 mins; *(1,2)*; hourly (half hourly during June, July, August and September). The company is also planning to establish a new service been Headford and Oughterard in Country Galway, across Lake Corrib. The vessel would be cable operated and accommodate up to 24 cars. It is unlikely to start before 2004/5.

1	SHANNON BREEZE	611t	00	10.0k	80.8m	350P	60C	-	BA	IR
2	SHANNON DOLPHIN	501t	95	10.0k	71.9m	350P	52C	-	BA	IR

SHANNON BREEZE, SHANNON DOLPHIN Built at Appledore, UK for *Shannon Ferry Ltd*.

SHETLAND ISLANDS COUNCIL

THE COMPANY *Shetland Islands Council* is a British Local Government authority.

MANAGEMENT Divisional Manager - Ferry Operations Ken Deurden, **Marine Superintendents** Capt William MacTear and Capt William Clark.

ADDRESS Port Administration Building, Sella Ness, Mossbank, Shetland ZE2 9QR.

TELEPHONE Administration +44(0)1806 244262, 244252, **Reservations/Voicebank**

Bressay Not Bookable/+44 (0)7626 980317, ***Fair Isle*** +44 (0)1595 760222/+44 (0)7626 986763 ***Foula*** +44 (0)1595 753226/+44 (0)7626 986763, ***Papa Stour*** +44 (0)1595 810460/+44 (0)7626 986763, ***Skerries*** +44 (0)1806 515226/+44 (0)7626 983633, ***Whalsay*** +44 (0)1806 566259/+44 (0)7626 983633, ***Yell, Unst, Fetlar*** +44 (0)1957 722259/+44 (0)7626 980735/980209.

FAX +44 (0)1806 244232.

INTERNET Emails: Ken.Duerden@sic.shetland.gov.uk William.MacTear@sic.shetiand.gov.uk, Bill.Clark@sic.shetland.gov.uk Lara.Jamieson@sic.shetland.gov.uk

Website: www.shetland.gov.uk/ferryinfo/ferry.htm *(English)*

ROUTES OPERATED Toft (Mainland) - Ulsta (Yell) (20 mins; *(1,8)*; up to 26 per day), Gutcher (Yell) - Belmont (Unst) (10 mins; *(3,4)*; 30 per day), Gutcher - Oddsta (Fetlar) (25 mins; *(3,4)*; 6 per day), Lerwick (Mainland) - Maryfield (Bressay) (5 mins; *(10)*; 19 per day), Laxo/Vidlin (Mainland) - Symbister (Whalsay) (30-45 mins; *(5,11)*; 17 per day), Lerwick (Mainland) - Skerries (3 hrs; *(13 (later 2))*; 2 per week), Vidlin (Mainland) - Out Skerries (1 hr 30 mins; *(13 (later 2))*; 7 per week), Grutness (Mainland) - Fair Isle (3 hrs; *(6)*; 2 per week), West Burrafirth (Mainland) - Papa Stour (40 mins; *(9 (later 13))*; 7 per week), Walls/Scalloway (Mainland) - Foula (3 hrs; *(12)*; 2 per week).

1	BIGGA	274t	91	11.0k	33.5m	96P	21C	4L	BA	UK
2	FILLA	351t	03	12.0k	35.5m	30P	10C	2L	BA	UK
3	FIVLA	230t	85	11.0k	29.9m	95P	15C	4L	BA	UK
4	FYLGA	147t	75	8.5k	25.3m	93P	10C	2L	BA	UK
5	GEIRA	226t	88	10.8k	29.9m	95P	15C	4L	BA	UK
6	GOOD SHEPHERD IV	76t	86	10.0k	18.3m	12P	1C	0L	C	UK
7	GRIMA	147t	74	8.5k	25.3m	93P	10C	2L	BA	UK
8	HENDRA	225t	82	11.0k	33.8m	100P	18C	4L	BA	UK
9	KOADA	35t	69	8.0k	14.6m	12P	1C	0L	C	UK
10	LEIRNA	420t	92	9.0k	35.1m	100P	20C	4L	BA	UK
11	LINGA	400t	01	11.0k	35.8m	100P	16C	2L	BA	UK
12	NEW ADVANCE	25t	96	8.7k	9.8m	12P	1C	0L	C	UK
13	SNOLDA	130t	83	9.0k	24.4m	12P	6C	1L	A	UK
14•	THORA	147t	75	8.5k	25.3m	93P	10C	2L	BA	UK

BIGGA Built at St Monans, UK. Used on the Toft - Ulsta service.

FILLA Built at Gdansk, Poland for the Lerwick /Vidlin - Out Skerries service.

FIVLA Built at Troon, UK. Used on the Gutcher - Belmont service.

FYLGA Built at Tórshavn, UK. Used on the Gutcher - Oddsta service.

GEIRA Built at Hessle, UK. Used on the Laxo - Symbister route.

GOOD SHEPHERD IV Built at St Monans, UK. Used on the service between Grutness (Mainland) and Fair Isle. Vehicles conveyed by special arrangement and generally consist of agricultural vehicles. She is pulled up on marine slip on Fair Isle at the conclusion of each voyage.

GRIMA Built at Bideford, UK. Used on the Lerwick (Mainland) - Maryfield (Bressay) service until 1992 when she was replaced by the LEIRNA and became a spare vessel.

HENDRA Built at Bromborough, Birkenhead, UK for the Laxo - Symbister service. In 2002 transferred to the Toft - Ulsta service.

KOADA Built at Bideford, UK. Built as an inshore trawler and bought by the shareholders on Fair Isle to operate to Shetland and named the GOOD SHEPHERD III. In 1986 the service was taken over by *Shetland Islands Council* and she was replaced by GOOD SHEPHERD IV. She was however acquired by the *Shetland Islands Council* and renamed the KOADA. Until 2003, she operated between West Burrafirth (Mainland) and Papa Stour (operation to Foula having ceased following the delivery of the NEW ADVANCE). Car carrying capacity used occasionally. Later in 2003 to be replaced by the SNOLDA and laid up.

LEIRNA Built at Port Glasgow, UK. Used on the Lerwick - Maryfield (Bressay) service.

LINGA Built at Gdansk, Poland. Used on the Laxo - Symbister service.

NEW ADVANCE Built at Penryn, UK for the Foula service. Although built at Penryn, she was completed at Stromness in Orkney. She has a Cygnus Marine GM38 hull and is based on the island where she can be lifted out of the water. Vehicle capacity is to take new vehicles to the island - not for tourist vehicles. Mainland ports used are Walls and Scalloway.

SNOLDA Built at Flekkefjord, Norway as the FILLA. Used on the Lerwick (Mainland) - Out Skerries and Vidlin (Mainland) - Out Skerries services. At other times she operates freight and charter services around the Shetland Archipelago. She resembles a miniature oil rig supply vessel. Passenger capacity was originally 20 from 1st April to 31st October inclusive but is now 12 all year. In 2003 renamed the SNOLDA; to be replaced by the new FILLA, and transferred to the West Burrafirth - Papa Stour route, replacing the KOADA. A new pier and linkspan is being built on the island.

THORA Built at Tórshavn, Faroe Islands. Sister vessel to the FYLGA and the GRIMA. After a period as a spare vessel, in 1998 she took over the Laxo - Symbister service from the withdrawn KJELLA.

Geira *(Miles Cowsill)*

Linga *(Miles Cowsill)*

SECTION 2 – DOMESTIC SERVICES

Withdrawn in 2001. Now a spare vessel.

Under Construction

| 15 | NEWBUILDING 1 | - | 04 | 12.0k | 61m | 145P | 30C | 4L | BA | UK |
| 16 | NEWBUILDING 2 | - | 04 | 12.0k | 61m | 145P | 30C | 4L | BA | UK |

NEWBUILDING 1, NEWBUILDING 2 To be built in Poland to replace the BIGGA and HENDRA on Yell Sound. These vessels will be used as spares and the THORA and GRIMA will be sold. New terminals are to be constructed at Toft and Ulsta on Yell Sound.

STRANGFORD LOUGH FERRY SERVICE

THE COMPANY The *Strangford Lough Ferry Service* is operated by the *DRD (Department for Regional Development)*, a Northern Ireland Government Department.

MANAGEMENT Ferry Manager D Pedlow.

ADDRESS Strangford Lough Ferry Service, Strangford, Co Down BT30 7NE.

TELEPHONE Administration +44 (0)28 4488 1637, **Reservations** Not applicable.

FAX Administration +44 (0)28 4488 1249, **Reservations** Not applicable.

ROUTE OPERATED Strangford - Portaferry (County Down) (10 mins; *(1,2)*; half hourly).

| 1 | PORTAFERRY II | 312t | 01 | 12.0k | 38.2m | 260P | 28C | - | BA | UK |
| 2 | STRANGFORD FERRY | 186t | 69 | 10.0k | 32.9m | 263P | 20C | - | BA | UK |

PORTAFERRY II Built at Bromborough, Birkenhead, UK for *DRD (Northern Ireland)*.

STRANGFORD FERRY Built at Cork, Irish Republic for *Down County Council*. Subsequently transferred to the *DOE (Northern Ireland)* and then the *DRD (Northern Ireland)*. Following delivery of the PORTAFERRY II, she became reserve ferry.

C TOMS & SON LTD

THE COMPANY *C Toms & Son Ltd* is a British private sector company.

MANAGEMENT Managing Director Mr Allen Toms.

ADDRESS East Street, Polruan, Fowey, Cornwall PL23 1PB.

TELEPHONE Administration +44 (0)1726 870232.

FAX Administration +44 (0)1726 870318.

ROUTE OPERATED Fowey - Bodinnick (Cornwall) (5 mins; *(1,2)*; frequent).

1	GELLAN	-	03	4.5k	36.0m	50P	10C	-	BA	UK
2	JENACK	60t	00	4.5k	36.0m	50P	15C	-	BA	UK
3•	NO 4	-	75	-	15.8m	48P	8C	-	BA	-

GELLAN, JENACK Built at Fowey, UK by *C Toms & Sons Ltd*. Self propelled and steered.

NO 4 Built at Fowey, UK by *C Toms & Son Ltd*. Float propelled by motor launch. No longer used.

VALENTIA ISLAND FERRIES

THE COMPANY *Valentia Island Ferries Ltd* is an Irish Republic private sector company.

MANAGEMENT Manager Richard Foran.

ADDRESS Valentia Island, County Kerry, Republic of Ireland.

TELEPHONE Administration +353 (0)66 76141, **Reservations** Not applicable.

FAX Administration +353 (0)66 76377, **Reservations** Not applicable.

INTERNET Email reforan@indigo.ie **Website** www.kerrygems.ie/valentiaferry/ *(English)*

ROUTE OPERATED Reenard (Co Kerry) - Knightstown (Valentia Island) (5 minutes; *(1)*; frequent service, 1st April - 30th September).

1	GOD MET ONS III	95t	63	-	43.0m	95P	18C	-	BA	IR

GOD MET ONS III Built at Millingen, Netherlands for *FMHE Res* of the Netherlands for a service across the River Maas between Cuijk and Middelaar. In 1987 a new bridge was opened and the service ceased. She was latterly used on contract work in the Elbe and then laid up. In 1996 acquired by *Valentia Island Ferries* and inaugurated a car ferry service to the island. Note: this island never had a car ferry service before. A bridge was opened at the south end of the island in 1970; before that a passenger/cargo service operated between Reenard Point and Knightstown.

WESTERN FERRIES

THE COMPANY *Western Ferries (Clyde) Ltd* is a British private sector company.

MANAGEMENT Managing Director Kenneth C Cadenhead.

ADDRESSES Hunter's Quay, Dunoon PA23 8HJ.

TELEPHONE Administration +44 (0)1369 704452, **Reservations** Not applicable.

FAX Administration +44 (0)1369 706020, **Reservations** Not applicable.

INTERNET Email enquiries@western-ferries.co.uk **Website** www.western-ferries.co.uk *(English)*

ROUTE OPERATED McInroy's Point (Gourock) - Hunter's Quay (Dunoon) (20 mins; *(1,2,3,4)*; half hourly).

1	SOUND OF SANDA	403t	64	10.0k	48.4m	220P	37C	4/5L	BA	UK
2	SOUND OF SCALPAY	403t	61	10.0k	48.4m	220P	37C	4/5L	BA	UK
3	SOUND OF SCARBA	489t	01	11.0k	49.5m	220P	40C	4/5L	BA	UK
4	SOUND OF SLEAT	466t	61	10.0k	39.9m	296P	30C	4/5L	BA	UK

SOUND OF SANDA Built at Walsum, Germany as the G24 for *Amsterdam City Council* and operated from Centraal Station to the other side of the River IJ. In 1996 purchased by *Western Ferries* and renamed the SOUND OF SANDA.

SOUND OF SCALPAY Built at Arnhem, Netherlands as the G23 for *Amsterdam City Council*. In 1995 sold to *Western Ferries* and renamed the SOUND OF SCALPAY.

SOUND OF SCARBA Built at Port Glasgow, UK for *Western Ferries*.

SOUND OF SLEAT Built at Hardinxveld, Netherlands as the DE HOORN for the service between Maassluis and Rozenburg, across the 'Nieuwe Waterweg' (New Waterway) in The Netherlands. In 1988 she was purchased by *Western Ferries* and renamed the SOUND OF SLEAT.

Under Construction

5	SOUND OF SHUNA	489t	03	11.0k	49.5m	220P	40C	4/5L	BA	UK

SOUND OF SHUNA Under construction at Port Glasgow, UK for *Western Ferries*. Due to enter service in September 2003.

St Clare *(John Hendy)*

Caedmon *(John Hendy)*

WIGHTLINK

THE COMPANY *Wightlink* is a British private sector company, owned by the management. The routes and vessels were previously part of *Sealink* but were excluded from the purchase of most of the *Sealink* operations by *Stena Line AB* in 1990. They remained in *Sea Containers'* ownership until purchased by *CINVen* Ltd, a venture capital company. The company was the subject of a management buy-out in 2001.

MANAGEMENT Chairman Michael Aiken, **Head of Marketing** Janet Saville.

ADDRESS PO Box 59, Portsmouth PO1 2XB.

TELEPHONE Administration +44 (0)23 9281 2011, **Reservations** 08705 827744 (from UK only), +44 (0)23 9281 2011 (from overseas).

FAX Administration & Reservations +44 (0)23 9285 5257, **Telex** 86440 WIGHTLG.

INTERNET Email info@wightlink.co.uk **Website** www.wightlink.co.uk *(English)*

ROUTES OPERATED Conventional Ferries Lymington - Yarmouth (Isle of Wight) (approx 30 mins; *(1,2,3)*; half hourly), Portsmouth - Fishbourne (Isle of Wight) (approx 35 mins; *(8,9,10,11,12)*; half hourly or hourly depending on time of day). **Fast Passenger Ferries** Portsmouth - Ryde (Isle of Wight) (passenger only) (approx 15 mins; *(4,5,6,7)*; half hourly/hourly).

1	CAEDMON	764t	73	9.5k	57.9m	512P	58C	6L	BA	UK
2	CENRED	761t	73	9.5k	57.9m	512P	58C	6L	BA	UK
3	CENWULF	761t	73	9.5k	57.9m	512P	58C	6L	BA	UK
4»p	FASTCAT RYDE	478t	96	34.0k	40.0m	361P	0C	0L	-	UK
5»p	FASTCAT SHANKLIN	478t	96	34.0k	40.0m	361P	0C	0L	-	UK
6»p	OUR LADY PAMELA	312t	86	28.5k	29.5m	410P	0C	0L	-	UK
7»p	OUR LADY PATRICIA	312t	86	28.5k	29.5m	410P	0C	0L	-	UK
8	ST CATHERINE	2038t	83	12.5k	77.0m	771P	142C	12L	BA	UK
9	ST CECILIA	2968t	86	12.5k	77.0m	771P	142C	12L	BA	UK
10	ST CLARE	3500t	01	13.0k	86.0m	800P	180C	-	BA	UK
11	ST FAITH	3009t	90	12.5k	77.0m	771P	142C	12L	BA	UK
12	ST HELEN	2983t	83	12.5k	77.0m	771P	142C	12L	BA	UK

CAEDMON Built at Dundee, UK for *Sealink* for the Portsmouth - Fishbourne service. In 1983 transferred to the Lymington - Yarmouth service.

CENRED, CENWULF Built at Dundee, UK for *Sealink* for the Lymington - Yarmouth service.

FASTCAT RYDE Kværner Fjellstrand Flyingcat 40m built at Singapore as the WATER JET 1 for *Waterjet Netherlands Antilles* and operated in the Philippines. In 1999 withdrawn from service and renamed the SUPERCAT 17. In summer 2000 sold to *Wightlink* and renamed the FASTCAT RYDE. After modifications, entered service on the Portsmouth - Ryde route in autumn 2000.

FASTCAT SHANKLIN Kværner Fjellstrand Flyingcat 40m built at Singapore as the WATER JET 2 for *Waterjet Netherlands Antilles* and operated in the Philippines. In 1999 withdrawn from service and renamed the SUPERCAT 18. In summer 2000 sold to *Wightlink* and renamed the FASTCAT SHANKLIN. After modifications, entered service on the Portsmouth - Ryde route in autumn 2000.

OUR LADY PAMELA, OUR LADY PATRICIA InCat 30 m catamarans built at Hobart, Tasmania, Australia for *Sealink* for the Portsmouth - Ryde service. Now spare vessels.

ST CATHERINE, ST HELEN Built at Leith, UK for *Sealink* for the Portsmouth - Fishbourne service.

ST CECILIA, ST FAITH Built at Selby, UK for *Sealink* for the Portsmouth - Fishbourne service.

ST CLARE Built at Gdansk, Poland for *Wightlink* for the Portsmouth - Fishbourne service. She is a double ended ferry with a central bridge.

WOOLWICH FREE FERRY

THE COMPANY The *Woolwich Free Ferry* is operated by the *London Borough of Greenwich*, a British municipal authority.

MANAGEMENT Ferry Manager Capt P Deeks.

ADDRESS New Ferry Approach, Woolwich, London SE18 6DX.

TELEPHONE Administration +44 (0)20 8921 5786, +44 (0)20 8921 5967, **Reservations** Not applicable.

FAX Administration +44 (0)20 8316 6096, **Reservations** Not applicable.

INTERNET Email peter.deeks@greenwich.gov.uk

Website www.greenwich.gov.uk/council/strategicplanning/ferry.htm (English)

ROUTE OPERATED Woolwich - North Woolwich (free ferry) (5 mins; *(1,2,3)*; every 9 mins (weekdays - two ferries in operation), every 16 mins (weekends - one ferry in operation)). Note: one ferry is always in reserve/under maintenance.

1	ERNEST BEVIN	738t	63	8.0k	56.7m	310P	32C	6L	BA	UK
2	JAMES NEWMAN	738t	63	8.0k	56.7m	310P	32C	6L	BA	UK
3	JOHN BURNS	738t	63	8.0k	56.7m	310P	32C	6L	BA	UK

ERNEST BEVIN, JAMES NEWMAN, JOHN BURNS Built at Dundee, UK for the *London County Council* who operated the service in 1963. In 1965 ownership was transferred to the *Greater London Council*. Following the abolition of the *GLC* in April 1986, ownership was transferred to the *Department of Transport* and in 2001 to *Transport for London*. The *London Borough of Greenwich* operate the service on their behalf. An alternative loading is 6m x 18m articulated lorries cars and 14 cars; lorries of this length are too long for the nearby northbound Blackwall Tunnel.

FastCat Shanklin *(John Hendy)*

Red Jet 3 *(John Hendy)*

LEANDER

Oleander *(Mike Louagie)*

section 3 freight only services
gb & ireland

BRITTANY FERRIES

THE COMPANY *See section 1.* The freight division of *Brittany Ferries* traded as *Truckline Ferries* until 2002.

MANAGEMENT Managing Director David Longden, **Freight Director** John Clarke.

ADDRESS New Harbour Road, POOLE, Dorset BH15 4AJ.

TELEPHONE Administration & Enquiries +44 (0)8709 013300, **Reservations** +44 (0)8709 040200.

FAX Administration & Reservations +44 (0)1202 679828, **Telex** 41744, 41745.

INTERNET Website www.truckline.co.uk *(English)*

ROUTES OPERATED Cherbourg (***Winter*** *dep: 09.30 Wed, Fri, Sun, 18.30 Tue, Thu, Sat, 23.45 Mon, Wed, Fri, Sun,* ***Summer*** *02.00 Mon, Sat, Sun, 09.30 Tue, Thu, 14.30 Fri, Sat, Sun, 18.30 Mon, Wed, 23.45 Tue, Thu)* - Poole (***Winter*** *dep: 16.00 Mon, Wed, Fri, Sun, 08.30, 23.45 Tue, Thu, Sat,* ***Summer*** *dep: 16.00 Tue, Thu, 08.30, 23.45 Mon, Wed, 07.30, 23.45 Fri, Sat, Sun)* (4 hrs 30 mins; *(1)*; 1/2 per day). Note Operates with the passenger vessel BARFLEUR to provide three or four sailings every 24 hrs.

1	COUTANCES	6507t	78	17.0k	125.2m	58P	-	58T	BA	FR

COUTANCES Built at Le Havre, France for *Truckline Ferries* for their Cherbourg - Poole service. In 1986 lengthened to increase vehicle capacity by 34%.

CALEDONIAN MACBRAYNE

THE COMPANY, MANAGEMENT , ADDRESS , TELEPHONE & INTERNET See section 2.

ROUTE OPERATED Ullapool - Stornoway (Lewis) (3 hours; *(1)*; 1 per day) (no fixed schedule - run according to demand).

1	MUIRNEAG	5801t	79	15.5k	105.6m	0P	-	54T	AS	UK

MUIRNEAG Built at Frederikshavn, Denmark as the MERCANDIAN CARRIER II for *Mercandia* of Denmark and used on a variety of services. In 1983 she was briefly renamed ALIANZA and between 1984 and 1985 she carried the name CARRIER II. In 1985 sold to *P&O*, renamed the BELARD and used on *Northern Ireland Trailers* services between Ardrossan and Belfast (later Larne), subsequently becoming part of *Pandoro*. In 1993 she was chartered to *IOMSP* subsidiary *Mannin Line* to inaugurate a new service between Great Yarmouth and IJmuiden. In 1994 she was purchased by *IOMSP*; however, in 1995 the *Mannin Line* service ceased and she was chartered back to *Pandoro*. At the end of 1995 she was returned to *IOMSP*. In 1996, after deputising for the PEVERIL, she was briefly chartered to *Exxtor Ferries* (operating between Immingham and Rotterdam) and then laid up. In 1997, she again deputised for the PEVERIL, followed by a short period of charter to *P&O European Ferries*. In 1997 she returned to *IOMSP* and replaced the PEVERIL as the main freight vessel. In 1998 she was sold to the *Aabrenaa Rederi* and operated between Åbenrå and Klaipeda. This service ended in 199 and she was used on a number of short term charters. In spring 2002 chartered to *Ferryways* and operated between Ipswich and Ostend. In autumn 2002 she was chartered to *Caledonian MacBrayne*, renamed the MUIRNEAG and placed on the Ullapool – Stornoway service, replacing the HASCOSAY (see *NorthLink*).

Muirneag *(Rob de Visser)*

Commodore Goodwill *(Brian D. Smith)*

SECTION 3 – FREIGHT ONLY FERRIES

CETAM

THE COMPANY *CETAM* (*Compagnie Européenne de Transport Automobile par Mer*) is a French company, owned by the *Hual Group* of Norway.

MANAGEMENT Managing Director: Geir Berger, **General Manager Southampton Agents:** Roger Thornton.

ADDRESS 923:21 rue du Faubourg St Honoré, BP 16.08 75363 Paris Cedex 08, **UK Agents** Wainwright Bros & Co Ltd, Bowling Green House, Orchard Place, Southampton SO14 3PX.

TELEPHONE Administration and Reservations *France* + 33 1 53 30 85 80, *UK* +44 (0)23 80 223671.

FAX Administration & Reservations: *France* + 33 1 53 30 75 95, *UK* +44 (0)23 80 330880.

TELEX *France* 285 130 AUTOPAR

INTERNET Email *France* g.berger@cetam.fr *UK* r.thornton@wainwrightgroup.com

Websites www.cetam.fr www.wainwrightgroup.com *(English)*

ROUTE OPERATED Southampton *(dep: 12.00 Wed)* - Santander (Spain) *(dep: 16.00 Fri)* (1 per week; *(1)*; 35/40 hours).

1	CETAM VICTORIAE	10100t	77	17.5k	142.3m	12P	-	105T	A	FI

CETAM VICTORIAE Built at Fredrikstad, Norway as the BORE SKY for *Bore Line* of Finland and used on services between Finland, Northern Europe and Britain; subsequently sold and chartered back. In 1991 *Bore Line* began to pull out of regular shipping services, the charter ceased and she was renamed the BLUE SKY. In 1992 she was chartered to *Transfennica* and renamed the BORDEN. She was used on a service between Finland and Harwich (Navyard). She was later moved to other Transfennica routes. In summer 2001 she was chartered to *SeaWind Line* to provide extra capacity on their Stockholm - Turku service. In 2002 chartered to *ArgoGood* to operate Hull - Cuxhaven - Hanko - Helsinki. She is now owned by *Rederi AB Engship*. In autumn 2002 chartered to *CETAM* and renamed the CETAM VICTORIAE, replacing the previous CETAM VICTORIAE (ex SEAHAWK, 2002).

COBELFRET FERRIES

THE COMPANY *Cobelfret Ferries nv* is a Belgian private sector company, a subsidiary of *Cobelfret nv* of Antwerp.

MANAGEMENT Operations Manager (Belgium) Marc Vandersteen, **UK** *Purfleet and Dagenham services* Cobelfret Ferries UK Ltd - **General Manager, Line & Agency Division** Nick Kavanagh, *Immingham Services* Cobelfret Ferries UK Ltd (Immingham Branch) - **General Manager** Peter Kirman.

ADDRESS *Belgium* B-8380 Zeebrugge, Belgium, *UK Purfleet* Purfleet Thames Terminal, London Road, Purfleet, Essex RM19 1RP, *UK Immingham* Cobelfret Ferries UK Ltd (Immingham Branch), Manby Road, Immingham, South Humberside DN40 3EG.

TELEPHONE Administration & Reservations *Belgium* +32 (0)50 502243, *UK (Purfleet)* +44 (0)1708 891199, *(Immingham)* +44 (0)1469 573115.

FAX Administration & Reservations *Belgium* +32 (0)50 502219, *UK (Purfleet)* +44 (0)1708 890853, *(Immingham)* +44 (0)1469 573739.

INTERNET Email *Zeebrugge* pur.cobzee@cobelfretferries.be

Purfleet nick.kavanagh@cobelfretfrerries.co.uk **Website:** www.cobelfret.com *(English)*

ROUTES OPERATED Zeebrugge *(dep: 04.00 Tue-Fri, 10.00 Mon-Fri, 16.00 Mon-Fri, 22.00 Mon-Fri)* - Purfleet *(dep: 06.00 Tue-Fri, 12.00 Mon-Fri, 18.00 Mon-Fri, 23.00 Mon-Fri (Note: weekend service run subject to demand and are liable to vary)* (9 hrs; *(3,8,14,19,20)*; 4 per day), Vlissingen *(dep: 02.00 Tue-Fri, 10.00 Mon-Fri, 18.00 Mon-Fri)* - Dagenham *(dep 01.00 Tue-Fri, 09.00 Mon-Fri, 17.00*

Mon-Fri) (contract service for Ford Motor Company) (13 hrs; *(5,6,17,18)*; 3 per day), Rotterdam (Brittanniehaven) *(dep: 17.00 Sat, 20.00 Mon-Fri)* - Purfleet *(dep: 16.00 Sat, 19.00 Mon-Fri)* (14 hrs; *(1,8)*; 1 per day (Note: if the service is carrying imported Ford cars, the ship will, after discharge at Purfleet, continue to Dagenham to unload there), Zeebrugge *(dep: 17.00 Sat, 19.00 Mon-Fri)* - Immingham *(17.00 Sat, 19.00 Mon-Fri (plus unadvertised extra sailings))* (14 hrs; *(4,11)* *(Sunday sailings as required))*; 1/2 per day), Rotterdam (Brittanniehaven) *(dep: 17.30)* - Immingham *(dep: 17.30)* (14 hrs; *(7,9)*; 1 per day), Zeebrugge *(dep: 06.00 Sun, 09.00 Mon, 12.00 Tue, 18.00 Wed, 18.00 Thu, 22.00 Fri)* - Gothenburg *(dep: 16.00 Sun, 00.01 Tue, 00.01 Wed, 04.00 Thu, 13.00 Fri, 13.00 Sat)* (33-38 hrs; *(12,14,15)*; 6 per week) (this service is operated by *Wagenborg* of the Netherlands for the *Stora-Enso* paper and board group, for the conveyance of their products. *Cobelfret Ferries* act as handling agents at Zeebrugge and market the surplus capacity on the vessels, which is available for general ro-ro traffic. Although this route is strictly outside the scope of this book it is included for the sake of completeness). The Dagenham - Zeebrugge service was moved the Vlissingen in spring 2003. Correct at 23rd May 2003; ships are quite frequently moved between routes so the above may have changed by the time this book is published.

1	AMANDINE	14715t	78	14.5k	172.9m	12P	-	133T	A	BS
2	CATHERINE	21287t	02	20.0k	182.2m	12P		200T	A2	SW
3	CELANDINE	23986t	00	18.0k	162.5m	12P	630C	157T	A	BS
4	CLEMENTINE	23986t	97	17.8k	162.5m	24P	630C	157T	A	LX
5	CYMBELINE	11866t	92	14.5k	147.4m	8P	350C	100T	A2	LX
6	EGLANTINE	10035t	89	14.5k	147.4m	8P	350C	100T	A2	LX
7	EVA ODEN	16950t	79	15.0k	170.3m	12P	180C	160T	A	SW
8	HOBURGEN	9082t	86	15.0k	121.5m	12P	-	100T	A	BS
9	LOUISE RUSS	18400t	00	23.5k	174.0m	12P	-	171T	A	GI
10	MARABOU	10931t	78	17.0k	161.4m	12P	-	102T	A2	BZ
11	MELUSINE	23987t	99	18.0k	162.5m	12P	630C	157T	A	LX
12	SCHIEBORG	21005t	00	17.0k	183.4m	12P	-	180T	A	NL
13	SEA CRUSADER	23986t	96	17.8k	162.5m	24P	630C	157T	A	UK
14	SEAHAWK	10171t	75	18.5k	137.5m	12P	-	94T	BA	NO
15	SLINGEBORG	21005t	00	17.0k	183.4m	12P	-	180T	A	NL
16	SPAARNEBORG	21005t	00	17.0k	183.4m	12P	-	180T	A	NL
17	SYMPHORINE	10030t	88	14.5k	147.4m	8P	350C	100T	A2	LX
18	UNDINE	11854t	91	14.5k	147.4m	8P	350C	100T	A2	LX
19	VALENTINE	23987t	99	18.0k	162.5m	12P	630C	157T	A	BS
20	VICTORINE	23987t	00	18.0k	162.5m	12P	630C	157T	A	BS

AMANDINE Built at Kiel, Germany as the MERZARIO PERSIA for *Merzario Line* of Italy and used on services between Italy and the Middle East. In 1986 she was chartered to *Grimaldi* of Italy and renamed the PERSIA, continuing on Middle East services. In 1988 she was sold to *Eimskip* of Iceland and renamed the BRUARFOSS. She was used on their service between Reykjavik, Immingham, Hamburg and Rotterdam. In 1996, the ro-ro service was replaced by a container only service and she was withdrawn. She was renamed the VEGA and was placed a number of short term charters including *Suardiaz* of Spain and *Fred. Olsen Lines*. In 1998, she was sold to *Cobelfret* and renamed the AMANDINE. Used mainly on the Rotterdam - Immingham service until 2002 when she was transferred to the Rotterdam - Purfleet route.

CATHERINE Built as the ROMIRA at Zhonghua , China for *Dag Engström Rederi* of Sweden. For six months engaged on a number of short term charters, including *Cobelfret Ferries* who used her on both the Rotterdam - Immingham and Zeebrugge - Purfleet routes. In September 2002 purchased by *Cobelfret Ferries* and in November 2002, renamed the CATHERINE and stared on the Rotterdam - Immingham service. In 2003 chartered to the *US Defense Department* to convey materials to the Persian Gulf.

CELANDINE, VALENTINE, VICTORINE Built at Sakaide, Japan for *Cobelfret*. Similar to the CLEMENTINE. The CELANDINE was originally to be called the CATHERINE and the VICTORINE the CELANDINE. The names were changed before delivery. They are generally used on the Zeebrugge - Purfleet service.

Valentine *(Philippe Holthof)*

Symphorine *(Philippe Holthof)*

CLEMENTINE Built at Sakaide, Japan for *Cobelfret*. Currently used on the Zeebrugge - Immingham service.

CYMBELINE ,EGLANTINE, SYMPHORINE, UNDINE Built at Dalian, China for *Cobelfret*. Used on the Dagenham - Vlissingen route.

EVA ODEN Built at Landskrona, Sweden as the EVA ODEN for *AB Norsjöfrakt* (later *Bylock & Norsjöfrakt*) of Sweden and chartered to *Oden Line* of Sweden for North Sea services, in particular associated with the export of Volvo cars and trucks from Gothenburg. In 1980 *Oden Line* was taken over by *Tor Lloyd AB*, a joint venture between *Tor Line* and *Broströms AB* and the charter transferred to them, moving to *Tor Line* in 1981 when *DFDS* took over. In 1987 she was enlarged and on re-entry into service in early 1988 was renamed the TOR BELGIA and became regular vessel on the Gothenburg - Ghent (Belgium) service. In 1998 renamed the EVA ODEN and in 1999 the charter was terminated. In 2000 she was chartered to *Cobelfret Ferries*. Until 2003, generally used on the Zeebrugge - Purfleet service. In 2003 transferred to the Rotterdam - Immingham service, replacing the CATHERINE. May return when she returns for her Gulf charter.

HOBURGEN Launched at Galatz, Romania as the BALDER RA for *K/S A/S Balder RO/RO No 2* of Norway. On completion acquired by *Navrom* of Romania, renamed the BAZIAS 5 and used on Mediterranean services; subsequently transferred to *Romline* of Romania. In 1995 she was chartered to *Grimaldi* of Italy and renamed the PERSEUS; she was later chartered to *Sudcargos* of France. In 1996 she was chartered to *Dart Line* and renamed the DART 5. In 1999 she was arrested in respect of a claim against *Romline* and laid up in Zeebrugge. In 2000 she was sold at auction to *Rederi AB Gotland* of Sweden. She was placed on the charter market. In 2001 she was chartered to *Cobelfret Ferries* and placed on the Purfleet - Rotterdam service, initially on a short term basis and, after a short break, on a longer term basis.

LOUISE RUSS Launched at Hamburg, Germany as the LOUISE RUSS for *Ernst Russ* of Germany. On completion, renamed the PORTO EXPRESS and chartered to *ROROExpress* to operate between Southampton, Oporto and Tangier. The service ceased in autumn 2001 and she was returned to her owners and resumed the name LOUISE RUSS. In 2002 chartered to *Cobelfret Ferries* and placed on the Rotterdam - Immingham service, replacing the AMANDINE.

MARABOU Built at Lödöse, Sweden as the VALLMO for the *Johansson Group* of Sweden and undertook a variety of charters. In 1982 she was sold to *Cobelfret* and renamed the MATINA. In 1984 renamed the LOVERVAL. In recent years has been chartered out for periods. In 2003 sold and renamed the MARABOU. Chartered back.Currently used on the Zeebrugge - Purfleet service.

MELUSINE Built at Sakaide, Japan for *Cobelfret*. Similar to the CLEMENTINE. Normally used on the Zeebrugge - Immingham service.

SCHIEBORG, SLINGEBORG, SPAARNEBORG Built at Lübeck, Germany for *Wagenborg* of the Netherlands and time chartered to *Stora-Enso* to operate between Zeebrugge and Gothenburg.

SEA CRUSADER Built at Sakaide, Japan as the CELESTINE. In 1996 chartered to the *British MoD* and renamed the SEA CRUSADER. She was originally expected to return to *Cobelfret Ferries* in early 2003 and resume the name CELESTINE; however the charter was extended because of the Iraq crisis. At time of going to press still on charter to the *MoD* but my return during summer 2003. If she does return, she is likely to be used on the Zeebrugge - Purfleet service.

SEAHAWK Launched at Kristiansand, Norway as the TOR CALEDONIA for *Tor Line* of Sweden (of the same design as *DFDS Tor Line's* TOR GOTHIA class). Delivered to *DSR* of the former DDR as the FICHTELBERG. She was used on services between the DDR and Cuba and also performed a number of charters. In 1991 she was chartered to *Dublin Ferries* for a new Dublin - Liverpool service and in 1992 she was renamed the SPIRIT OF DUBLIN. Later in 1992 the service ceased and, after a brief period with her owners, resuming the name FICHTELBERG, she was chartered to *North Sea Ferries* and placed on the Hull - Rotterdam service, being renamed NORCLIFF. The charter ended in autumn 1993 and she returned to her owners and resumed her previous name. In 1994 she was chartered to *DFDS* to provide additional capacity on the Immingham - Cuxhaven service following the ending of *DSR's* service between Hull and Hamburg. In 1995 she was renamed the DANA MINERVA. In early

1996 she was transferred to the *DFDS Baltic Line* service to operate between København/Malmö and Klaìpeda (Lithuania). In December 1996 she was chartered to *Pandoro* and renamed the SEAHAWK. She operated between Liverpool and Dublin. In 1997 she was sub-chartered to *Suardiaz* of Spain. In 1998 she returned and the charter was transferred to *P&O European Ferries (Portsmouth)* and she operated between Portsmouth and Cherbourg. The charter ended later in the year. She was then chartered to *Lineas Suardiaz* of Spain and was used mainly for the conveyance of new cars. In May 2002 chartered to *CETAM*, renamed the CETAM VICTORIAE and operated between Southampton and Santander. Charter ended in autumn 2002 and she was renamed the SEAHAWK. In 2003 chartered to *Cobelfret Ferries*. Now used on the Zeebrugge - Purfleet route. Charter may end when the CATHERINE returns from her Gulf charter.

COMMODORE FERRIES

THE COMPANY, MANAGEMENT & ADDRESS See Section 1.

TELEPHONE Administration & Reservations +44 (0)1481 728620.

FAX Administration & Reservations +44 (0)1481 728521.

INTERNET Email jvidamour@comferries.com

ROUTE OPERATED Portsmouth *(dep: 09.30*, 20.00)* - Guernsey *(dep: 04.00, 17.30*)* (6 hrs 30 min) - Jersey *(dep: 08.00, 21.30*)* (10 hrs 30 min; *(1)*; 2 per day) (*operated by ro-pax ferry COMMODORE CLIPPER - see Section 1), Guernsey *(dep: 07.00 Sat)* - Jersey *(dep: 11.00 Sat)* - St Malo *(arr: 14.00 Sat, dep: 17.00 Sat)* - Jersey *(arr: 06.00 Sun)* - Guernsey *(arr: 03.00 Mon)*; *(1)*; 1 per week).

1	COMMODORE GOODWILL	11166t	96	18.3k	126.4m	12P	-	92T	A	BS

COMMODORE GOODWILL Built at Vlissingen, Netherlands for *Commodore Ferries*.

DART LINE

THE COMPANY *Dart Line Ltd* is a British private sector company owned by *Bidcorp plc*. It took over the Dartford - Vlissingen service from *Sally Ferries* in 1996.

MANAGEMENT Managing Director Ron Herman, **Commercial Director** Ronny Daelman, **Continental Sales Director** Helmut Walgræve.

ADDRESS Crossways Business Park, Thames Europort, Dartford, Kent DA2 6QB.

TELEPHONE Administration & Reservations +44 (0)1322 281122.

FAX Administration & Reservations +44 (0)1322 281133.

INTERNET Email sales@dartline.co.uk **Website** www.dartline.co.uk *(English)*

ROUTES OPERATED Dartford *(dep: 3.30 Tue-Fri, 05.00 Sat, 07.30 Mon-Fri, 20.30 daily)* - Zeebrugge *(dep: 09.30 Tue-Fri, 16.30 Mon-Sat, 21.00 Mon, 20.30 Daily)* (8 hrs 30 mins; *(1,2,4)*; up to 3 per day), Dartford *(dep: 01.00 Fri, 10.00 Sun, 11.00 Tue-Fri, 21.00 Sun, Mon, Sat, 22.00 Tue, 23.00 Wed, 23.59 Thu)* - Vlissingen *(dep: 10.00 Tue-Fri, 11.00 Sun, 22.00 Sun-Fri)* (9 hrs 30 mins; *(2,8)*; 2 per day), Dartford *(dep: 06.30 Tue-Fri, 06.30 Sat+, 23.59 Sun)* - Dunkerque *(dep: 20.30 Mon-Fri, 20.30 Sat+ (+ = optional depending on volumes))* (6 hrs 45 min; *(River Lune (see Norse Merchant Ferries)*; 1 per day).

1	BAZIAS 1	9071t	84	15.0k	121.5m	12P	-	90T	A	RO
2	DART 2	9082t	84	15.0k	121.5m	12P	-	90T	A	BS
3	DART 3	9088t	85	15.0k	121.5m	12P	-	90T	A	BD
4	DART 4	9088t	85	16.5k	121.5m	12P	-	90T	A	BD
5	DART 8	22748t	80	18.0k	178.5m	12P	-	155T	A	BD
6	DART 9	22748t	80	18.0k	178.5m	12P	-	155T	A	BD
7	DART 10	22748t	80	18.0k	178.5m	12P	-	155T	A	UK

| 8 | NORTHERN STAR | 11086t | 91 | 20.8k | 136.0m | 12P | - | 86T | A | CY |
| 9 | VARBOLA | 7800t | 98 | 17.0k | 122.3m | 12P | - | 84T | A | ES |

BAZIAS 1 Built at Galatz, Romania as the BALDER FJORD for *K/S A/S Balder RO/RO No 2* of Norway. In 1986 acquired by *Navrom* of Romania and renamed the BAZIAS 1. In 1990 transferred to *Romline* of Romania and subsequently sold to *Octogon Shipping* of Romania. In 1996 chartered to *Ignazio Messina* of Italy and later renamed the JOLLY ARANCIONE. In late 1997 chartered to *Dart Line* and renamed the DART 1. In late 1999 charter ended, and she was briefly chartered to *Merchant Ferries*, although she was taken back on short term charter by *Dart Line* in February 2000. In 2001 renamed the BAZIAS 1 and in April chartered to *Cobelfret Ferries* to operate between Rotterdam and Purfleet. In autumn she transferred to the Zeebrugge -Purfleet service. In March 2002 chartered to *Dart Line* to operate between Dartford and Dunkerque (not inter-worked with the Vlissingen service). In summer 2002 charter ended. Re-chartered in autumn 2002 and worked additional sailings from Dartford to Zeebrugge. From November 2002 she has operated a triangular Dartford - Dunkerque - Zeebrugge - Dartford service. From January 2003 resumed service between Dartford and Zeebrugge only.

DART 2 Built at Galatz, Romania as the BALDER HAV for *K/S A/S Balder RO/RO No 2* of Norway. In 1985 acquired by *Navrom* of Romania, renamed the BAZIAS 2 and used on Mediterranean services. In 1995 chartered to *Dart Line* and renamed the DART 2. Operations began in 1996. Later in 1996 she was sold to *Jacobs Holdings*. Now operates on the Dartford - Dartford - Dunkerque/Vlissingen routes (alternating between the two routes on a daily basis). In 2003 began operating between Dartford and Dunkerque only but later switched to the Dartford - Vlissingen route.

DART 3 Built at Galatz, Romania as the BALDER STEN for *K/S A/S Balder RO/RO No 2* of Norway (part of the *Parley Augustsson* group). In 1995 acquired by *Navrom* of Romania and renamed the BAZIAS 3. In 1991 chartered to *Sally Ferries* for the Ramsgate - Ostend freight service and subsequently purchased by a joint *Sally Ferries/Romline* company. In 1993 renamed the SALLY EUROROUTE and re-registered in The Bahamas. In October 1996 she was chartered to *Belfast Freight Ferries* and renamed the MERLE. In 1997 *Sally Ferries'* interests in her were purchased by *Jacobs Holdings*. In January 2000 she joined *Dart Line* and was placed on the Vlissingen service, being renamed the DART 3. In autumn 2000 she was chartered to *NorseMerchant Ferries* and placed again on the Heysham - Belfast service. In autumn 2001 returned to *Dart Line* to operate with the DART 2 on the Dartford - Dunkerque/Vlissingen routes (alternating between the two routes on a daily basis). In 2003 transferred to the Dartford – Zeebrugge route.

DART 4 Built at Galatz, Romania as the BALDER BRE for *K/S A/S Balder RO/RO No 2* of Norway. Later in 1985 acquired by *Navrom* of Romania and renamed the BAZIAS 4. In 1991 chartered to *Sally Ferries* for the Ramsgate - Ostend freight service and subsequently purchased by *Rosal SA*, a joint *Sally Ferries/Romline* company. In 1993 renamed the SALLY EUROLINK and re-registered in The Bahamas. In 1997 *Sally Ferries'* interests in her were purchased by *Jacobs Holdings*. She was later transferred to *Dart Line* and renamed the DART 4. In 1998 she was chartered to *Belfast Freight Ferries*. She returned to *Dart Line* in February 1999 and operated on the Dartford - Vlissingen route. In 2003 transferred to the Dartford - Zeebrugge route.

DART 8 Built at Sakaide, Japan as the XI FENG KOU, a deep sea ro-ro/container ship for *China Ocean Shipping Company* of the People's Republic of China for service between the USA, Australia and New Zealand. In 1999, purchased by *Jacobs Holdings*. After delivery, she was converted in Nantong, China to short sea ro-ro specification, including the fitting of a stern ramp (replacing the quarter ramp) and luxury accommodation for 12 drivers and entered service in August 1999 on the Dartford - Zeebrugge service. In 2003 chartered to the *British MoD* for service in the Persian Gulf.

DART 9 Built at Sakaide, Japan as the GU BEI KOU. As the DART 8. She entered service in September 1999 on the Dartford - Zeebrugge service. In 2003 chartered to the *British MoD* for service in the Persian Gulf.

DART 10 Built at Sakaide, Japan as the ZHANG JIA KOU. As the DART 8. Rebuilt as the DART 10. On completion of rebuilding, chartered to *Sudcargos* of France and renamed the MONT VENTOUX and operated between France and North Africa. In December 2000 the charter ended. In January 2001 she briefly ran on the Dartford - Zeebrugge route in place of the DART 8. After two brief

Stena Gothica *(John Bryant)*

Louise Russ *(Mike Louagie)*

charters to the *British MoD* she was refitted and renamed the DART 10. She then entered long tem charter with the *British MoD*.

NORTHERN STAR Built at Kawajiri, Japan as the KOSEI MARU for *Kanko Kisen KK Line* of Japan for domestic services. In 1998 she was sold to *Jay Management Corporation* of Cyprus and renamed the IOLAOS. In November 1998 she was chartered to *East Coast Ferries*, renamed the LOON-PLAGE and placed on their Hull - Dunkerque service. The service ceased in January 1999 and after a brief charter to *DFDS Tor Line*, she was renamed the CELTIC STAR, chartered *to P&O European Ferries (Irish Sea)* and placed on the Liverpool - Dublin route. In January 2002 she was renamed the NORTHERN STAR and inaugurated a new Liverpool - Larne service. In 2003 chartered to *Dart Line* to replace the DART 8; placed on the Dartford - Vlissingen route.

VARBOLA Built at Huelva, Spain as the VARBOLA for *Estonian Shipping Company*. On completion, chartered to *Dart Line* and placed on the Dartford - Vlissingen route. In 1999 she was renamed the DART 6. At the end of August 1999, the charter was terminated and she was renamed the VARBOLA. She undertook a number of short term charters, including *Merchant Ferries*. In 2000 long-term chartered to *Merchant Ferries* to operate between Heysham and Dublin. In 2003 sub-chartered to *Dart Line* to replace the DART 9; placed initially on the Dartford - Vlissingen route but later transferred to the Dartford - Dunkerque route in May 2003 returned to *NMF*.

DFDS TOR LINE

THE COMPANY *DFDS Tor Line* is primarily a ro-ro operator on the North Sea and Baltic Sea. The Parent company *DFDS A/S* was formed in 1866 and is today quoted on the Copenhagen Stock Exchange. The *DFDS Tor Line* group consists of companies in Denmark, Sweden, Norway, the United Kingdom, the Netherlands, Belgium, Germany and Lithuania. 1,200 people are employed at sea and ashore and ro-ro, lo-lo and ro-pax vessels are operated to 18 destinations.

MANAGEMENT Managing Director Ole Frie, **Managing Director UK** Ebbe K Pedersen.

ADDRESS *Denmark (Head Office)* Sankt Annæ Plads 30, DK-1295 Copenhagen K, Denmark, *UK* Nordic House, Western Access Road, Immingham Dock, Immingham, South Humberside DN40 2LZ.

TELEPHONE Administration & Reservations *Denmark (Head Office)* +45 33 42 33 00, *UK* +44 (0)1469 575231.

FAX Administration & Reservations *Denmark* +45 33 42 33 01, *UK* +44 (0)1469 552690.

INTERNET Email info@dfdstorline.com **Website** www.dfdstorline.com *(English)*

ROUTES OPERATED Esbjerg *(dep: 19.00* Tue, Thu, Sat)* - Harwich *(dep 18.00* Sun, Wed, Fri, 14.00 Sat)* (17hrs; *Ro-pax vessel DANA SIRENA (see *DFDS Seaways*, Section 1), *(2/4 (alternate weeks))*; 3 per week southbound, 4 per week northbound (Note: Ro-pax service operates alternate days rather than 3 per week during peak summer period), Esbjerg *(dep: 19.00, 22.00+ Mon, 21.00 Tue, 03.00 Thu, 19.00 Fri, 12.00, 21.00 Sat)* - Immingham *(dep: 18.00 Sun, 15.00 Mon, 22.30 Tue, 22.30*, 23.59 Wed, 16.00 Fri, 23.00 Sat)* (21 hrs (+44 hrs 30 mins, *55 hrs 30 min (via Cuxhaven)); *(10/14)*; 5 per week, Cuxhaven *(dep: 19.00 Mon, 19.00 Tue, 01.00 Thu, 20.00+ Fri, 08.00 Sat)* - Immingham *(dep: 10.00 Sun, 18.00* Sun, 21.30 Tue, 22.30 Wed, 03.00 Fri)* (22 hrs (+40 hrs, *36 hrs (via Esbjerg)); *(7, 12)*; 5 per week), Gothenburg *(dep: 19.00 Thu, 15.00+ Sat)* - Harwich *(dep: 19.00 Tue, 14.00 Sat)* (36 hrs (+ 43 hrs via Esbjerg)); *(2/4)*; 2 per week), Gothenburg *(dep: 21.00 Sun-Fri, 19.00+ Tue, 18.00 Sat)* - Immingham *(dep: 04.00 Sun-Fri, 16.00+ Thu, 10.00 Sat)* - (26 hrs (+38 hrs); *(6,18,19,+2/4 (alternate weeks))*; 8 per week), Rotterdam (Waalhaven) *(dep: 19.00 Mon, 18.00 Tue-Fri, 17.00 Sat)* - Immingham *(dep: 18.15 Mon-Fri, 17.00 Sat)* (14 hrs 30 mins); *(13,15)*; 6 per week), Gothenburg *(dep: 03.00 Tue-Thu, 01.00 Fri, 03.00, 23.00 Sat)* - Brevik (Norway) *(dep: 10.00 Sun, 16.00, 15.00)* - Ghent (Belgium) *(dep: 00.01 Sun, 03.00 Tue-Sat (Brevik served Wed*, Fri and Sun)* (Gothenburg 42 hrs, Brevik 35 hrs; *(5,8,9,17)*; 6 per week) (*calls at Gothenburg before Brevik), Brevik *(dep: 03.00 Mon, 20.00 Thu)* - Kristiansand *(dep: 11.00 Mon, 02.30 Thu)* - Immingham *(dep: 20.30 Tue, 14.00 Sat)* (approx 27-29 hours Norwegian Port - Immingham; *(11)*; 2 per week) (**Note** Tue ex Immingham operates Immingham - Kristiansand - Brevik - Immingham, Sat ex Immingham operates Immingham - Brevik - Kristiansand - Immingham), Fredericia *(dep: 22.00 Tue, Thu, 02.30 Sat)* – Copenhagen *(dep: Mon 12.00, Wed 09.00, Sat 15.00)* - Klaìpeda (Lithuania) *(dep: 21.00 Sun, 22.00 Sun 13.00 Thu) (15); 3 per week), ((1,16); 3 per week).*

DFDS Tor Lines also operates a Ro-pax service between Lubeck and Riga. See Section 6.

Space is also used for freight on *DFDS Seaways'* passenger vessels between Harwich and Esbjerg, Cuxhaven and Harwich (3 per week or alternate days during the summer), Gothenburg and Kristiansand/Newcastle (2-3 per week) and IJmuiden - Newcastle (daily).

Note Non-UK routes shown above are strictly outside the scope of this book but are shown for the sale of completeness.

1	PANEVEZYS	6884t	86	15.0k	125.9m	12P	-	50T	A	LB
2	STENA GOTHICA	14406t	75	16.0k	188.7m	12P	-	148T	A	SW
3	TOR ANGLIA	17492t	77	15k	171.9m	12P	-	184T	A	SW
4	TOR BALTICA	14374t	78	18.0k	163.6m	12P	-	150T	A	UK
5	TOR BELGIA	21491t	78	18.0k	193.2m	12P	200C	184T	AS	SW
6	TOR BRITANNIA	24200t	00	21.1k	197.5m	12P	-	206T	A	DK
7	TOR CIMBRIA	12189t	86	17.0k	145.0m	12P	-	154T	A	DK
8	TOR DANIA	21850t	78	18.0k	193.3m	12P	200C	184T	AS	DK
9	TOR FLANDRIA	33652t	82	19.0k	193.6m	12P	300C	212T	A	SW
10	TOR FUTURA	18469t	96	20.0k	183.1m	12P	-	170T	AS	DK
11	TOR GOTHIA	12259t	71	17.0k	163.6m	12P	-	116T	A	UK
12	TOR HOLLANDIA	12254t	73	15.5k	163.6m	12P	-	122T	A	UK
13	TOR HUMBRIA	20165t	78	18.5k	183.1m	12P	-	158T	A	SW
14	TOR MAXIMA	17068t	78	17.0k	176.2m	12P	-	206T	A	NO
15	TOR MINERVA	21213t	78	18.0k	183.1m	12P	-	158T	A	DK
16	TOR NERINGA	12494t	75	19.0k	167.6m	12P	-	126T	A	LT
17	TOR SCANDIA	33652t	82	19.0k	193.6m	12P	300C	212T	A	SW
18	TOR SELANDIA	24196t	98	21.1k	197.5m	12P	-	206T	A	SW
19	TOR SUECIA	24200t	99	21.1k	197.5m	12P	-	206T	A	SW

PANEVEZYS Built at Rostock, Germany (DDR) as the KOMPOZITOR MUSORGISKY for *Baltic Shipping Company* of the Soviet Union. In 1997 sold to the *Lithuanian Shipping Company* and renamed the PANEVEZYS. In May 2002 chartered to *DFDS Tor Line* to operate on their Trelleborg - Gdansk service (a route which ceased when the *DFDS Seaways* Copenhagen - Trelleborg - Gdansk service started). In October transferred to the Fredericia - Copenhagen - Klaìpeda route.

STENA GOTHICA Built at Sandefjord, Norway as the MELBOURNE TRADER for *Australian National Line* for services in Australia. She was of the same design as *Tor Line's* TOR GOTHIA class. In 1987 sold to *Forest Shipping*. In 1988 she was chartered to *Elbe-Humber RoLine* and renamed the RAILRO 2. Later in 1988 she was sold to *Stena Line*, renamed the STENA PROJECT and was chartered by them to *CoTuNav* of Tunisia and renamed the MONAWAR L. In 1990, following the start of a joint *Stena Line/DFDS Tor Line* service between Gothenburg and Harwich (operated by *DFDS Tor Line*) she was renamed the STENA GOTHICA, lengthened by 31m and chartered to *DFDS Tor Line*, operating on a combined Gothenburg - Immingham/Harwich service. In 1999 the Immingham and Harwich services were separated. She initially operated between Gothenburg and Immingham but was then transferred to the Gothenburg - Harwich service. Now operates between Gothenburg and both Harwich and Immingham.

TOR ANGLIA Built at Kiel, Germany as the MERZARIO GALLIA and chartered to *Merzario Line* of Italy for services between Italy and Saudi Arabia. In 1981 she was chartered to *Wilhelmsen*, renamed the TANA and used between USA and West Africa. In 1983 she was chartered to *Salenia AB* of Sweden and renamed the NORDIC WASA. In 1987 she had a brief period on charter to *Atlantic Marine* as the AFRICAN GATEWAY and in 1988 she was sold to *Tor Line* and renamed the TOR ANGLIA. In 1989 an additional deck was added. In recent years she operated on the Gothenburg - Ghent service but in late 1998 she was switched to the Immingham - Rotterdam service. In 2001 transferred back to the Gothenburg - Ghent service. In January 2003 chartered to the *British MoD* for three months.

Flanders Way *(John Hendy)*

Varbola *(Miles Cowsill)*

TOR BALTICA Built at Ulsan, South Korea as the ELK for *Stena Rederi* of Sweden and chartered to *P&O Ferrymasters* for use on services from Middlesbrough to Gothenburg and Helsingborg. Purchased by *P&O* in 1981 and lengthened in 1986; she was managed by *P&O North Sea Ferries Ltd.* In 2001 she was sold to *DFDS Tor Line*, who took over management of the vessel. *P&O Ferrymasters'* services ceased in May 2001. She was renamed the TOR BALTICA and transferred to the *DFDS Tor Line* Gothenburg - Harwich route. Now operates between Gothenburg and both Harwich and Immingham.

TOR BELGIA Built at Dunkerque, France as the VILLE DU HAVRE for *Société Française de Transports Maritimes* of France. Between 1979 and 1981 she was chartered to *Foss Line*, renamed the FOSS HAVRE and operated between Europe and the Middle East. In 1987 she was renamed the KAMINA. In 1990 she was chartered to *Maersk Line* of Denmark, renamed the MAERSK KENT and used on *Kent Line* services between Dartford and Zeebrugge. In 1992 she was chartered to and later purchased by *Tor Line*, placed on the Gothenburg - Immingham route and renamed the TOR BRITANNIA. In 1994 she was lengthened by 23.7m. In 1999 she was renamed the TOR BELGIA and was later transferred to the Gothenburg - Brevik -Ghent route.

TOR BRITANNIA Built at Ancona, Italy for *DFDS Tor Line*. Operates on the Gothenburg - Immingham route.

TOR CIMBRIA Built at Frederikshavn, Denmark. Launched as the MERCANDIAN EXPRESS II and immediately bare-boat chartered to *DFDS* for their North Sea freight services, being renamed the DANA CIMBRIA. Purchased by *DFDS* in 1989. Until 1996, generally used on Immingham and North Shields - Esbjerg services; between 1996 and 1998 she operated between Immingham and Esbjerg. In 1998 she was transferred to the Immingham - Cuxhaven service. In 2001 renamed the TOR CIMBRIA. In 2002 sold to Norwegian interests and chartered back to *DFDS Tor Line*.

TOR DANIA Built at Dunkerque, France as the VILLE DE DUNKERQUE for *Société Française de Transports Maritimes* of France. Between 1979 and 1981 she was chartered to *Foss Line*, renamed the FOSS DUNKERQUE and operated between Europe and the Middle East. In 1986 she was chartered to *Grimaldi* of Italy and renamed the G AND C EXPRESS. In 1988 she was briefly chartered to *Elbe-Humber RoLine* and renamed the RAILRO. She was then chartered to *DFDS* where she was renamed the DANIA HAFNIA. The following year she was chartered to *Maersk Line* of Denmark, renamed the MAERSK ESSEX and used on *Kent Line* services between Dartford and Zeebrugge. In 1992 she was chartered to and later purchased by *DFDS* and renamed the TOR DANIA. In 1993 she was renamed the BRIT DANIA but later in the year reverted to her original name. She was generally used on the Harwich - Esbjerg service, working in consort with the passenger ferry DANIA ANGLIA (see *DFDS Seaways*). In 1994 she was lengthened by 23.7m. and chartered to *Tor Line* and placed on the Gothenburg - Immingham route. She now operates on the Gothenburg - Brevik - Ghent route.

TOR FLANDRIA Built at Malmö, Sweden as the FINNCLIPPER for the *Johansson Group* of Sweden and chartered out. In 1983 she was sold to *Zenit Shipping* and renamed the ZENIT CLIPPER. She was chartered to *Foss Line* and used on services between Northern Europe and the Middle East. In 1986 she was sold to *Crowley American Transport* of the USA and chartered to the US Military. She was renamed the AMERICAN FALCON and used for military transport purposes across the world. In 1998 sold to *Stena Rederi* and was renamed the STENA PARTNER. She was then chartered to *Tor Line* and renamed the TOR FLANDRIA; part of her charter conditions are that she be purchased at the end of the five year charter period; however, she was purchased in 2001. She is normally used on the Gothenburg - Brevik - Ghent route. In 2002 she was sold to *Norwegian Scandinavian Ro/Ro KS* and chartered back for 5.5 years.

TOR FUTURA Built at Donada, Italy as the DANA FUTURA for *DFDS*. In 2001 she was renamed the TOR FUTURA. Initially operated mainly between Esbjerg and Harwich, but now operates between Esbjerg and Immingham.

TOR GOTHIA Built at Sandefjord, Norway for *Tor Line*. Lengthened in 1977. She was usually used on the Immingham - Rotterdam service. In 1999 transferred to the Norway - UK service and in 2000 to the Norway - UK/Netherlands service. In 2001 she was moved to the Rotterdam - Immingham route. Now operates on the Immingham - Kristiansand - Brevik route.

TOR HOLLANDIA Built at Sandefjord, Norway as the TOR DANIA for charter to *Tor Line*. In 1975 she was chartered to *Salenrederierna* for service in the Middle East and renamed the BANDAR ABBAS EXPRESS. In 1977 she was lengthened and, in 1978, returned to *Tor Line* and resumed the name TOR DANIA. Purchased by *Tor Line* in 1986. In 1992 she was renamed the TOR DAN and in 1993 the TOR HOLLANDIA. She was usually used on the Immingham - Rotterdam service. In 1999 transferred to the Norway - UK/Netherlands services (Netherlands services ceased in 2001). In 2002 moved to the Norway - Immingham route. Now operates between Immingham and Cuxhaven.

TOR HUMBRIA Built at Oskarshamn, Sweden as the EMIRATES EXPRESS for *A/S Skarhamns Oljetransport* of Norway and chartered to *Mideastcargo* for services between Europe and the Middle East. In 1981 chartered to *OT West Africa Line* for services between Europe and West Africa and renamed the ABUJA EXPRESS. In 1983 chartered to *Foss Line*, renamed the FOSSEAGLE and returned to Middle East service. In 1985 she was renamed the FINNEAGLE, chartered briefly to *Finncarriers* and then to *Fred. Olsen Lines*. In 1987 they purchased her and renamed her the BORAC. In 1999 purchased by *DFDS Tor Line* and renamed the TOR HUMBRIA. In 2000 she was chartered to *Costa Container Lines spa* of Italy, operating between Savano and Catania. This service ended in early 2001 and she was then chartered to *CoTuNav* of Tunisia. Returned in April 2001. In 2003 sold to Norwegian interests and chartered back. She currently operates on the Rotterdam - Immingham service.

TOR MAXIMA Built at Osaka, Japan as the DANA MAXIMA for *DFDS* for their North Sea services. Until 1996, generally used on the Esbjerg - Grimsby and North Shields services. In summer 1995 she was lengthened to increase trailer capacity. In December 2000 she was renamed the TOR MAXIMA. In December 2001 sold to *Per Sand* of Norway and chartered back for 3 years. She currently operates between Esbjerg and Immingham.

TOR MINERVA Built at Oskarshamn, Sweden as the BANDAR ABBAS EXPRESS for *A/S Skarhamns Oljetransport* of Norway and chartered out. In 1980 renamed the SAUDI EXPRESS. During the early eighties she undertook a number of charters including *Mideastcargo* for services between Europe and the Middle East, *Atlanticargo* for services from Europe to USA and Mexico and *OT West Africa Line* from Europe to West Africa. In 1983 she was chartered to *Ignazio Messina* of Italy, renamed the JOLLY AVORIO and used on services from Italy to the Middle East. In 1986 this charter ended and she briefly reverted to the name the SAUDI EXPRESS before being chartered again to *OT West Africa Line* and renamed the KARAWA. In 1987 she was sold to *Fred. Olsen Lines* who renamed her the BORACAY; she operated between Norway and Northern Europe. In 1998 she was sold to *DFDS*, renamed the DANA MINERVA and placed on the Esbjerg - Immingham route. In 2001 she was renamed the TOR MINERVA. She now operates between Immingham and Rotterdam.

TOR NERINGA Built at Florø, Norway as the BALDUIN for *Fred. Olsen Lines*. In 1999 purchased by *DFDS Tor Line* and renamed the TOR NORVEGIA. Initially used on Norway - UK/Netherlands services; in 2001 moved to the Fredericia - Copenhagen - Klaìpeda (Lithuania) service. In 2001 December 2001 sold to *Lisco Baltic Service* of Lithuania, renamed the TOR NERINGA and chartered back to *DFDS Tor Line*.

TOR SCANDIA Built at Malmö, Sweden as the KUWAIT EXPRESS for the *Johansson Group* of Sweden and chartered to *NYK Line* of Japan for services between Japan and the Arabian Gulf. In 1983 she was sold to *Zenit Shipping* and renamed the ZENIT EXPRESS. She was chartered to *Foss Line* and used on services between Northern Europe and the Middle East. In 1984 she was sold to *Crowley American Transport* of the USA and chartered to the US Military. She was reamed the AMERICAN CONDOR and used for military transport purposes across the world. In 1998 she was sold to *Stena Rederi* and renamed the STENA PORTER. Later she was sold to *Tor Line* and renamed the TOR SCANDIA. She is used on the Gothenburg - Brevik - Ghent route. In 2002 she was sold to Norwegian Scandinavian Ro/Ro KS and chartered back for 5.5 years.

TOR SELANDIA, TOR SUECIA Built at Ancona, Italy for *DFDS Tor Line*. They operate on the Gothenburg - Immingham route.

Under Construction

20	TOR MAGNOLIA	32400t	03	22.4k	199.8m	12P	-	260T	AS	DK
21	NEWBUILDING 2	32400t	04	22.4k	199.8m	12P	-	260T	AS	DK

Dart 8 *(Nick Widdows)*

Tor Hollandia *(Andrew Cooke)*

22	NEWBUILDING 3	32400t	04	22.4k	199.8m	12P	-	260T	AS	DK
23	NEWBUILDING 4	32400t	04	22.4k	199.8m	12P	-	260T	AS	DK
24	NEWBUILDING 5	32400t	04	22.4k	199.8m	12P	-	260T	AS	DK

TOR MAGNOLIA, NEWBUILDING 2, NEWBUILDING 3, NEWBUILDING 4, NEWBUILDING 5 Under construction at Flensburg, Germany for *DFDS Tor Line*. The first three will operate on the Gothenburg - Immingham route, the existing vessels being deployed elsewhere. The fourth and fifth will operate between Esbjerg and Immingham. The first ship is due to enter service in September 2003.

FERRYWAYS

THE COMPANY *Ferryways nv* is a Belgian company.

MANAGEMENT Managing Director J Dewilde, **Marketing Manager** Martin Gouwy.

ADDRESS *Ostend* Esplanadestraat 10, B-8400 Ostend, Belgium. *Ipswich* West Bank Terminal, Wherstead Road, Ipswich IP2 8NB.

TELEPHONE Administration & Reservations *Ostend* +32 (0)59 34 22 20, *Ipswich* +44 (0)1473 696200.

FAX Administration & Reservations *Ostend* +32 (0)59 34 22 29, *Ipswich* +44 (0)1473 696201.

INTERNET Email *Ostend* info@ferryways.com *Ipswich* info@ferryways.co.uk

Website www.ferryways.co.uk *(English)*

ROUTE OPERATED Ostend *(dep: 11.00 Mon -Fri, 11.30 Sat,16.00 Sat, 17.00 Mon-Fri, 21.30 Sun, 22.00 Mon-Fri,)* - Ipswich *(dep: 03.00 Tue-Sat, 09.30 Mon-Fri, 11.00 Sat, 22.00 Mon-Fri, 21.30 Sun)* (7 hrs; *(1,2,4)*; 3 per day), Ostend *(dep: 02.00 Sun, Tue-Sat)* - Killingholme *(dep: 01.00 Sun, Tue-Sat)* (14/19 hrs; *(3,5)*; 1 per day).

1	ANGLIAN WAY	7635t	78	15.0k	141.3m	12P	55C	84T	A	PA
2	FLANDERS WAY	7628t	77	16.0k	141.3m	12P	55C	84T	A	PA
3	IPSWICH WAY	6568t	80	15.0k	136.0m	12P	-	84T	A	SW
4	OSTEND WAY	6568t	80	15.0k	136.1m	12P	-	84T	A	SW
5	VILJA	9698t	78	16.0k	152.3m	12P	-	95T	A	NO

ANGLIAN WAY Built at Bremerhaven, Germany as the THOMAS WEHR for *Wehr Transport* of Germany as THOMAS WEHR but on delivery chartered to *Wacro Line* and renamed the WACRO EXPRESS. In 1978 charter ended and she was renamed the THOMAS WEHR. Over the next few years she was chartered to several operators. In 1982 she was chartered to *Tor Lloyd* (later *Tor Line*) for North Sea service and renamed the TOR NEERLANDIA. In 1985 the charter was transferred to *DFDS* and she was renamed the DANA GERMANIA. This charter terminated in 1985 and she resumed her original name. In early 1986 she was chartered to *North Sea Ferries* for their Hull - Zeebrugge service. This charter ended in summer 1987. Subsequent charters included *Cobelfret* and *Elbe-Humber RoLine* and a twelve month period with *North Sea Ferries* again - this time on the Hull - Rotterdam and Teesport - Zeebrugge routes. In 1993 she was renamed the MANA, then the SANTA MARIA and finally chartered to *TT-Line* and renamed the FULDATAL. 1994 she was chartered to *Horn Line* for service between Europe and the Caribbean and renamed the HORNLINK. Later that year she was chartered to *P&O European Ferries* for the Portsmouth - Le Havre freight service and resumed the name THOMAS WEHR. In late 1995 transferred to the Felixstowe - Zeebrugge freight service. In autumn 1999 the charter was ended. In 2000 she was chartered to *Ferryways*. In 2001 she was purchased by *Ferryways* and renamed the ANGLIAN WAY.

FLANDERS WAY Built at Bremerhaven, Germany as the GABRIELE WEHR for *Wehr Transport* of Germany and chartered to several operators. In 1982, chartered to *Tor Lloyd* (later *Tor Line*) for North Sea service and renamed the TOR ANGLIA. This charter terminated in 1985 when she resumed her original name and, in early 1986, she was chartered to *North Sea Ferries* for their Hull - Zeebrugge service. This charter ended in summer 1987 when the lengthened NORLAND and

NORSTAR entered service. Subsequent charters included *Kent Line* and *Brittany Ferries*. In 1989 she was chartered to *P&O European Ferries* for the Portsmouth - Le Havre freight service. Her charter was terminated following the transfer of the EUROPEAN TRADER to the route in late 1992 but in 1993 it was renewed, following the transfer of the EUROPEAN CLEARWAY (now the EUROPEAN PATHFINDER) to *Pandoro*. In 1996, she was transferred to the Felixstowe - Zeebrugge service. In autumn 1999 the charter was ended. In 2000 she was chartered to *Ferryways*. In 2001 she was purchased by *Ferryways* and renamed the FLANDERS WAY.

IPSWICH WAY Built at Karslkrona, Sweden as the BALDER DONA for *Dag Engström Rederi* of Sweden and undertook a number of charters in the Caribbean and Mediterranean. In 1984 she was renamed the RODONA and chartered to *Seaboard Shipping* of the USA and used on Caribbean services. In 1987 she was chartered to the *Ford Motor Company* for conveyance of privately owned trailers between Dagenham and Zeebrugge. In 1995 *Cobelfret Ferries* took over the operation of this service and she was used on both the Purfleet - Zeebrugge and Dagenham - Zeebrugge services. In 1999 she was chartered to *P&O North Sea Ferries* to operate between Felixstowe and Zeebrugge. In 2002 this service ceased and she was chartered to *Ferryways* to operate between Killingholme and Ostend. In 2003 purchased by *Ferryways* and renamed IPSWICH WAY.

OSTEND WAY Built at Karlskrona, Sweden as the BALDER VINGA for *Dag Engström Rederi* of Sweden and undertook a number of charters in the Caribbean and Mediterranean. In 1984 she was renamed the ROVINGA and chartered to *Seaboard Shipping* of the USA and used on Caribbean services. In 1985 she was renamed the AZUA. In 1987 she briefly reverted to the name ROVINGA before being renamed the SAPPHIRE and chartered to the *Ford Motor Company* for conveyance of privately owned trailers between Dagenham and Zeebrugge. Since 1995, as the RODONA. Normally operates on the Ipswich service. In 2003 purchased by *Ferryways* and renamed OSTEND WAY.

VILJA Built at Krimpen aan den IJssel, Rotterdam, Netherlands as the ANZERE for *Keller Shipping* and chartered to *Nautilus Line* for services between Europe and West Africa. In 1991 she was sold to *AS Tiderø* of Norway and renamed the TIDERO STAR. She was initially chartered to *Fred. Olsen Lines* and later to *Arimure Line* for service in the Far East. In 1994 chartered to *Fred. Olsen Lines* again. In early 1996 she was briefly chartered to *North Sea Ferries* for their Hull - Rotterdam service and then chartered to *Pandoro* and placed on the Liverpool - Dublin service. In 1997, chartered to *P&O Ferrymasters* operating between Middlesbrough and Gothenburg. Later in 1997 she was chartered again to *P&O North Sea Ferries* and placed on the Middlesbrough - Rotterdam service. The charter ended in 1999. After that she undertook a number of short term charters including *Lineas Suardiaz* and NATO. In early 2002 she was renamed the VILJA and entered service with *Ferryways* on their Ostend - Killingholme service.

FINNLINES

THE COMPANY *Finnlines PLC* is a Finnish private sector company. Services to the UK are marketed by *Finanglia Ferries*, a joint operation between *Finnlines* and *Andrew Weir Shipping*, (owners of the *United Baltic Corporation*), a British private sector company. From 1st January 2001, *Finncarriers* was merged into the parent company, trading as *Finnlines Cargo Service*.

MANAGEMENT *Finnlines* **President** Antti Lageroos, **Vice-President** Simo Airas.

ADDRESS *Finnlines* PO Box 197, Salmisaarenkatu 1, FIN-00181 Helsinki, Finland, *Finanglia Ferries* 8 Heron Quay, London E14 4JB.

TELEPHONE Administration & Reservations *Finnlines* +358 (0)10 34350, *Finanglia Ferries* +44 (0)20 7519 7300.

FAX Administration *Finnlines* +358 (0)10 3435200, *Finanglia Ferries* +44 (0)20 7536 0255.

INTERNET Email *Finnlines* info@finnlines.fi *Finanglia Ferries* london@finnlines.co.uk

Websites www.finnlines.fi *(English, Finnish)* www.finanglia.co.uk *(English)*

ROUTES OPERATED Hanko *(dep: 11.00 Mon)* - Helsinki (Finland) *(dep: 22.00 Mon, 23.00 Fri)* - Hamina (Finland) *(dep: 23.00 Tue, 20.00 Thu)* - Felixstowe *(arr: 08.00 Tue, 20.00 Fri, dep: 18.00 Tue, 07.00 Sat)* - Amsterdam *(arr: 08.00 Wed, dep: 15.00 Thu)* - Zeebrugge *(arr: 14.00 Mon, 12.00*

Sat, dep: 18.00 Mon, 18.00 Sat) - Helsinki (arr: 16.00 Mon, 11.00 Tue) - Hamina (arr: 06.00 Tue, Wed) - Hanko (arr: 07.00 Mon); (4,13,23); 1/2 per week), Kemi (dep: 16.00 Mon, 23.00 Thu) - Oulu (dep: 22.00 Tue, Fri) - Felixstowe (arr: 08.00 Wed, Sat, dep: 14.00 Wed, 18.00 Sat) - Antwerp (arr: 08.00 Sun, 14.00 Tue, dep: 16.00 Sun, 22.00 Tue) - Helsinki (arr: 07.00 Wed, 07.00 Sat) - Kemi (arr: 08.00 Mon, 16.00 Thu) (5,6,7); 2 per week (3 ships operate 2 round trips every 3 weeks), Hamina (dep: 23.00 Thu) - Helsinki (arr: 07.00 Fri, dep: 15.00 Fri) - Hull (arr: 07.00 Mon, dep: 18.00 Mon) - Hamina (arr: 12.00 Thu) (3 days; (17); 1 per week), Rauma (dep: 20.00 Wed) - Hull (arr: 07.00 Sat, dep: 20.00 Sat) - Helsinki (arr: 08.00 Tue, dep: 15.00 Tue) - Rauma (arr: 07.00 Wed), (3/4 days; (14); 1 per week) (3 days; (12); 1 per week).

In view of the fact that ships are liable to be transferred between routes, the following is a list of all *Finnlines Cargo* ro-ro vessels, including those which currently do not serve the UK. Ro-pax vessels (none of which normally serve the UK) are listed in Section 6.

1	ANTARES	5989t	88	20.3k	157.6m	18P	-	154T	A	NO
2	ASTREA	7380t	91	15.0k	129.1m	0P	-	60T	A	FI
3	AURORA	20391t	82	18.5k	155.0m	12P	-	160T	A	NO
4	BALTIC EIDER	20865t	89	19.0k	157.7m	0P	-	160T	A	IM
5	BIRKA CARRIER	12251t	98	20.0k	155.5m	12P	-	124T	A2	FI
6	BIRKA EXPRESS	12251t	97	20.0k	154.5m	12P	-	124T	A2	FI
7	BIRKA TRADER	12251t	98	20.0k	154.5m	12P	-	124T	A2	FI
8	FINNBIRCH	15396t	78	17.0k	155.9m	0P	-	155T	A	SW
9	FINNFOREST	15525t	78	17.0k	155.9m	0P	-	155T	A	SW
10	FINNHAWK	11530t	01	20.0k	162.2m	12P	-	140T	A	UK
11	FINNKRAFT	11530t	00	20.0k	162.2m	12P	-	140T	A	UK
12	FINNMASTER	11530t	00	20.0k	162.2m	12P	-	140T	A	UK
13	FINNMERCHANT	21195t	82	17.0k	154.9m	12P	-	160T	A	FI
14	FINNMILL	11400t	02	20.0k	184.8m	12P	-	230T	A	IR
15	FINNOAK	7953t	91	16.5k	139.5m	0P	-	94T	A	FI
16	FINNPULP	11400t	02	20.0k	184.8m	12P	-	230T	A	IR
17	FINNREEL	11530t	00	20.0k	162.2m	12P	-	140T	A	UK
18	FINNRIDER	20077t	84	18.9k	186.5m	12P	-	140T	A	GY
19	FINNRUNNER	20729t	90	18.9k	189.7m	12P	-	144t	A	GY
20	MIRANDA	10471t	99	20.3k	153.5m	12P	-	120T	A2	FI
21	NORCLIFF	8407t	94	14.5k	125.2m	0P	-	78T	A	NO
22	POLARIS	7944t	88	14.7k	122.0m	0P	500C	38T	A	GY
23	TRANSBALTICA	21224t	90	19.0k	157.7m	0P	-	163T	A	CY
24	TRANSFINLANDIA	19524t	81	18.5k	157.8m	12P	-	172T	A	GY
25	VASALAND	20203t	84	14.0k	155.0m	0P	-	160T	A	FI

ANTARES Built at Gdansk, Poland as the FINNFORREST for *Neste* of Finland and chartered to *Finncarriers*. In 1988 renamed the ANTARES. In 2002 chartered to *Stena Line* to operate between Harwich and Rotterdam. In 2003 chartered to the *British MoD* for service to the Gulf.

ASTREA Built at Tomrefjord, Norway for *Finncarriers*. Operates between Finland and Spain - Portugal via Antwerp.

AURORA Built at Rauma, Finland as the ARCTURUS for *EFFOA* of Finland and chartered to *Finncarriers*. In 1991 renamed the AURORA. Used on the Uusikaupunki - Rauma - Gdynia - Rostock - Lübeck - Travemünde service.

BALTIC EIDER Built at Ulsan, South Korea for *United Baltic Corporation*. Used on the Hanko - Helsinki - Hamina - Felixstowe - Amsterdam - Zeebrugge service.

BIRKA CARRIER, BIRKA TRADER Built at Rissa, Norway as the UNITED CARRIER and UNITED TRADER for *Birka Shipping* of Finland and chartered to *Transfennica*. During 2000 they were used on their Kemi - Oulu - Antwerp - Felixstowe service. In 2001 the route and vessels used were transferred to *Finnlines*. In 2002 renamed the BIRKA CARRIER and BIRKA TRADER.

Holyhead Port, North Wales (Miles Cowsill)

BIRKA EXPRESS Built at Rissa, Norway for *United Shipping* of Finland as the UNITED EXPRESS and chartered to *Transfennica*. During 2000 she was used on their Kemi - Oulu - Antwerp - Felixstowe service. In 2001 the route and vessel used was transferred to *Finnlines*. In 2002 *United Shipping* was renamed *Birka Cargo* and the ship renamed the BIRKA EXPRESS.

FINNBIRCH Laid down at Ulsan, South Korea as the STENA PROSPER and completed as the ATLANTIC PROSPER for *Stena Rederi* and chartered to *ACL* of Great Britain for service between Britain and Canada. In 1981 chartered to *Merzario Line* of Italy for services between Italy and Saudi Arabia and renamed, initially, the STENA IONIA and then the MERZARIO IONIA. In 1982 she reverted to the name STENA IONIA and was chartered to *OT West Africa Line* for services between Europe and Nigeria. In 1985 she was renamed the STENA GOTHICA and used on *Stena Portlink* services. In 1988 she was chartered to *Bore Line* of Finland and renamed the BORE GOTHICA. In 1992 chartered to *Finncarriers*. In 1996 renamed the FINNBIRCH. In 1997 she began operating a service between Hull and Zeebrugge on charter to *P&O North Sea Ferries* in the course of her normal two week circuit from Finland. This ceased in 1999. In 2000 transferred to the Helsinki - Århus service.

FINNFOREST Laid down at Ulsan, South Korea as the STENA PROJECT and completed as ATLANTIC PROJECT for *Stena Rederi* and chartered to *ACL* (see above). In 1981 chartered to *Merzario Line* of Italy for services between Italy and Saudi Arabia and renamed the MERZARIO HISPANIA. In 1983 returned to *Stena Line* and renamed the STENA HISPANIA. In 1984 chartered to *Kotka Line* of Finland, renamed the KOTKA VIOLET and used on their services between Finland, UK and West Africa. This charter ended in 1985 and she was again named the STENA HISPANIA. In 1986 she was renamed the STENA BRITANNICA and used on *Stena Portlink* (later *Stena Tor Line*) service between Sweden and Britain. In 1988 she was chartered to *Bore Line* of Finland, renamed the BORE BRITANNICA and used on services between Finland and Britain. In 1992 chartered to *Finncarriers*. In 1997 renamed the FINNFOREST. In 1997 she began operating a service between Hull and Zeebrugge on charter to *P&O North Sea Ferries* in the course of her normal two week circuit from Finland. This ceased in 1999. In 2000 transferred to the Helsinki - Århus service.

FINNHAWK Built at Nanjing, China for *Finnlines*. Currently operating on the Uusikaupunki - Kemi - Oulu - Lübeck route.

FINNKRAFT Built at Nanjing, China for *Forest Terminals* and chartered to *Finncarriers*. Currently operates on the Rauma - Gdynia - Rostock - Lübeck - Helsinki route.

FINNMASTER Built at Nanjing, China for *Forest Terminals* and chartered to *Finncarriers*. Operates on Helsinki - Rauma -Hull route.

FINNMERCHANT Built at Rauma, Finland for *Finnlines*. Operates on the Hanko - Helsinki - Hamina - Felixstowe - Amsterdam - Zeebrugge service.

FINNMILL Built at Nanjing, China for *Forest Terminals* and chartered to *Finnlines*. Operate on the Helsinki - Kotka - Rauma - Lübeck route.

FINNOAK Built at Rissa, Norway as the AHTELA for *Holming Shipping* of Finland and chartered to *Transfennica*. In 1997 renamed the FINNOAK and chartered to *Finncarriers*. Used on the *Polfin Line* service between Helsinki - Kotka and Gdynia - Szczecin (joint with *Euroafrica Shipping* of Poland).

FINNPULP Built at Nanjing, China for *Forest Terminals* and chartered to *Finnlines*. Currently used on the Helsinki - Kotka - Rauma - Lübeck service.

FINNREEL Launched as the FINNMAID but renamed before delivery. Built at Nanjing, China for *Forest Terminals* and chartered to *Finncarriers*. Currently operating on the Hamina - Helsinki - Hull service.

FINNRIDER Built at Bremerhaven, Germany as the RAILSHIP II for *Railship*, later taken over by Finnlines. In 2002 renamed the FINNRUNNER. Operates between Travemünde and Turku.

FINNRUNNER Built at Bremerhaven, Germany as the RAILSHIP III for *Railship*, later taken over by Finnlines. In 2002 renamed the FINNRUNNER. Operates between Travemünde and Turku.

MIRANDA Built at Hamburg, Germany for *Godby Shipping A/S* of Finland. Initially chartered to *Transfennica*. In 2000 she was chartered to *Finnlines*. Currently used on the Helsinki - Copenhagen - Helsingborg service.

NORCLIFF Built at Trogir, Croatia for *Sea-Link AB* of Sweden but due to delays order cancelled before completion. On delivery, renamed the BRAVO and chartered to the *Stora Paper Group*. In 1995 chartered to *North Sea Ferries* and renamed the NORCLIFF. She became second vessel on the Middlesbrough - Rotterdam service. The charter ended in 1996 when the service reverted to a single ship operation. She kept her *NSF* name and was chartered to a number of operators including *Finnlines (Finncarriers)*. In 2001 again chartered to *Finnlines* and is currently used on the Finland to Spain - Portugal via Antwerp service.

POLARIS Built at Hamburg, Germany for *Pohl Shipping* and chartered to Finncarriers. Currently operating between Finland and Spain - Portugal via Antwerp.

TRANSBALTICA Built at Ulsan, South Korea as the AHLERS BALTIC the for *Ahlers Line* and chartered to *Finncarriers*. In 1995 acquired by *Poseidon Schiffahrt AG* of Germany and renamed the TRANSBALTICA. She continued to be chartered to *Finncarriers* and was acquired by them when they purchased *Poseidon Schiffahrt AG* (now *Finnlines Deutschland AG*) in 1997. Currently operating on the Helsinki - Hamina - Felixstowe - Zeebrugge - Antwerp service.

TRANSFINLANDIA Built at Lübeck, Germany for *Poseidon Schiffahrt AG* of Germany. Currently operating on the Helsinki - Kotka - Turku - Rauma - Lübeck service.

VASALAND Built at Rauma, Finland as the OIHONNA for *Finncarriers*. In 2003 sold to *Stena RoRo*. Later sold to *Imperial RoRo*, chartered back to *Stena RoRo* and then time chartered to *Finnlines*. Currently operating on the Lübeck - Malmö - Hanko - Kotka - Rostock service.

MANN LINES

THE COMPANY *Mann Lines* is owned by *Mann & Son (London) Ltd* of Great Britain. It replaced in 2001 *ArgoMann Ferry Service*, a joint venture between *Argo Reederei* of Germany and *Mann & Son*.

MANAGEMENT Managing Director Bill Binks.

ADDRESS *UK* Mann & Son (London) Ltd, The Naval House, Kings Quay Street, Harwich CO12 3JJ, Germany Mann Lines GmbH, Birkenstrasse 15, 28195 Bremen.

TELEPHONE Administration & Reservations *UK* +44 (0)1255 245200, *Germany* +49 (0)421 163850

FAX Administration & Reservations *UK* +44 (0)1255 245219, *Germany* +49 (0)421 1638520

INTERNET Email enquiry@mannlines.co.uk **Website** www.mannlines.com *(English)*

ROUTE OPERATED Harwich (Navyard) *(dep: 22.00 Fri)* - Cuxhaven *(arr: 17.00 Sat, dep: 19.00 Sat)* - Tallinn (Paldiski) *(arr: 15.00 Mon, dep: 21.00 Mon)* - Turku *(arr: 08.00 Tue, dep: 17.30 Tue)* - Bremerhaven *(arr: 18.00 Thu, dep: 21.00 Thu)* - Harwich *(arr: 16.00 Fri); (1); one per week)*, Turku *(dep: 23.00 Fri)* - Tallinn (Paldiski) *(arr: 12.00 Sat, dep: 19.00 Sat)* - Gdansk *(arr: 21.00 Sun, dep: 04.00 Mon)* - Kiel *(arr: 05.00 Tue, dep: 10.00 Tue)* - Bremerhaven *(arr: 01.00 Wed, dep: 06.00 Wed)* - Kiel *(arr: 22.00 Wed, dep: 03.00 Thu)* - Turku *(arr: 18.00 Fri); (2); one per week)*.

1	ESTRADEN	18205t	99	20.0k	162.7m	12P	130C	170T	A	FI
2	TRADEN	8188t	77	14.5k	129.2m	10P	-	92T	A	FI

ESTRADEN Built at Rauma, Finland as the ESTRADEN for *Rederi Ab Engship* of Finland and chartered to *ArgoMann*. Later in 1999 renamed the AMAZON. In 2001 charter was taken over by *Mann Lines* and later in the year she resumed the name ESTRADEN.

TRADEN Built at Rauma, Finland as the ABHA. In 1979 sold to *Bore Line* of Finland and renamed the BORE SONG. In 1991 chartered to *Erikson Rederi AB* of Åland and renamed the KEY BISCAYNE. Later that year she was sub-chartered to *Seaboard Marine* of the USA and renamed the SEABOARD HORIZON. She was used on services in the Caribbean. In 1993 she returned to *Bore Line* and was renamed the BORE SONG. She was chartered to *Finncarriers*. In 1997 she was renamed the TRANSNORDICA. In 2000 she was sold to *Rederi AB Engship* of Finland and renamed the TRADEN. She was chartered to *Botnia Link*. In 2001 she was replaced by the larger TRANSPARADEN. In 2002 she was again chartered to *Finnlines* and placed on their new Hull - Gdynia service. Later in 2002 she was chartered to *Mann Lines*.

Estraden *(John May)*

Maersk Flanders *(Andrew Cooke)*

SECTION 3 – FREIGHT ONLY FERRIES

NORFOLKLINE

THE COMPANY, MANAGEMENT, ADDRESS, TELEPHONE & INTERNET See Section 1.

ROUTES OPERATED Felixstowe *(dep: 06.00 Tue-Fr, 12.00 Daily, 19.00 Mon-Fri, 23.59 Daily)* - Scheveningen *(dep: 07.00 Tue-Fri, 13.00 Sun, 14.00 Mon-Sat, 19.30 Mon-Sat, 22.00 Sun, 23.59 Mon-Fri)* (7 hrs; *(1,2,3,4)*; 4 per day), Immingham - Esbjerg (5 per week), Harwich - Esbjerg (6/7 per week). UK - Denmark services operated in conjunction with *DFDS Tor Line* who provide all vessels.

1	MAERSK ANGLIA	13017t	00	18.6k	142.5m	12P	-	114T	A	NL
2	MAERSK EXPORTER	13017t	96	18.6k	142.5m	12P	-	114T	A	NL
3	MAERSK FLANDERS	13073t	00	18.6k	142.5m	12P	-	114T	A	NL
4	MAERSK IMPORTER	13017t	96	18.6k	142.5m	12P	-	114T	A	NL

MAERSK ANGLIA Built at Guangzhou, China for *Norfolkline*. Entered service as the GUANGZHOU 7130011 (unofficially the 'China II') but renamed shortly afterwards. Operates on the Scheveningen - Felixstowe service.

MAERSK EXPORTER, MAERSK IMPORTER Built at Shimizu, Japan for *Norfolkline*. Used on the Felixstowe - Scheveningen service.

MAERSK FLANDERS Built at Guangzhou, China for *Norfolkline*. Used on the Felixstowe - Scheveningen service.

NORSEMERCHANT FERRIES

THE COMPANY, MANAGEMENT AND ADDRESS. See Section 1.

TELEPHONE Administration +44 (0)28 9077 9090, **Reservations Belfast (Liverpool service)** +44 (0)870 6099 299, **(Heysham service)** +44 (0) +44 (0)870 6099 299, **Liverpool (Belfast service)** +44 (0) +44 (0)870 6099 299, **(Dublin service)** +44 (0) +44 (0)870 6099 299, **Heysham** +44 (0)1524 865050, **Dublin** +353 (0)1 819 2955.

FAX Administration Belfast +44 (0)28 9077 1286, **Reservations Belfast (Liverpool service)** +44 (0)28 9077 5520, **(Heysham service)** +44 (0)28 9078 6073, **Heysham** +44 (0)1524 865070, **Liverpool (Belfast service)** 44 (0)151 906 2718, **(Dublin service)** 44 (0)151 906 2718, **Dublin** +353 (0)1 819 2941.

INTERNET Email enquiries@norsemerchant.com **Website** www.norsemerchant.com *(English)*

ROUTES OPERATED Port of Liverpool (Twelve Quays River Terminal, Birkenhead) *(dep: 11.00 Tue-Sat, 22.00 Sun, 22.45 Mon-Sat)* - Dublin *(dep: 10.30 Tue-Sat, 22.00 Sun, 22.45 Mon-Sat)* (7 hrs; *(1,4)*; 2 per day), Heysham *(dep: 09.00 Tue-Sat, 21.00 Daily)* - Dublin *(dep: 09.00 Tue-Sat, 21.00 Daily)* (8 hrs; *(6, VARBOLA (See **Dart Line***); 2 per day), Heysham *(dep: 09.00 Tue-Sat, 21.00 Daily)* - Belfast *(dep: 09.00 Tue-Sat, 21.00 Daily)* (8 hrs; *(2,3)*; 2 per day.

NorseMerchant Ferries also operate passenger/freight services from Liverpool to Belfast. See Section 1.

1	LINDA ROSA	17428t	96	19.7k	183.1m	12P	-	144T	AS	IT
2	MERCHANT BRAVERY	9368t	78	17.0k	133.0m	12P	-	94T	A	BS
3	MERCHANT BRILLIANT	9368t	79	17.0k	133.0m	12P	-	94T	A	BS
4	NORSE MERSEY	13500t	95	19.5k	174.5m	61P	-	160T	A	IT
5	RIVER LUNE	7765t	83	15.0k	121.4m	12P	-	90T	A	BS
6	SAGA MOON	7746t	84	15.0k	134.8m	12P	-	66T	A	GI

LINDA ROSA Built at Donanda, Italy for *Levantina Trasporti* of Italy. Chartered to *CoTuNav* of Tunisia for service between Tunisia and Italy. In 2002 chartered to *NorseMerchant Ferries* to operate additional sailings between Liverpool and Belfast. In 2003 transferred to the Birkenhead – Dublin service, replacing the ro-pax BRAVE MERCHANT (see section 1) which had been chartered to the *British MoD*.

MERCHANT BRAVERY Built at Oslo, Norway. Launched as the STEVI for *Steineger & Wiik* of Norway and, on delivery, chartered to *Norient Line* of Norway, being renamed the NORWEGIAN CRUSADER. In 1980 chartered to *Ignazio Messina* of Italy for Mediterranean service and renamed the JOLLY GIALLO. In 1982 the charter ended and she was briefly renamed the NORWEGIAN CRUSADER before being purchased by *Ignazio Messina* and resuming the name JOLLY GIALLO. In 1993 sold to *Merchant Ferries*, renamed the MERCHANT BRAVERY and placed on the Heysham - Warrenpoint (Dublin since 1995) service. In 1999 transferred to *Belfast Freight Ferries'* Heysham - Belfast service.

MERCHANT BRILLIANT Built at Kyrksæterøra, Norway as the NORWEGIAN CHALLENGER *for Steineger & Wiik* of Norway and chartered to *Norient Line* of Norway. In 1982, chartered to *Ignazio Messina* of Italy for Mediterranean service and renamed the JOLLY BRUNO. Later in 1982 she was purchased by *Ignazio Messina*. In 1993 sold to *Merchant Ferries*, renamed the MERCHANT BRILLIANT and placed on the Heysham - Warrenpoint (Dublin since 1995) service. In 1999 transferred to *Belfast Freight Ferries'* Heysham - Belfast service.

NORSE MERSEY Built at Donanda, Italy for *Levantina Trasporti* of Italy. On delivery, chartered to *Norse Irish Ferries* and named the NORSE MERSEY (replacing another vessel with the same name). In 1997 chartered to *P&O Ferrymasters* and operated between Middlesbrough and Gothenburg. In 1999 she was chartered to *DFDS Tor Line* to operate between Immingham and Rotterdam until mid 2000. In 2001 she had a brief periods with *Stena Line* between Gothenburg and Travemünde and the British *MoD* and was then chartered to *CETAM*, operating between Marseilles and Tunis. In early 2002 she was renamed the CETAM MASSALIA. In September 2002 she was chartered to *NorseMerchant Ferries* to operate between Birkenhead and Dublin in freight only mode in lieu of the DAWN MERCHANT which had been chartered to *Norfolkline*. She resumed the name NORSE MERSEY.

RIVER LUNE Built at Galatz, Romania for *Almira Shipping* of Liberia (part of the Norwegian *Balder* group) as the BALDER VIK and initially used on services between Italy and the Middle East. Subsequently she was employed on a number of charters including *North Sea Ferries* and *Norfolk Line*. In 1986 she was acquired by *Navimpex* of Romania, renamed the BAZIAS 7 and initially used on Mediterranean and Black Sea services. In 1987 she was chartered to *Kent Line* for service between Chatham and Zeebrugge. In 1988 she was sold to *Stena Rederi AB* of Sweden and chartered for service between Finland and Germany. In 1989 she was briefly renamed the STENA TOPPER before being further renamed the SALAR. During the ensuing years she undertook a number of charters. In 1993 she briefly resumed the name STENA TOPPER before being chartered to *Belfast Freight Ferries* and renamed the RIVER LUNE. In October 1996 she was sold to *Belfast Freight Ferries*. In 1999 she was transferred to *Merchant Ferries'* Heysham - Dublin service. In 2000 she returned to the Heysham - Belfast route. In January 2003 replaced the VARBOLA on the Heysham – Dublin service. In May 2003 chartered to *Dart Line*.

SAGA MOON Built at Travemünde, Germany as the LIDARTINDUR for *Trader Line* of the Faroe Islands for services between Tórshavn and Denmark. In 1986 chartered to *Belfast Freight Ferries* renamed the SAGA MOON. In 1990 she was purchased by *Belfast Freight Ferries*. In 1995 she was lengthened by 18m to increase trailer capacity from 52 to 72 units and trade cars from 25 to 50; the lift was replaced by an internal fixed ramp. In 1998 she was transferred to *Merchant Ferries'* Heysham - Dublin service and in 2001 back to the Heysham - Belfast service. Resumed service between Heysham and Dublin in 2002.

Hascosay *(Miles Cowsill)*

Norcape *(Philippe Holthof)*

NORSE ISLAND FERRIES

THE COMPANY *Norse Island Ferries* is a UK private sector company jointly owned by *Gulf Offshore, Cenargo, Jim Backenridge Transport, Shetland Transport* and *Northwards.*

MANAGEMENT Managing Director Managing Prentice, **Marketing Manager** Stephen Struthers.

TELEPHONE Administration & Reservations 01224 594881

FAX Administration & Reservations 01224 594882.

INTERNET Email stephen@norseif.co.uk **Website** www.norseif.co.uk (English)

ROUTE OPERATED Aberdeen *(dep: 17.30 Mon-Fri)* – Lerwick (Shetland) *(dep: 19.00 Mon-Fri)* (13 hours; *(1,2)*; 5 per week), Aberdeen *(dep: 23.00 Sat)* - Kirkwall *(arr: 08.00, dep: 11.00 Sun)* - Lerwick *(arr: 18.00 Sun)*; ((1,2); 1 per week), Lerwick *(dep: 12.00 Sun)* - Kirkwall *(arr: 20.00, dep: 22.00 Sun)* - Aberdeen *(arr: 07.00 Mon)* ((1,2); 1 per week). Full timetable not operated at time of going to print as the MERCHANT VENTURE is out of service.

1	MERCHANT VENTURE	6056t	79	17.0k	119.4m	12P	-	48T	A	IM
2	ST ROGNVALD	5297t	70	16 k	103.8m	12P	-	41L	A	UK

MERCHANT VENTURE Built at Castelo, Portugal as the FARMAN and chartered to *GNMTC* of Italy for Mediterranean services. In 1982 she was sold to *Medlines* for similar service and renamed the MED ADRIATICO. In 1985 she was sold, renamed the ARGENTEA and chartered to *SGMAT*, continuing to operate in the Mediterranean. In 1987 sold to *Cenargo* and chartered to *Merchant Ferries* who renamed her first the MERCHANT ISLE and then the MERCHANT VENTURE. She was purchased by *Merchant Ferries* in 1993. Until 1993 she was used on the Fleetwood - Warrenpoint service; in 1993 the UK terminal was moved to Heysham and in 1995 the Irish terminal was moved to Dublin. In autumn 1998 she was placed on the charter market. In Autumn 1999 she was chartered to *P&O Irish Sea* and used on the Fleetwood - Larne service. She was later replaced by EUROPEAN NAVIGATOR and then used on Cairnryan – Larne service until end of 1999 when her charter ended and she was returned to her owners. In 2000 she operated for *Merchant Ferries* between Heysham and Belfast until the autumn when she was replaced by the DART 3 (see *Dart Line*) and laid up. In August 2002 transferred to *Norse Island Ferries.*

ST ROGNVALD Built at Lübeck, Germany. Launched as the RHONETAL but renamed the NORCAPE on delivery and chartered to *North Sea Ferries* for their Hull - Rotterdam service; in 1972 she inaugurated their Hull - Zeebrugge service. In 1974 she returned to her owners and resumed the name RHONETAL. In 1975 sold to *Meridional D'Armements* of France for services to Corsica and renamed the RHONE. In 1987 sold to *Conatir* of Italy for Mediterranean services and renamed the MARINO TORRE. In 1989 taken on six months charter to *P&O Scottish Ferries.* In 1990 she was purchased by them and renamed the ST ROGNVALD. She initially operated alongside and then replaced the ST MAGNUS (1206t, 1970). Earlier calls at Leith, Hanstholm (Denmark) and Stavanger (Norway) were discontinued. In August 2002 *P&O Scottish Ferries'* service ceased and she was chartered to *Norse Island Ferries.*

NORTHLINK FERRIES

THE COMPANY, MANAGEMENT, ADDRESS, TELEPHONE, FAX & INTERNET See Section 1.

ROUTES OPERATED Aberdeen - Kirkwall (Orkney) *(8 hours; (1))*, Aberdeen - Lerwick (Shetland) *(13 hours; (1))*. Timetable varies according to demand

1	HASCOSAY	6136t	71	17.0k	118.4m	12P	-	50T	A	NO

HASCOSAY Built Kristiansand, Norway as the JUNO. In 1979 sold to *Finnfranline* of France, renamed the NORMANDIA and chartered to *Finncarriers* for service between Finland and France. In 1982 chartered to *Sudcargo* and used on services between France and Algeria and the Middle East. In 1986 sold to *Mikkola* of Finland, renamed the MISIDIA and chartered to *Transfennica* for services between Finland and Northern Europe. In 1990 sold to *Kristiania Eiendom* of Norway and renamed the EURO NOR. In 1991 she was chartered to *Commodore Ferries* and renamed the COMMODORE CLIPPER. In 1996 she was replaced by the COMMODORE GOODWILL and renamed the SEA CLIPPER. She was placed on the charter market. In 1998 she was chartered to the *Estonian Shipping Company (ESCO)* and operated between Germany and Estonia; she was renamed the TRANSBALTICA. In 2001 she resumed the name SEA CLIPPER and chartered to *Fjord Line.* In 2002 she was sold to *NorthLink* and renamed the HASCOSAY. She was modified to enable her to accommodate *NorthLink's* cassette system for livestock transport in addition to commercial vehicles. She was chartered to *Caledonian MacBrayne* to operate between Ullapool and Stornoway during summer 2002. In October 2002 entered service with *NorthLink*.

P&O FERRIES

THE COMPANY, MANAGEMENT, ADDRESS, TELEPHONE See Section 1.

INTERNET Website www.poferriesfreight.co.uk *(English)*

ROUTES OPERATED Dover *(dep: 01.30, 06.30, 11.15, 15.45, 20.15)* – Calais *(dep: 05.00, 10.00, 14.30, 19.00, 23.30)* (1 hr 15 min; *(1)*; 5 per day (+ up to 35 sailings by multi-purpose vessels (see Section 1)), Hull *(dep: 16.00 Thu, 21.00* Daily, 21.00 Wed)* - Rotterdam dep *(21.00* Daily, 23.30 Wed)* (Wed ex Hull: 2, Wed ex Rotterdam, Thu ex Hull: 4, *passenger vessels), Hull *(dep: 19.00* Daily, 21.00 Mon, Wed+, Fri)* - Zeebrugge *(dep: 19.00* Daily, 21.00 Tue, Sat, 22.00 Thu)* (13 hrs (+23 hrs via Rotterdam); *(2, *passenger vessels)*; 10 per week), Middlesbrough (Teesport) *(dep: 21.00 Mon-Wed, Fri, 17.00 Sat)* - Rotterdam (Beneluxhaven, Europoort) *(dep: 23.00 Mon-Tue, Thu-Fri, 19.00 Sat)* (15 hrs; *(3,4)*; 5 per week), Middlesbrough (Teesport) *(dep: 21.00 Mon-Fri, 17.00 Sat)* - Zeebrugge *(dep: 20.30 Mon-Sat)* (15 hrs; *(5,6)*; 6 per week).

1	EUROPEAN SEAWAY	22986t	91	21.0k	179.7m	200P	-	120L	BA2	UK
2	NORCAPE	14807t	79	19.4k	151.0m	12P	-	124T	A	NL
3	NORKING	17884t	80	19.0k	170.9m	12P	-	155T	A	FI
4	NORQUEEN	17884t	80	19.0k	170.9m	12P	-	155T	A	FI
5	NORSKY	19992t	99	20.0k	180.0m	12P	-	194T	A	NL
6	NORSTREAM	19992t	99	20.0k	180.0m	12P	-	194T	A	NL

EUROPEAN SEAWAY Built at Bremerhaven, Germany for *P&O European Ferries* for the Dover - Zeebrugge freight service. In 2000 a regular twice daily freight only Dover-Calais service was established, using this vessel, which continued to operate to Zeebrugge at night. In 2001 passengers (not foot or coach passengers) began to be conveyed on the Dover - Zeebrugge service. In 2003 the Zeebrugge service ended and she now operates only between Dover and Calais in a freight only mode.

NORCAPE Built at Tamano, Japan. Launched as the PUMA but, on completion chartered to *B&I Line* and renamed the TIPPERARY for their Dublin - Liverpool service. In 1989 sold to *North Sea Ferries*, renamed the NORCAPE and introduced onto the Ipswich - Rotterdam service. In 1995 that service ceased and she was moved to the Hull - Zeebrugge freight service. She retains Dutch crew and registry.

NORKING, NORQUEEN Built at Rauma, Finland as the BORE KING and the BORE QUEEN for *Bore Line* of Finland for Baltic services. In 1991 chartered to *North Sea Ferries* for their Teesport - Zeebrugge service and renamed the NORKING and NORQUEEN respectively. During winter 1995/96 they were lengthened by 28.8 metres and re-engined. In 1999 transferred to the Teesport - Rotterdam service.

NORSKY, NORSTREAM Built at Rauma, Finland for *Bore Line* of Finland and chartered to *P&O North Sea Ferries.* They operate on the Teesport - Zeebrugge service.

P&O IRISH SEA

THE COMPANY AND ADDRESS See Section 1.

MANAGEMENT Chairman Russ Peters, **Managing Director** J H Kearsley, **Commercial Manager** Philip Simpson.

TELEPHONE Administration +44 (0)1253 615700, **Reservations** *UK* 0870 6000 868, *Irish Republic* +353 (0)1 855 0522.

FAX Administration & Reservations *Cairnryan* +44 (0)1581 200282, *Larne* +44 (0)28 2827 2477, *Fleetwood* +44 (0)1253 615740.

INTERNET Website www.poisfreight.com *(English)*

ROUTES OPERATED Troon *(dep: 02.30 Mon-Sat, 12.00 Sun)* - Larne *(dep: 08.30 Sat, 19.00 Sun-Fri)* (4 hrs 30 mins; *(3)*; 1 per day), Fleetwood *(dep: 03.00 Tue-Sat, 10.00 Daily, 22.00 Daily)* - Larne *(dep: 10.00 Daily, 16.00 Mon-Fri, 22.00 Daily)* (7 hrs; *(2,4,5)*; 3 per day), Liverpool *(dep: 10.30 Tue-Sat, 22.30 Daily)* - Dublin *(dep: 10.30 Tue-Sat, 22.00 Mon-Sat, 23.00 Sun)* (8 hrs; *(6,7)*; 2 per day), Rosslare *(dep: 22.00 Tue, 21.30 Thu, 16.00 Sat)* - Cherbourg *(dep: 14.00 Sun, 22.00 Wed, 19.00 Fri)* (18 hrs; *(1)*; 3 per week). Note: Cairnryan – Larne sailings are no longer shown as this is now a full passenger service. Vessels are sometimes moved between routes. A limited number of private cars and their passengers is conveyed on the day sailings between Fleetwood and Larne and Liverpool and Dublin and on all sailings between Rosslare and Cherbourg under the 'Value Route' branding.

1	EUROPEAN DIPLOMAT	16776t	78	17.0k	151.0m	74P	-	122T	A2	UK
2	EUROPEAN LEADER	12879t	75	17.0k	157.2m	50P	-	114T	A	BD
3	EUROPEAN MARINER	5897t	77	15.0k	116.3m	12P	-	62T	A	BS
4	EUROPEAN PIONEER	14387t	75	17.7k	141.8m	76P	-	114T	A	BD
5	EUROPEAN SEAFARER	10957t	75	18.0k	141.8m	50P	-	80T	A	BD
6	NORBANK	17464t	93	22.0k	166.7m	114P	-	150T	A	NL
7	NORBAY	17464t	94	22.0k	166.7m	114P	-	150T	A	UK

EUROPEAN DIPLOMAT Built at Ulsan, South Korea as the STENA TRANSPORTER, for *Stena Rederi* of Sweden. In 1979 she was renamed the FINNROSE and chartered to *Finnlines*. She later served with *Atlanticargo* on their service between Europe and USA/Mexico. In 1980 she returned to *Stena Line* and resumed her original name. Later in 1980 she was chartered to *European Ferries* for their Felixstowe - Rotterdam freight-only service and renamed the BALTIC FERRY. In 1982 she served in the Falkland Islands Task Force. In 1986 she was converted to ro-pax format and moved to the Felixstowe - Zeebrugge passenger service. In 1992 she was renamed the PRIDE OF SUFFOLK. In 1994 she was purchased by *P&O European Ferries*. In 1995 the Felixstowe - Zeebrugge passenger service ceased, most of her additional passenger accommodation was removed, passenger capacity was reduced and she was transferred to the Felixstowe - Rotterdam freight service. In 2001 transferred to the *P&O Irish Sea's* Liverpool - Dublin route and renamed the EUROPEAN DIPLOMAT. In 2002 transferred to the Rosslare - Cherbourg route.

EUROPEAN LEADER Built at Hamburg, Germany for *Stena Line* as the BUFFALO and due to be chartered to *P&O* for *Pandoro* Irish Sea services. Before completion she was purchased by *P&O*. In 1989 she was lengthened by 12.5m and in 1998 she was further lengthened by 15m and renamed the EUROPEAN LEADER. She is now used on the Fleetwood - Larne service.

EUROPEAN MARINER Built at Bremerhaven, Germany as the SALAHALA and chartered to *Gilnavi* of Italy for Mediterranean services. In 1990 she was purchased by *Cenargo* and chartered to *Merchant Ferries* who renamed her the MERCHANT VALIANT. She was used on their Fleetwood - Warrenpoint service until 1993 when she was chartered to *Pandoro* and placed on their Ardrossan - Larne service. Purchased by *P&O* in 1995 and renamed the LION. In early 1998 renamed the EUROPEAN HIGHLANDER. In July 2001, the service moved to Troon and she was renamed the EUROPEAN MARINER. In 2002 replaced by the EUROPEAN NAVIGATOR. After a brief charter to *Seatruck Ferries* she went on a two month charter to *Color Line*, operating between Kristiansand and Hirtshals. On return she went on a short charter to *Commodore Ferries* and in late September was transferred to the Larne - Troon route replacing the EUROPEAN NAVIGATOR. Later she was chartered to *Norse*

Island Ferries; she returned to *P&O Irish Sea* in late 2002.

EUROPEAN PIONEER Built at Hamburg, Germany for *Stena Line* as the BISON and due to be chartered to *P&O* for *Pandoro* Irish Sea services. Before completion she was purchased by *P&O*. Between 1989 and 1993 she was operated by *B&I Line* of Ireland on a joint service with *Pandoro* between Dublin and Liverpool. An additional deck was added in 1995. In late 1997 she was renamed the EUROPEAN PIONEER. She is now used on the Fleetwood - Larne service.

EUROPEAN SEAFARER Built at Hamburg, Germany. Ordered by *Stena Line* as the UNION TRADER but completed as the UNION MELBOURNE for the *Northern Coasters Ltd* of the UK and lengthened before entering service. Chartered to the *Union Steamship Company* of New Zealand and used on services to Australia. In 1980 she was sold to another *P&O* subsidiary and renamed the PUMA. In early 1998 she was renamed the EUROPEAN SEAFARER. Used on the Fleetwood - Larne service in recent years, in 2001 she was transferred to the Rosslare - Cherbourg service. In 2002 replaced by the EUROPEAN DIPLOMAT and returned to the Fleetwood - Larne service.

NORBANK Built at Krimpen aan den IJssel, Rotterdam, Netherlands for *North Sea Ferries* for the Hull - Rotterdam service. She was originally owned by *Nedlloyd* and in 1996 was sold to *P&O* but retains Dutch crew and registry. In May 2001 moved to the Felixstowe - Europoort route. In January 2002 transferred to *P&O Irish Sea* and operated on the Liverpool – Dublin route.

NORBAY Built at Krimpen aan den IJssel, Rotterdam, Netherlands for *North Sea Ferries* for the Hull - Rotterdam service. Owned by *P&O*. In January 2002 transferred to *P&O Irish Sea* and operated on the Liverpool – Dublin route.

SCA TRANSFOREST

THE COMPANY *SCA Transforest* is a Swedish company.

MANAGEMENT Managing Director (UK) Bo Frölander.

ADDRESS Interforest Terminal London Ltd, 44 Berth, Tilbury Dock, Essex RM18 7HR.

TELEPHONE Administration & Reservations +44 (0)1375 48 85 00.

FAX Administration & Reservations +44 (0)1375 48 85 03.

INTERNET Email bo.frolander@sca.com **Website** www.transforest.sca.se *(English)*

ROUTE OPERATED Umeå *(dep: 11.00 Mon, 16.00 Thu)* - Husum *(dep: 20.00 Mon, 22.00 Thu)* - Sundsvall *(dep: 12.00 Tue, 12.00 Fri)* - Iggesund *(dep: 19.00 Tue, 19.00 Fri)* - Tilbury *(arr: 11.00 Tue, 13.00 Sat, dep: 16.00 Tue, 18.00 Sat)* - Rotterdam (Eemhaven) *(dep: 13.00 Sun, 12.00 Wed)* - Helsingborg *(arr: 07.00 Fri)* (8/9 day round trip; *(1,2,3)*; 2 per week).

1	OBBOLA	20171t	96	16.0k	170.6m	0P	-	-	A	SW
2	ORTVIKEN	20171t	97	16.0k	170.4m	0P	-	-	A	SW
3	ÖSTRAND	20171t	96	16.0k	170.6m	0P	-	-	A	SW

OBBOLA, ORTVIKEN, ÖSTRAND Built at Seville, Spain for *Gorthon Lines* and chartered to *SCA Transforest*. They are designed for the handling of forest products in non-wheeled 'cassettes' but can also accommodate ro-ro trailers; however no trailer capacity is quoted. The ORTVIKEN was lengthened during autumn 2000 and the OBBOLA and ÖSTRAND were lengthened during 2001

Norstream *(Philippe Holthof)*

European Mariner *(John Hendy)*

SEA-CARGO

THE COMPANY *Sea-Cargo AS* of Norway is a joint venture between *Nor-Cargo AS* (a Norwegian company jointly owned by *Ofotens og Vesteraalen Dampskipsselskab, Det Stavargerske Dampskipsselskab* and *Troms Fylkes Dampskipsselskab*) and *SeaTrans DS* of Norway.

MANAGEMENT *Sea-Cargo UK Ltd* **Managing Director** Barry Jenks.

ADDRESS *Norway* Sea-Cargo AS, PO Box 353, Nesttun, N-5853 Bergen, Norway, *Grimsby* Sea-Cargo UK, 1 Prince Albert Gardens, Grimsby DN31 3HT, *Aberdeen* Nor-Cargo Ltd, Matthews Quay, Aberdeen Harbour, Aberdeen, AB11 5PG.

TELEPHONE Administration & Bookings *Bergen* +47 55 10 84 84, *Grimsby* +44 (0)1472 251269, *Aberdeen* +44 (0)1224 596481.

FAX Administration & Reservations *Bergen* +47 55 91 22 33, *Grimsby* +44 (0)1472 267966, *Aberdeen* +44 (0)1224 582360.

INTERNET Email mail@sea-cargo.no **Website** www.sea-cargo.no *(English, Norwegian)*

ROUTES OPERATED Circuit 1 Bergen *(dep: Sat)* - Tanager *(dep: Sat)* - Grimsby *(arr/dep: Mon)* - Amsterdam *(arr/dep: Tue)* – Tananger *(arr: Thu)* - Haugesund *(arr: Thu)* - Odda *(arr: Fri)* - Bergen *(arr: Sat)* (1 week; *(1)*; weekly), **Circuit 2** Bergen *(dep: Tue, Fri)* - Tananger *(dep: Wed, Sat)* - Aberdeen *(arr/dep: Thu, Sun)* - Tananger *(arr: Fri, Mon)* - Bergen *(arr: Fri, Mon)* (3 days; *(2)*; 2 per week), **Circuit 3** Bergen *(dep: Tue)* - Husnes *(dep: Wed)* Karmoy *(dep: Wed)* - Tanager *(dep: Wed)* - Amsterdam *(arr/dep: Fri)* - Grimsby *(arr/dep: Sat)* - Tanager *(arr: Mon)* - Bergen *(arr: Mon)* (1 week; *(3)*; weekly).

1	COMETA	4610t	81	16.0k	102.2m	0P	-	26T	AS	NO
2	SC ABERDEEN	4234t	79	15.5k	109.0m	0P	-	24T	AS	NO
3	TRANS CARRIER	8407t	93	14.5k	125.2m	0P	-	78T	A	BS

COMETA Built at Rissa, Norway for *Nor-Cargo*.

SC ABERDEEN Built at Rissa, Norway for *Nor-Cargo*. Launched as the ERIC JARL but renamed the ASTREA before entering service. In 1986 she sank and, after raising and refitting she was, in 1992, renamed the TUNGENES. In 2001 she was renamed the SC ABERDEEN.

TRANS CARRIER Built at Kraljevica, Croatia as the KORSNÄS LINK for *SeaLink AB* of Sweden and due to be time chartered to *Korsnäs AB*, a Swedish forest products company. However, due to the war in Croatia, delivery was seriously delayed and she was offered for sale. In 1994 sold to the *Swan Group* and renamed the SWAN HUNTER. She was placed on the charter market. In 1997 she was chartered to *Euroseabridge* and renamed the PARCHIM. In 1999 the charter ended and she resumed the name SWAN HUNTER. In 1999 she was sold to *SeaTrans* and renamed the TRANS CARRIER.

SEAFRANCE

THE COMPANY, MANAGEMENT & ADDRESS See Section 1.

TELEPHONE Reservations +44 (0)1304 203030.

FAX Reservations +33 321 464861

INTERNET Email freightdover@wanadoo.fr **Website** www.seafrancefreight.com *(English, French)*

ROUTE OPERATED Calais *(dep: 01.45 Mon-Sat, 05.45 Mon-Sat, 09.45 Tue-Sat, 13.45, 17.45, 21.45 Sun-Fri)* - Dover *(dep: 02.45 Mon-Sat, 06.45 Mon-Sat, 10.45 Tue-Sat, 14.45, 18.45, 22.45 Sun-Fri)* (1 hr 30 mins; *(1)*; 6 per day).

1	SEAFRANCE NORD PAS-DE-CALAIS	13727t	87	21.5k	160.1m	80P	-	102L	BA2	FR

SEAFRANCE NORD PAS-DE-CALAIS Built as the NORD PAS-DE-CALAIS at Dunkerque, France for *SNCF* for the Dunkerque (Ouest) - Dover train ferry service. Before being used on this service (which required the construction of a new berth at Dover (Western Docks)) in May 1988, she operated road freight services from Calais to Dover Eastern Docks. The train ferry service continued to operate following the opening of the Channel Tunnel in 1994, to convey road vehicles and dangerous loads which were banned from the tunnel. However, it ceased in December 1995 and, after a refit, in February 1996 she was renamed the SEAFRANCE NORD PAS-DE-CALAIS and switched to the Calais - Dover service, primarily for road freight vehicles and drivers but also advertised as carrying up to 50 car passengers. Since the entry into service of a third multi-purpose ferry, she has operated on a freight-only basis.

SEATRUCK FERRIES

THE COMPANY *Seatruck Ferries Ltd* is a British private sector company, owned by *Crescent plc*.

MANAGEMENT Managing Director Kevin Hobbs, **Sales Director** Alastair Eagles.

ADDRESS *Warrenpoint (HQ)* Seatruck House, The Ferry Terminal, Warrenpoint, County Down BT34 3JR. *Heysham* North Quay, Heysham Port, Heysham, Morecambe, Lancs LA3 2UL.

TELEPHONE Administration +44 (0)28 4175 4411, **Reservations** *Warrenpoint* +44 (0)28 4175 4400, *Heysham* +44 (0)1524 853512.

FAX Administration +44 (0)28 4175 4545, **Reservations** *Warrenpoint* +44 (0)28 4177 3737, *Heysham* +44 (0)1524 853549.

INTERNET Email alistair@seatruck-ferries.co.uk **Website** www.seatruckferries.com *(English)*

ROUTES OPERATED Heysham *(dep: 08.00 Tue-Sat, 21.00 Daily)* - Warrenpoint *(dep: 08.00 Tue-Sat, 17.00 Sun, 20.00 Mon-Sat)* (8 hrs; *(1,2)*; 2 per day).

1	MOONDANCE	5881t	78	15.0k	116.3m	12P	-	62T	A	BS
2	RIVERDANCE	6041t	77	15.0k	116.3m	12P	-	62T	A	BS

MOONDANCE Built at Bremerhaven, Germany as the EMADALA for *Emadala Shipping* and chartered to *Gilnavi Line* of Italy for Mediterranean service. In 1987 she was purchased by *Gilnavi Line*. In 1990 sold to *Cenargo* of Great Britain and chartered to *Merchant Ferries* for their Heysham - Warrenpoint service and renamed the MERCHANT VICTOR. She was withdrawn from that service in 1993 and was chartered out to a number of operators. In 1997 she was chartered to *Seatruck Ferries* and renamed the MOONDANCE. In 1998 she was purchased by *Seatruck Ferries*. Following collapse of ramp at Warrenpoint in January 2001, she briefly operated between Heysham and Larne.

RIVERDANCE Built at Bremerhaven, as the MASHALA for *Mashala Shipping* and chartered to *Gilnavi* of Italy for Mediterranean services. After a long period out of service in the mid-nineteen eighties, in 1987 she was sold, renamed the HALLA and chartered for Caribbean service. In 1988 she was renamed the TIKAL. In 1989 she was sold to *Schiaffino Line* of France, renamed the SCHIAFFINO and put into service between Ramsgate and Ostend. In 1990 the company was taken over by *Sally Ferries* and in 1991 she was chartered to *Belfast Freight Ferries*. In 1993 she was renamed the SALLY EUROBRIDGE. In January 1994, she was chartered to *North Sea Ferries* to operate between Hull and Zeebrugge and renamed the EUROBRIDGE. In summer 1994 she returned to *Sally Ferries*, resumed the name SALLY EUROBRIDGE and became the second vessel on the Ramsgate - Vlissingen service; in the autumn the British terminal was switched to Dartford. In 1995 she was chartered to *Norfolk Line*, renamed the EUROBRIDGE and also sold by *Sally Ferries*. In 1996 she was chartered to *Seatruck Ferries* and renamed the RIVERDANCE. In 1997 she was purchased by *Seatruck Ferries*. Following collapse of ramp at Warrenpoint in January 2001, she briefly operated between Heysham and Larne.

Stena Transporter *(Rob de Visser)*

Stena Britannica *(John Bryant)*

SEAWHEEL

THE COMPANY *Seawheel Ltd* is a UK company, part of the *Simon Group plc.*

MANAGEMENT Managing Director Alan Jones, **Marketing Manager** Richard Beales, **Killingholme Manager** Robin Anson.

ADDRESS *Seawheel HO* Western House, Hadleigh Road, Ipswich, Suffolk IP2 0HB, *Local Office* Seawheel Limited, CCTL Division, Humber Sea Terminal, Clough Lane, North Killingholme, North Lincolnshire, DN40 3JP.

TELEPHONE *Seawheel HO* **Administration and Reservations** +44 (0)1473 222000, *Local Office* +44 (0)1469 540 689.

FAX *Seawheel HO* **Administration & Reservations** +44 (0)1473 230083, *Local Office* +44 (0)1469 540 687.

INTERNET Email RAnson@seawheel.com **Website** www.seawheel.com *(English)*

ROUTE OPERATED Killingholme *(dep: 21.30 Mon-Thu, Sat)* - Rotterdam (Prins Johan Frisohaven) *(dep: 21.00 Mon-Fri)* (14 hrs; *(1,2)*; 4 per week), Killingholme *(dep: 22.00 Sun, 07.00 Thu, 21.00 Fri)* – Hamburg *(dep: 07.00 Sun, 17.00 Tue, 22.00 Fri)* (30-33 hrs; *(2,3)*; 6 per week).

1	SEAWHEEL HUMBER	14738t	79	18.0k	137.5m	12P	-	116T	A	GR
2	SEAWHEEL RHINE	10279t	77	17.5k	142.3m	8P	-	95T	A	SW
3	ZERAN	15414t	87	15.0k	147.0m	0P	-	84T	A	MA

SEAWHEEL HUMBER Built in Rauma, Finland as the BALTIC EAGLE for *United Baltic Corporation* and used on *Finanglia Ferries* services between the UK and Finland (joint with *Finncarriers*). In 1999 chartered to *Crowley American Transport Inc* for Caribbean service. In 2002 sold to *Jay Management Corporation* of the UK and renamed the OLYMPIC STAR. Later in 2002 chartered to *Seawheel* to inaugurate a Killingholme – Rotterdam service and renamed the SEAWHEEL HUMBER. Normally operates between Killingholme and Rotterdam.

SEAWHEEL RHINE Built at Naantali, Finland as the ROLITA for *Merivienti* of Italy. In 1979 chartered to *Finncarriers* of Finland, renamed the FINNFOREST and used on services between Finland and North West Europe. In 1982 sold to *EFFOA* of Finland and renamed the CANOPUS. In 1992 sold to *B&N* of Sweden and chartered to *Stora Line* for services from Sweden to NW Europe. She was renamed the CUPRIA. In 1995, chartered to *North Sea Ferries* to inaugurate a new service between Middlesbrough and Rotterdam and renamed the NORCOVE. In 1999 she was chartered to *Finncarriers* and renamed the CUPRIA. She was used on services from Finland to Spain via Antwerp. In 2001 she was chartered to *Cobelfret Ferries* for the Purfleet - Rotterdam service. In 2002 chartered to *SeaWind Line* to operate additional freight only sailings between Stockholm and Turku before the SKY WIND was delivered in September 2002. In September 2002 chartered to *Seawheel*, renamed the SEAWHEEL RHINE and placed on the Killingholme – Rotterdam service. Since January 2003 has also operated on the Killingholme – Hamburg service, operating the Friday out, Sunday back trip.

ZERAN Built at Gdansk, Poland for *Polish Ocean Lines* and operated on services between Poland and Northern Europe and the Mediterranean. In 2003 chartered to *Seawheel*. May be renamed the SEAWHEEL ELBE. Normally operates between Killingholme and Hamburg.

SMYRIL LINE

THE COMPANY, MANAGEMENT, ADDRESS, TELEPHONE, FAX & INTERNET See Section 1.

ROUTES OPERATED Tórshavn (Faroes) *(dep: 22.00 Tue)* – Lerwick (Shetland) *(arr: 12.00 Wed, dep: 14.00 Wed)* – Klasvik (Faroes) *(arr: 08.00 Thu, dep: 14.00 Fri)* - Tórshavn *(arr: 15.30 Fri, dep: 18.00 Fri)* – Drelnes (Faroes) *(arr: 20.30 Fri, dep: 21.00 Fri)* - Lerwick *(arr: 12.00 Sat, dep: 12.30 Sat)* - Hanstholm (Denmark) *(arr: 14.00 Sun, 17.00 Sun)* - Drelnes *(arr: 06.00 Tue, dep: 06.30 Tue)* - Tórshavn *(arr: 09.00 Tue)*. Note: because of the very low level of driver accompanied freight on this service, up to 12 passengers can be conveyed.

1	CLARE	5617t	72	17.0k	114.9m	12P	-	62T	A	NO

CLARE Built at Bremerhaven, Germany as the WESERTAL for *Reinecke* of Germany. After delivery she was renamed the MEYER EXPRESS and resumed the name WESERTAL in 1973. She was chartered out to a number of operators including *North Sea Ferries* and *Olau Line*. In 1998 she was briefly renamed the. In 1993 she was sold to Italian Interests and renamed the VINZIA E. She was chartered to *Stena Sealink Line* and operated between Newhaven and Dieppe. In 1994 she was chartered to DFDS subsidiary *Dan-Let Line* (later *DFDS Baltic Line*) and renamed the DANA BALTICA. She operated between Denmark and Lithuania. In 1996 she was renamed the CLARE and again placed on the charter market. 1997 she briefly served on *NorSea Link*, a joint venture between *Scandlines (DSB Rederi)* and *Norse Irish Ferries* between Kristiansand and Eemshaven in the north of the Netherlands. In 1998 she was again chartered to *DFDS* to institute freight only services between Newcastle and IJmuiden. After further brief charters she was, in 1999, briefly chartered to *CargoConnect Transport + Logistics* and placed on a new service between Hull and Hamburg. In 2001, she was chartered to *Smyril Line* to operate between Tórshavn and Hanstholm. In 2002, Lerwick was added to her winter itinerary. From September 2002 Aberdeen was added to a year round roster but dropped at the beginning of 2003.

STENA LINE

THE COMPANY, MANAGEMENT, ADDRESS, TELEPHONE AND INTERNET See Section 1.

ROUTE OPERATED Harwich *(dep:05.00 (Tue-Sat), 11.00 (Mon-Sat), 22.45 (Sun-Fri)* - Rotterdam *(dep: 11.30 (Mon-Fri), 19.00 (Mon-Fri), 23.45 (Sun-Fri))* (7 hrs 45 mins; *(1,4,5)*; 3 per day), Killingholme *(dep: 19.00)* - Hoek van Holland *(dep: 19.15)* (13 hrs; *(2,3)*; 1 per day).

1	STENA PARTNER	21162t	77	16.5k	184.6m	166P	-	180T	A2	UK
2	STENA SEARIDER	21019t	69	17.0k	178.9m	120P	-	198T	AS2	IM
3	STENA SEATRADER	17991t	73	17.5k	181.6m	221P	-	174T	AS2	UK
4	STENA TRANSFER	21162t	77	16.5k	184.6m	166P	-	180T	A2	UK
5	STENA TRANSPORTER	16776t	78	17.0k	151.0m	74P	-	122T	A2	UK

STENA PARTNER Built at Ulsan, South Korea for *Stena Rederi* as the ALPHA ENTERPRISE and chartered to *Aghiris Navigation* of Cyprus. In 1979 she was renamed the SYRIA and chartered to *Hellas Ferries* for services between Greece and Syria. In 1981 she was lengthened by 33.6m. In 1982 she was chartered to *European Ferries* and used on freight services between Felixstowe and Rotterdam. In 1983 she was renamed the STENA TRANSPORTER and in 1986 the CERDIC FERRY. In 1992 she was renamed the EUROPEAN FREEWAY and, in 1994, purchased by *P&O European Ferries*. In 2002 sold to *Stena Line* and renamed the FREEWAY. She initially operated between Felixstowe and Rotterdam and later Harwich and Rotterdam. In early 2003 she was renamed the STENA PARTNER.

STENA SEARIDER Built at Helsinki, Finland as the FINNCARRIER for *Finnlines* of Finland for service between Finland, Denmark and Germany. In 1975 renamed the POLARIS. In 1984 sold to *Rederi AB Nordö* of Sweden to operate between Malmö (Sweden) and Travemünde (Germany) and renamed the SCANDINAVIA. In 1987 she was rebuilt to increase capacity from 122 trailers to 200. In 1989 the name of the company was changed to *Nordö Link* and she was renamed the SCANDINAVIA LINK. In 1990 she was sold to *Stena Line*, renamed the STENA SEARIDER and used on their Gothenburg (Sweden) - Travemünde service. In 1991 she was chartered out for service in the Caribbean and renamed the SEARIDER. In 1992 she was chartered to *Norse Irish Ferries* and renamed the NORSE MERSEY. In 1995 she was replaced by a new vessel of the same name and returned to *Stena Line*, resumed the name STENA SEARIDER and resumed operating between Gothenburg and Travemünde and Gothenburg and Kiel. In May 1997, she was transferred to the Harwich - Hoek van Holland service. In autumn 2000 she inaugurated (with the chartered ROSEBAY - see the TRANSPARADEN, *Botnia Link*) a new service from Hoek van Holland to Killingholme (near Immingham).

STENA SEATRADER Built at Nakskov, Denmark as the SVEALAND for *Lion Ferry AB* of Sweden and chartered to *Statens Järnvägar (Swedish State Railways)* for the train ferry service between Trelleborg (Sweden) and Sassnitz (Germany (DDR)). The charter ceased in 1980 and in 1982 she was sold to *Rederi AB Nordö* of Sweden. She was lengthened by 33.7 metres, renamed the SVEALAND AV MALMÖ and used on their lorry/rail wagon service between Malmö and Travemünde. In 1986 she was rebuilt with a higher superstructure and in 1987 she was renamed the SVEA LINK, the service being renamed *Nordö Link*. In 1990 she was sold to *Stena Line*, renamed the STENA SEATRADER and introduced onto the Hoek van Holland - Harwich service. In spring 2001 she replaced the chartered ROSEBAY on the Hoek van Holland - Killingholme service.

STENA TRANSFER Built at Ulsan, South Korea. Launched as the STENA RUNNER by *Stena Rederi* of Sweden. On completion, renamed the ALPHA PROGRESS and chartered to *Aghiris Navigation* of Greece. In 1979 renamed the HELLAS and operated by *Soutos-Hellas Ferry Services* on services between Greece and Syria. In 1982 she was lengthened by 33.6m. In 1982 she was chartered to *European Ferries* and used on freight services between Felixstowe and Rotterdam. The following year she was returned to *Hellas Ferries*. In 1985 she returned to *European Ferries* and the Rotterdam service. In 1986 she was renamed the DORIC FERRY. In 1992 she was renamed the EUROPEAN TIDEWAY and, in 1994, purchased by *P&O European Ferries*. In 2001 replaced by the NORBANK and laid up. In 2002 returned to the Felixstowe - Rotterdam route when the NORBANK was transferred to *P&O Irish Sea*. In 2002 sold to *Stena Line* and renamed the IDEWAY. She initially operated between Felixstowe and Rotterdam and later Harwich and Rotterdam. Later in 2002 she was renamed the STENA TRANSFER.

STENA TRANSPORTER Built at Ulsan, South Korea as the MERZARIO ESPANIA for *Stena Rederi* of Sweden and immediately chartered to *Merzario Line* for their service between Italy and Saudi Arabia. In the same year she was renamed the MERZARIO HISPANIA. In 1979 she was chartered to *European Ferries* for their ro-ro freight service between Felixstowe and Rotterdam and renamed the NORDIC FERRY. In 1982 she served in the Falkland Islands Task Force. In 1986 she was modified to carry 688 passengers and, with sister vessel the BALTIC FERRY (now EUROPEAN DIPLOMAT), took over the Felixstowe - Zeebrugge passenger service. In 1992 she was renamed the PRIDE OF FLANDERS. In 1994, purchased by *P&O European Ferries*. In 1995 the Felixstowe - Zeebrugge passenger service ceased, her additional passenger accommodation was removed, passenger capacity was reduced and she was transferred to the Felixstowe - Rotterdam freight service. In 2002 sold to *Stena Line* and renamed the FLANDERS. She initially operated between Felixstowe and Rotterdam and later Harwich and Rotterdam. In autumn 2002 chartered to *Scandlines AB* of Sweden to operate between Travemünde and Trelleborg whilst the SVEALAND was undergoing a major rebuild. Later in 2002, after a refit, she returned to the Harwich - Rotterdam route and was renamed the STENA TRANSPORTER.

TRANSEUROPA FERRIES

THE COMPANY *TransEuropa Ferries NV* is a Belgian subsidiary of *TransEuropa Shipping Lines*, a Slovenian private sector company. Channel operations started in 1997, in conjunction with *Sally Ferries*, replacing them on November 1998. The company traded as *TESL* until 2000. Note that all the owning companies listed here are associated companies of *TESL*.

MANAGEMENT *TransEuropa Shipping* **Managing Director** Stergulc Rihard, *TransEuropa Ferries NV*, **General Manager Belgium & UK** Mr Dominique Penel, **Sales Manger, Europe** Mr Peter Sys.

ADDRESS *TSL Slovenia* Vojkovo nabrezje 38, 6000 Koper, Slovenia, *TEF UK* Ferry Terminal, Ramsgate New Port, RAMSGATE, Kent CT11 8RP *TEF Belgium* Slijkensesteenweg 2, 8400 Ostend, Belgium.

TELEPHONE *TSL Slovenia* +386 (0)5 664 17 77, *TEF UK* +44 (0)1843 853833, *TEF Belgium* +32 (0)59 34 02 50.

FAX *TSL Slovenia* +386 (0)5 639 50 36, *TEF UK* +44 (0)1843 853668, *TEF Belgium* +32 (0)59 34 02 51.

INTERNET Website www.t-s-l.si *(English)*

ROUTE OPERATED Ramsgate *(dep: 01.00 Tue-Sat, 01.30 Mon, 02.30 Tue-Sat, 05.00 Tue-Sat, 09.30 Tue-Fri, 10.00 Sun, 11.30 Mon, 13.30 Sun-Fri, 15.30 Sun-Fri, 17.30 Mon-Fri, 18.30 Sun, 20.30 Mon-Sat, 21.30 Sun,*

Primrose *(Mike Louagie)*

Seawheel Rhine *(Rob de Viser)*

22.30 Mon-Fri) - Ostend (Belgium) (dep: 01.00 Mon-Sat, 03.00 Tue-Fri, 05.00 Mon, 07.30 Sun, Tue-Thu, 10.00 Tue-Fri, 11.00 Mon, 11.30 Sun, 13.00 Sun-Fri, 16.00 Mon-Sat, 17.30 Sun, 18.00 Mon-Sat, 20.00 Sun, 20.30 Mon-Fri, 21.30 Sun, 22.30 Mon-Fri, 23.30 Sun) (4 hrs; (1,2,3,4,5,6); up to 9 per day).

1	BEGONIA	8023t	76	18.5k	118.1m	105P	-	52L	BA	SV
2	EUROVOYAGER	12110t	78	22.0k	118.4m	1250P	348C	45L	BA2	CY
3	GARDENIA	8097t	78	18.4k	118.1m	105P	-	52L	BA2	CY
4	LARKSPUR	14458t	76	17.5k	143.8m	1150P	314C	55L	BA2	BS
5	OLEANDER	13728t	80	23.0k	132.5m	1326P	350C	44L	BA2	CY
6	PRIMROSE	12046t	75	22.0k	118.4m	1250P	348C	45L	BA2	CY
7	ROSEANNE	7744t	82	17.0k	112.8m	12P	525C	85T	AS	SV

BEGONIA Built at Bremerhaven, Germany as the EUROPEAN CLEARWAY for *European Ferries* ro-ro freight services. She was built at to a standard design rather than custom-built. She was used on freight services between Dover and Calais and Dover and Zeebrugge. In 1992 she was moved to the Portsmouth - Le Havre route. In 1993 she was transferred to *Pandoro* to inaugurate a new Cherbourg - Rosslare service. In 1996 she was renamed the PANTHER. In early 1998 she was renamed the EUROPEAN PATHFINDER. In 2001 she was moved to the Cairnryan - Larne service to replace the EUROPEAN TRADER. In 2002 sold *ERATO Shipping* and renamed the REGINA I. Before delivery, resold to *Abbey Trading SA Trust Co* and renamed the BEGONIA. In 2003 to begin operating for *TransEuropa Ferries*.

EUROVOYAGER Built at Hoboken, Belgium as the PRINS ALBERT for *RMT* of Belgium for the Ostend - Dover service. During 1986 she had an additional vehicle deck added. In 1994 the British port became Ramsgate. Withdrawn after 28th February 1997 and laid up. In 1998 she was sold to *Hawthorn Shipping Co Ltd*, renamed the EUROVOYAGER. In July, she was chartered to *Sally Freight*. In November the *Sally Freight* service ended and she immediately began operating for *TSL*.

GARDENIA Built at Bremerhaven, Germany as the EUROPEAN ENTERPRISE for *European Ferries*. In 1988 she was renamed the EUROPEAN ENDEAVOUR. She was used on freight services between Dover and Calais and Dover and Zeebrugge. If space was available, a small number of passengers was sometimes conveyed on the Zeebrugge service, although the sailings were not advertised for passengers. This ceased with the withdrawal of passenger services on this route at the end of 1991. During the summer period she provided additional freight capacity on the Dover - Calais service and has also served on other routes. In autumn 1995 she was transferred to the Cairnryan - Larne service. In 1998 accommodation was raised to provide extra freight capacity. In March 1999 began also operating from Larne to Ardrossan but this ceased later in the year. Withdrawn from service in July 2002 and sold to *Odyssy Maritime Co Ltd* and renamed the GARDENIA. In 2003 she began operating for *TEF* between Ramsgate and Ostend.

LARKSPUR Built at Bremerhaven, Germany as the GEDSER for *Gedser-Travemünde Ruten* of Denmark for their service between Gedser (Denmark) and Travemünde (Germany). In 1986 she was purchased by *Thorsviks Rederi A/S* of Norway and chartered to *Sally Ferries*, re-registered in the Bahamas, renamed the VIKING 2 and entered service on the Ramsgate - Dunkerque service. In early 1989 she was renamed the SALLY SKY and during winter 1989/90 she was 'stretched' to increase vehicle capacity. At the end of 1996 she was withdrawn from the Dunkerque service. In 1997 she was renamed the EUROTRAVELLER, transferred to *Holyman-Sally Ferries* and, in March, was introduced onto the Ramsgate - Ostend route. In 1998, when *Holyman-Sally Ferries* came to an end, she operated in a freight-only role for *Sally Line* under the *Sally Freight* name. Passenger services were resumed in May, under the name of *Sally Direct*. All *Sally Line* operations ended in November 1998 and she was withdrawn for sale and laid up. In 1999 sold to *Forsythia Maritime Co Ltd* and renamed the LARKSPUR. She was given a major refit at Dunkerque, including the provision of 60 drivers' cabins with private facilities. She entered service with *TEF* in August 2000.

OLEANDER Built at Bremerhaven, Germany for *European Ferries (Townsend Thoresen)* as the PRIDE OF FREE ENTERPRISE for the Dover - Calais service, also operating on the Dover - Zeebrugge service during the winter. In 1988 she was renamed the PRIDE OF BRUGES and, following the delivery of the new PRIDE OF CALAIS, she was transferred all year to the Dover - Zeebrugge service. In 1992, after the closure of that routes to passengers, she returned to the Dover

- Calais route. Plans to operate her in a freight-only mode in 1997 were changed and she ran as a full passenger vessel. In 1998, transferred to *P&O Stena Line*; plans to transfer her to the Newhaven - Dieppe route were dropped and she remained at Dover. In 1999 renamed the P&OSL PICARDY. In early 2000 she was laid up for sale in Dunkerque. In 2001 she was sold to *Seaborne Navigation Co Ltd* and renamed the OLEANDER. Entered service with *TEF* in July 2002 after major renovation work in Dunkerque, including the provision of 60 drivers' cabins with private facilities.

PRIMROSE Built at Hoboken, Belgium as the PRINCESSE MARIE-CHRISTINE for *Regie voor Maritiem Transport* of Belgium for the Ostend - Dover service. During 1985 she had an extra vehicle deck added, increasing vehicle capacity. Passenger capacity was increased by 200 by the conversion of an upper deck 'garage' into passenger accommodation. In January 1994 the British port became Ramsgate. In 1994 chartered briefly to *Sally Ferries* and operated between Ramsgate and Dunkerque. Since then a spare vessel and withdrawn in early 1997. In 1998 sold to *Dianthus Maritime Co Ltd* of the UK and renamed the PRIMROSE. In 1999 she began operating for *TSL* between Ramsgate and Ostend after a major refit at Dunkerque.

ROSEANNE Built at Vigo, Spain as the REINA DEL CANTABRICO for *Labiad Andalusia* of Spain and chartered to *Matina Line* for services between Europe and West Africa. In 1983 renamed the SALAH LABIAD but resumed her original name in 1985. In 1987 she was sold, renamed the FAROY and chartered to *Elbe-Humber Roline* for their service between Immingham and Cuxhaven. In 1989 sold to *Chartwell Navigation Co Ltd* and renamed the ROSEANNE; she was chartered to *P&O European Ferries* and used on their Felixstowe - Zeebrugge service. In 1991 chartered to *Norfolk Line*. In 1996 this charter ended and she was chartered to *Lineas Suardiaz* of Spain. In 2000 chartered to *TSL* and placed on the Ostend - Ramsgate service. She has also been chartered to *Ferryways* for their Ostend - Ipswich and Killingholme services. In 2003 chartered to *Flota Suardiaz* for their car-carrying service between Vlissingen - Zeebrugge and Spain but may return to *TSL* in due course.

TRANSFENNICA

THE COMPANY *Transfennica Ltd* is a Finnish private sector company.

MANAGEMENT President Rolf G W Eriksson, **Director (UK)** Jim Deeprose, **Operations Manager (UK)** Andrew Prior.

ADDRESS *Finland* Eteläranta 12, FIN-00130 Helsinki, Finland, *UK* Finland House, 47 Berth, Tilbury Freeport, Tilbury, Essex RM18 7EH.

TELEPHONE Administration & Reservations *Finland* +358 (0)9 13262, *UK* +44 (0)1375 363 900.

FAX Administration & Reservations *Finland* +358 (0)9 652377, *UK* +44 (0)1375 840 888.

INTERNET Email *Finland* info@transfennica.com *UK* info.uk@transfennica.com

Website www.transfennica.com *(English)*

Rauma (dep: 18.00 Fri) - Tilbury (arr: 06.00 Wed, dep: 17.00 Wed or Thu) - Rauma (arr: 07.00 Thu) ((1,2,3); 1 per week), Hamina (dep: 09.00 Mon) - Tilbury (arr: 06.00 Fri, dep: 17.00 Fri) - Hamina (arr: 10.00 Mon) ((1,23); 1 per week), Hanko (dep: 18.00 Mon, 12.00 Wed or Thu) - Tilbury (arr: 13.00 Thu, 06.00 Tue or Wed, dep: 17.00 Thu, 17.00 Tue or Thu) -- Hanko (arr: 07.00 Mon, 07.00 Mon or Tue) ((1,2,3); 1 per week). Some services are via Antwerp. Note: 'dep' times are closure times for freight. Ship will actually leave a little later.

1	CAROLINE RUSS	10471t	99	21.0k	153.5m	12P	-	120T	A2	AT
2	PAULINE RUSS	10471t	99	21.0k	153.5m	12P	-	120T	A2	AT
3	SEAGARD	10471t	99	21.0k	153.5m	12P	-	134T	A2	FI

CAROLINE RUSS, PAULINE RUSS Built at Hamburg, Germany for *Ernst Russ* of Germany and chartered to *Transfennica*.

SEAGARD Built at Hamburg, Germany for *Bror Hussel* of Finland and chartered to *Transfennica*.

In addition to the ferries listed above, there are a number of short chain ferries, cable ferries and ferries operated by unpowered floats.

Norbay *(Miles Cowsill)*

GOSPORT QUEEN
PORTSMOUTH

Val de Loire and **Gosport Queen** *(John Bryant*

section 4 *chain, cable etc ferries*

gb & ireland

BOURNEMOUTH-SWANAGE MOTOR ROAD AND FERRY COMPANY

Address *Company* Shell Bay, Studland, Swanage, Dorset BH19 5BA. **Tel** +44 (0)1929 450203, **Fax** +44 (0)1929 450498), *Ferry* Floating Bridge, Ferry Way, Sandbanks, Poole, Dorset BH13 7QN. **Tel** +44 (0)1929 450203.

Route Sandbanks - Studland (Dorset).

1	BRAMBLE BUSH BAY	93	74.4m	400P	48C	BA

BRAMBLE BUSH BAY chain ferry, built at Hessle, UK for the *Bournemouth-Swanage Motor Road and Ferry Company.*

CUMBRIA COUNTY COUNCIL

Address Community, Economy & Environment Department, Lower Gaol Yard, The Courts, Carlisle CA3 8NA. **Tel** +44 (0)1228 606744, **Fax** +44 (0)1228 606577.

INTERNET Email john.robinson@cumbriacc.gov.uk **Website** www.cumbria.gov.uk *(English (County Council web site - little about ferry))*

Route Bowness-on-Windermere - Far Sawrey.

1	MALLARD	90	25.9m	140P	18C	BA

MALLARD Chain Ferry built at Borth, Dyfed for *Cumbria County Council.*

DARTMOUTH – KINGSWEAR FLOATING BRIDGE CO LTD

Address Dart Marina, Sandquay Road, Dartmouth, Devon TQ6 9PH. **Tel** +44 (0)1803 833351.

Route Dartmouth - Kingswear (Devon) across River Dart (higher route) (forms part of A379).

1	HIGHER FERRY	60	42.7m	136P	18C	BA

HIGHER FERRY Built by *Philip Ltd* at Dartmouth UK. Diesel electric paddle propelled vessel guided by cross-river cables.

ISLE OF WIGHT COUNCIL (COWES FLOATING BRIDGE)

Address Ferry Office, Medina Road, Cowes, Isle of Wight PO31 7BX. **Tel** +44 (0)1983 293041.

Route Cowes - East Cowes.

1	NO 5	76	33.5m	-	15C	BA

NO 5 Chain ferry built at East Cowes for *Isle of Wight County Council*, now *Isle of Wight Council.*

KING HARRY STEAM FERRY COMPANY

Address Feock, Truro, Cornwall TR3 6QJ. **Tel** +44 (0)1872 862312, **Fax** +44 (0)1872 863355.

INTERNET Email info@kingharry.fq.co.uk **Website** www.kingharry-info.co.uk *(English)*

Route Across River Fal, King Harry Ferry (Cornwall).

1	KING HARRY FERRY	74	44.2m	100P	28C	BA

KING HARRY FERRY Chain ferry built at Falmouth, UK for *King Harry Steam Ferry Company.*

REEDHAM FERRY

Address Reedham Ferry, Ferry Inn, Reedham, Norwich NR13 3HA. **Tel** +44 (0)1493 700429, **Fax** +44 (0)1493 700999.

Route Acle - Reedham - Norton (across River Yare, Norfolk).

1	REEDHAM FERRY	84	11.3m	12P	3C	BA

REEDHAM FERRY Chain ferry built at Oulton Broad, UK for *Reedham Ferry.* Maximum weight, 12 tons.

SOUTH HAMS DISTRICT COUNCIL

Address Lower Ferry Office, The Square, Kingswear, Dartmouth, Devon TQ6 0AA. **Tel** +44 (0)1803 752342, **Fax** +44 (0)1803 752227.

Route Dartmouth - Kingswear (Devon) across River Dart (lower route).

1	THE TOM AVIS	94	33.5m	50P	8C	BS
2	THE TOM CASEY	89	33.5m	50P	8C	BS

THE TOM AVIS Float propelled by tugs built at Fowey, UK for *South Hams District Council.*

THE TOM CASEY Float propelled by tugs built at Portland, UK for *South Hams District Council.*

TORPOINT FERRY

Address 2 Ferry Street, Torpoint, Cornwall PL11 2AX. **Tel** +44 (0)1752 812233, **Fax** +44 (0)1752 816873.

INTERNET Website www.torpointferry.org.uk *(English)*

Route Devonport (Plymouth) - Torpoint (Cornwall) across the Tamar. Pre-booking is not possible and the above number cannot be used for that purpose.

1	LYNHER	61	70.7m	350P	48C	BS
2	PLYM	68	70.7m	350P	54C	BS
3	TAMAR	60	70.7m	350P	48C	BS

LYNHER, PLYM, TAMAR Chain ferries built at Southampton, UK (PLYM built at Bristol) for the *Torpoint Ferry.* The three ferries operate in parallel, each on its own 'track'.

There are plans to order three new vessels which would each convey 350 passengers and 73 cars but, at the time of going to press, no orders had been placed.

WATERFORD CASTLE HOTEL

Address The Island, Waterford, Irish Republic. **Tel** +353 (0)51 78203.

INTERNET Email info@waterfordcastle.com **Website** www.waterfordcastle.com *(English (mainly about hotel; little about ferry))*

Route Grantstown - Little Island (in River Suir, County Waterford).

| 1 | LITTLE ISLAND FERRY | 68 | - | 24P | 6C | BS |

LITTLE ISLAND FERRY Chain ferry built at Cork, Irish Republic for *Waterford Castle Hotel*.

section **5** *major passenger only ferries*

gb & ireland

There are a surprisingly large number of passenger only ferries operating in the British Isles, mainly operated by launches and small motor boats. There are, however, a few 'major' operators who operate only passenger vessels (of rather larger dimensions) and have not therefore been mentioned previously.

Clyde Marine Services CRUISER (119t, 1974, 24.4m, 249 passengers (ex POOLE SCENE, 2001), FENCER (18t, 1976, 11.0m, 33 passengers), KENILWORTH (44t, 1936, 18.3m, 97 passengers (ex HOTSPUR II (Southampton - Hythe ferry) 1979)), ROVER (48t, 1964, 19.8m, 120 passengers), THE SECOND SNARK (45t, 1938, 22.9m, 120 passengers). **Route operated** Gourock - Kilcreggan - Helensburgh (generally the KENILWORTH is used on the ferry services and other vessels on excursions). **Tel** +44 (0)1475 721281, **Fax** +44 (0)1475 888023, **Websites** www.clyde-marine.co.uk www.secondsnark.co.uk *(English)*.

Dart Pleasure Craft EDGCUMBE BELLE (35t, 1957, 17.7m, 150 passengers), KINGSWEAR BELLE (43t, 1972, 18.0m, 257 passengers). **Route operated** Dartmouth - Kingswear. Note Pleasure craft owned by this operator are also used for the ferry service on some occasions. **Tel** +44 (0)1803 834488, **Fax** +44 (0)1803 835248, **Email** sales@riverlink.co.uk **Website** www.riverlink.co.uk *(English)*.

Doolin Ferry Company/O'Brien Shipping DONEMARK (70t, 1978, 19.8m, 65 pass), HAPPY HOOKER (77t, 1989, 19.8m, 96 passengers), QUEEN OF ARAN (113t, 1976, 20.1m, 96 passengers), ROSE OF ARAN (113t, 1976, 20.1m, 96 passengers), TRANQUILITY (62t, 1988, 15.8m, 96 passengers). **Route operated** Doolin - Inishere, Doolin - Inishmaan, Doolin - Inishmore. OILEAN ARANN (416t, 1992, 39.6m, 190 passengers). **Route operated** Galway - Inishere, Galway - Inishmaan, Galway - Inishmore. **Tel** +353 (0)65 7074455, **Fax** +353 (0)65 7074417, **Email** doolinferries@eircom.net **Web Site** www.doolinferries.com *(English)*

G&T Ferries (Lower Thames & Medway Passenger Boat Co Ltd) DUCHESS M (71t, 1956, 23.8m, 124 passengers) (ex VESTA 1979), PRINCESS POCAHONTAS (180t, 1962, 33.5m, 207 passengers (ex FREYA II 1989, LABOE I 1985, LABOE 1984 (excursion vessel)). **Route operated** Gravesend (Kent) - Tilbury (Essex), **Tel** +44 (0)1732 353448, **Direct Line to Ferry** +44 (0)7973 390124, **Email** enquiry@princess-pocahontas.com **Web Site** www.princess-pocahontas.com *(English)*

Gosport Ferry GOSPORT QUEEN (159t, 1966, 30.5m, 250 passengers), PORTSMOUTH QUEEN (159t, 1966, 30.5m, 250 passengers), SOLENT ENTERPRISE (274t, 1971, 32.0m, 250 passengers (ex GAY ENTERPRISE 1979), (mainly used on excursion work), SOLENT PRINCE (12t, 1981, 43m, 60 passengers) (ex JENNY ANN, ex WATER WYTCH) (mainly used on charter work), SPIRIT OF GOSPORT (250t, 2001, 32.6m, 300 passengers). **Route operated** Gosport - Portsmouth. **Tel** +44 (0)23 9252 4551, **Email** info@gosportferry.co.uk **Web Site** www.gosportferry.co.uk *(English)*

Hovertravel DOUBLE O SEVEN (1989, 25.4m, 98 passengers) (BHC AP1-88/100 hovercraft), FREEDOM 90 (1990, 25.4m, 98 passengers) (BHC AP1-88/100S hovercraft (converted from AP1-88/100 in 2000)), ISLAND EXPRESS (1985, 25.4m, 98 passengers) (BHC AP1-88/100S hovercraft (converted from BHC AP1-88/100 in 2001)) (ex FREJA VIKING 2002), LIV VIKING (1985, 25.4m, 82 passengers) (BHC AP1-88/100 hovercraft). **Route operated** Southsea - Ryde. **Tel** +44 (0)1983 811000, **Fax** +44 (0)1983 562216, **Email** info@hovertravel.co.uk, **Website** www.hovertravel.co.uk *(English)*

Island Ferries ARAN EXPRESS (117t, 1984, 27.4m, 180 passengers), ARAN FLYER (170t, 1988, 33.5m, 208 passengers), ARAN SEABIRD (164t, 1976, 27.7m, 181 passengers), CEOL NA FARRAIGE (200t, 2001, 35.4m, 294 passengers), DRAÍOCHT NA FARRAIGE (200t, 1999, 35.4m, 294 passengers). **Routes operated** Rossaveal (Co Galway) - Aran Islands. **Tel** +353 (0)91 568903 (572273 after 19.00), **Fax** +353 (0)91 568538, **Email** island@iol.ie, **Website** www.aranislandferries.com *(English)*

Lundy Company OLDENBURG (288t, 1958, 43.6m, 267 passengers). **Routes operated** Bideford - Lundy Island, Ilfracombe - Lundy Island. Also North Devon Coastal Cruises. **Tel** +44 (0)1271 863636, **Fax** +44 (0)1237 477779, **Email** info@lundyisland.co.uk **Web Site** www.lundyisland.co.uk *(English)*

Mersey Ferries ROYAL DAFFODIL (ex OVERCHURCH 1999) (468t, 1962, 46.6m, 860 passengers), ROYAL IRIS OF THE MERSEY (ex MOUNTWOOD 2002) (464t, 1960, 46.3m, 750 passengers), WOODCHURCH (464t, 1960, 46.6m, 750 passengers). **Routes operated** Liverpool (Pier Head) - Birkenhead (Woodside), Liverpool - Wallasey (Seacombe). Also regular summer cruises from Pier Head to Salford along Manchester Ship Canal. **Tel** *Admin* +44 (0)151 639 0609, *Reservations* +44 (0)151 330 1444, **Fax** +44 (0)151 639 0578, **Email** info@merseyferries.co.uk **Website** www.merseyferries.co.uk *(English)*

Nexus (trading name of Tyne & Wear PTE) PRIDE OF THE TYNE (222t, 1993, 24.0m, 350 passengers), SHIELDSMAN (93.2t, 1976, 24.0m, 350 passengers). **Route operated** North Shields - South Shields. Also cruises South Shields - Newcastle. **Tel** +44 (0)191 454 8183, **Fax** +44 (0)191 427 9510, **Web Site** www.nexus.org.uk *(English)*

Société de Navigation de Normandie (Connex) VICTOR HUGO (ex SALTEN 2003) (387t, 1997, 35.0m, 190 passengers) (catamaran), **Routes operated** Portbail or Carteret – Jersey, Guernsey and Sark, Dielette - Alderney - Guernsey, MARIN MARIE (ex AREMETI 3 2003) (608t, 1994, 40.0m, 356 passengers), **Route operated** Granville – Jersey.

Strathclyde Passenger Transport RENFREW ROSE (65t, 1984, 21.9m, 50 passengers), YOKER SWAN (65t, 1984, 21.9m, 50 passengers). **Route operated** Renfrew - Yoker. Note although this a passenger only service, the vessels are built as small front loading car ferries and are able to convey one vehicle if necessary. This facility is sometimes used for the conveyance of ambulances. **Tel** +44 (0)141 885 2123, **Fax** +44 (0)141 432 1025, **Email** liz.parkes@spt.co.uk **Website** www.spt.co.uk *(English)*

Thames Clippers (part of Collins River Enterprises) ABEL MAGWITCH (25.6t, 1999, 18.3m, 60 passengers (tri-maran)), HURRICANE CLIPPER (181t, 2002, 37.8m, 27.5k, 220 passengers), SKY CLIPPER (60t, 1992, 25.0m, 62 passengers) (ex VERITATUM 1995, SD10 2000), STORM CLIPPER (60t, 1992, 25.0m, 62 passengers) (ex DHL WORLDWIDE EXPRESS 1995, SD11 2000). **Routes operated** Savoy Pier (Embankment) - Canary Wharf, Canary Wharf - Rotherhithe (Hilton Hotel) (usually the ABEL MAGWITCH). **Tel** +44 (0)20 7977 6892, **Fax** +44(0) 20 7481 8300, **Email** sean@thamesclippers.com **Website** www.thamesclippers.com *(English)*

Waverley Excursions BALMORAL (735t, 1949, 62.2m, 800 passengers), WAVERLEY (693t, 1947, 73.2m, 950 passengers). **Routes operated** Excursions all round British Isles. However, regular cruises in the Clyde, Bristol Channel and south coast provide a service which can be used for transport purposes and therefore both vessels are, in a sense, ferries. The WAVERLEY is the only seagoing paddle steamer in the world. **Tel** +44 (0)141 221 8152, **Fax** +44 (0)141 248 2150, **Email** info@waverleyexcursions.co.uk **Website** www.waverleyexcursions.co.uk *(English)*

White Horse Ferries GREAT EXPECTATIONS (66t, 1992, 21.3m, 162 passengers) (catamaran), HOTSPUR IV (50t, 1946, 19.5m, 125 passengers). **Route operated** Southampton - Hythe (Hants). *Head Office* **Tel**. +44 (0)1793 618566, **Fax** +44 (0)1793 488428, *Local Office* **Tel** +44 (0)23 8084 0722, **Fax** +44 (0)23 8084 6611, **Email** post@hytheferry.co.uk **Website** www.hytheferry.co.uk *(English)*

TT-Line

Tom Sawyer *(Mike Louagie)*

section **6** *major passenger ferries*

northern europe

ÅNEDIN LINE

THE COMPANY *Ånedin Line* is the trading name of *Rederi AB Allandia*, a Swedish company.

MANAGEMENT Managing Director Magnus Straunch, **Marketing Manager** Torsten Sundberg.

ADDRESS PO Box 1151, S-11181 Stockholm, Sweden.

TELEPHONE Administration +46 (0)8-456 2200, **Reservations** +46 (0)8-456 2200.

FAX Administration & Reservations +46 (0)8-10 07 41.

INTERNET Email m.straunch@rederiallandia.se **Website** www.anedinlinjen.com *(Swedish)*

ROUTE OPERATED Cruises from Stockholm to Mariehamn (Åland) (22 hrs; *(1)*; 1 per day).

1	BIRGER JARL	3564t	53	15.0k	92.4m	400P	0C	0L	-	SW

BIRGER JARL Built at Stockholm, Sweden as the BIRGER JARL for *Stockholms Rederi AB Svea* of Sweden to operate between Stockholm and Turku and Stockholm and Helsinki. She was a crane loading car ferry with capacity for 25 cars, since removed. In 1973 she was sold to *Jacob Line*, to operate between Pietarsaari (Finland) and Skellefteå (Sweden); she was renamed the BORE NORD. In 1974 she started a service from Turku to Visby (Gotland) but this was short lived and, for a time, she served as an accommodation vessel at Stavanger. In 1977 she was sold to *Mini Carriers* of Finland who renamed her the MINISEA and announced plans for a new Finland - Sweden service. These plans did not materialise and in 1978 she was acquired by the *Caribbean Shipping Company* of Panama, chartered to *Rederi AB Allandia*, renamed the BALTIC STAR and started operating 24 hour cruises. In 1997, following changes to Swedish customs regulations, these became 22 hour cruises, allowing a regular departure time each day. In 2002 renamed the BIRGER JARL and re-registered in Sweden.

BASTØ FOSEN

THE COMPANY *Bastø Fosen* is a Norwegian private sector company, a subsidiary of *Fosen Trafikklag* of Trondheim.

MANAGEMENT Managing Director Olav Brein, **Operations Manager** Kirsti Been Tofte.

ADDRESS PO Box 94, 3191 Horten, Norway.

TELEPHONE Administration +47 33 03 17 40, **Reservations** not applicable.

FAX Administration & Reservations +47 33 03 17 49.

INTERNET Email basto@fosen.no **Website** www.basto-fosen.no *(Norwegian)*

ROUTE OPERATED Moss - Horten (across Oslofjord, Norway) (30 mins; *(1,2)*; up to every 45 mins).

1	BASTØ I	5505t	97	14.0k	109.0m	550P	220C	18L	BA	NO
2	BASTØ II	5505t	97	14.0k	109.0m	550P	220C	18L	BA	NO

BASTØ I, BASTØ II Built at Frengen, Norway for *Bastø Fosen*.

Baltic Star (renamed Birger Jarl in 2002) *(Miles Cowsill)*

Prinsesse Ragnhild *(John May)*

BIRKA CRUISES

THE COMPANY *Birka Cruises* is an Åland Islands company.

MANAGEMENT Managing Director Michael Larkner.

ADDRESS Box 15131, S-104 65 Stockholm, Sweden.

TELEPHONE Administration +46 (0)8-702 7200, **Reservations** +46 (0)8-702 7230.

FAX Administration & Reservations +46 (0)8-643 9246.

INTERNET Email info@birkacruises.com **Website** www.birkacruises.com *(Swedish, English)*

ROUTES OPERATED Stockholm - Mariehamn (Åland) - Stockholm (cruise) (22 hrs 45 mins; *(1)*; 1 per day (except when Riga/Gdynia/Tallinn cruises operate), Stockholm - Visby (Gotland) - Riga (Latvia) - Stockholm, Stockholm - Visby Gdynia (Poland) or Stockholm - Tallinn (Estonia) - Visby - Stockholm (70 hrs 45 mins (cruise); *(1)*; weekly, mid June to mid-August).

1p	BIRKA PRINCESS	22412t	86	21.0k	142.9m	1500P	0C	0L	-	FI

BIRKA PRINCESS Built at Helsinki, Finland for *Birka Cruises*. As built, she had capacity for 10 cars, loaded via a side door. During winter 1998/99 she was the subject of a major refit to modernise her, increase her passenger capacity and install catalytic converters on all engines to make her the most environmentally friendly cruise ferry in the world; the vehicle facility was removed.

Under Construction

2p	NEWBUILDING	33000t	04	21.0k	170m	1800P	0C	0L	-	FI

NEWBUILDING Under construction at Rauma, Finland for *Birka Cruises*.

BORNHOLMSTRAFIKKEN

THE COMPANY *BornholmsTrafikken* is a Danish state owned company.

MANAGEMENT Managing Director Mads Kofod, **Sales and Marketing Manager** Niels Kreutzmann.

ADDRESS Havnen, DK-3700 Rønne, Denmark.

TELEPHONE Administration +45 56 95 18 66, **Reservations** +45 56 95 18 66.

FAX Administration & Reservations +45 56 91 07 66.

INTERNET Email info@bornholmferries.dk **Website** www.bornholmferries.dk *(Danish, German, English)*

ROUTES OPERATED Conventional Ferries Rønne (Bornholm, Denmark) - Copenhagen (7 hrs; *(1,3)*; 1 or 2 per day). **Fast Ferry** Ystad (Sweden) - Rønne (1 hr 20 mins; *(4)*; up to 5 per day). **Freight Ferry** Rønne - Køge (7 hrs; *(2)*; 1 per day).

1	JENS KOFOED	12131t	79	19.5k	121.0m	1500P	262C	26T	BA	DK
2F	NORDHAV	5846t	80	15k	103.0m	12P	-	58T	A	NO
3	POVL ANKER	12131t	78	19.5k	121.0m	1500P	262C	26T	BA	DK
4»	VILLUM CLAUSEN	6402t	99	40.0k	86.6m	1000P	180C	-	BA	DK

JENS KOFOED, POVL ANKER Built at Aalborg, Denmark for *BornholmsTrafikken*. Used on the Rønne - Copenhagen, Rønne - Ystad and (until December 2002) Rønne - Sassnitz services.

NORDHAV Built at Kraljevica, Yugoslavia as the CRES for *Losinjska Plovidba* of Yugoslavia (later Croatia) and used on Mediterranean services. In 1998 she was sold to *Nor-Cargo* and renamed the NORDHAV. She operated between the west coast of Norway and the UK. In 2002 sold to *Cargoferry* of Norway to operate between Moss and Århus. In 2003 chartered to *BornholmsTrafikken* to operate between Rønne and Køge.

VILLUM CLAUSEN Austal Auto-Express 86 catamaran built at Fremantle, Australia for *BornholmsTrafikken*. Used on the Rønne - Ystad service.

COLOR LINE

THE COMPANY *Color Line ASA* is a Norwegian private sector stock-listed limited company. The company merged with *Larvik Scandi Line* of Norway (which owned *Larvik Line* and *Scandi Line*) in 1996. *Larvik Line's* operations were incorporated into *Color Line* in 1997; *Scandi Line* continued as a separate subsidiary until 1999, when it was also incorporated into *Color Line*. The marketing name *Color Scandi Line* was dropped at the end of 2000.

MANAGEMENT Managing Director Trond Kleivdal, **Marketing Manager** Elisabeth Anspach.

ADDRESS *Commercial* Postboks 1422 Vika, 0115 OSLO, Norway, *Technical Management* Color Line Marine AS, PO Box 2090, N-3210 Sandefjord, Norway.

TELEPHONE Administration +47 22 94 44 00, **Reservations** +47 810 00 811.

FAX Administration +47 22 83 04 30, **Reservations** +47 22 83 07 76.

INTERNET Website www.colorline.com *(Norwegian, English)*

ROUTES OPERATED Conventional Ferries Oslo (Norway) - Kiel (Germany) (19 hrs 30 mins; *(5,7)*; 1 per day), Oslo - Hirtshals (Denmark) (8 hrs 30 mins; *(3)*; 1 per day), Kristiansand (Norway) - Hirtshals (4 hrs 30 mins; *(2)*; 2 per day), Larvik (Norway) - Frederikshavn (Denmark) (6 hrs 15 mins; *(6,9)*; 2 or 3 per day), Sandefjord (Norway) - Strömstad (Sweden) (2 hrs 30 mins; *(1,3)*; up to 6 per day). **Fast Ferry (under the name 'Color Line Express') Summer only** Kristiansand - Hirtshals (2 hrs 30 mins; *(8)*; 3 per day).

1	BOHUS	8772t	71	19.5k	122.7m	1480P	280C	34T	BA	NO
2	CHRISTIAN IV	21699t	82	20.0k	153.1m	1860P	480C	56T	BAS2	NO
3	COLOR FESTIVAL	34314t	85	22.0k	168.0m	2000P	330C	80T	BA	NO
4	COLOR VIKING	19763t	85	17.5k	134.0m	2000P	320C	40T	BA2	NO
5	KRONPRINS HARALD	31914t	87	21.5k	166.3m	1432P	700C	90T	BA	NO
6	PETER WESSEL	29704t	81	19.0k	168.5m	2100P	570C	136T	BA	NO
7	PRINSESSE RAGNHILD	35438t	81	21.0k	205.3m	1875P	770C	70T	BA	NO
8»	SILVIA ANA L	7895t	96	41.0k	125.0m	1043P	238C	4L	A	BS
9	SKAGEN	12333t	75	20.0k	129.8m	1200P	430C	28Tr	BA2	NO

BOHUS Built at Aalborg, Denmark as the PRINSESSAN DESIREE for *Rederi AB Göteborg-Frederikshavn Linjen* of Sweden (trading as *Sessan Linjen*) for their service between Gothenburg and Frederikshavn. In 1981 the company was taken over by *Stena Line* and she became surplus to requirements. During 1981 she had a number of charters including *B&I Line* of Ireland and *Sealink* UK. In 1982 she was chartered to *Sally Line* to operate as second vessel on the Ramsgate - Dunkerque service between June and September. She bore the name VIKING 2 in large letters on her hull although she was never officially renamed and continued to bear the name PRINSESSAN DESIREE on her bow and stern. In September 1982 she returned to *Stena Line* and in 1983 she was transferred to subsidiary company *Varberg-Grenaa Line* for their service between Varberg (Sweden) and Grenaa (Denmark) and renamed the EUROPAFÄRJAN. In 1985 she was renamed the EUROPAFÄRJAN II. In 1986, following a reorganisation within the *Stena Line* Group, ownership was transferred to subsidiary company *Lion Ferry AB* and she was named the LION PRINCESS. In 1993 she was sold to *Scandi Line* and renamed the BOHUS. In 1999 *Scandi Line* operations were integrated into *Color Line*.

CHRISTIAN IV Built at Bremerhaven, Germany as the OLAU BRITANNIA for *Olau Line* of Germany for their service between Vlissingen (Netherlands) and Sheerness (England). In 1989 sold to *Nordström & Thulin* of Sweden for delivery in spring 1990. She was subsequently resold to *Fred. Olsen Lines* of Norway and, on delivery, renamed the BAYARD and used on their service between Kristiansand and Hirtshals. In December 1990 she was acquired by *Color Line* and in 1991 renamed the CHRISTIAN IV. She continues to operate on that route.

COLOR FESTIVAL Built at Helsinki, Finland as the SVEA for *Johnson Line* for the *Silja Line* Stockholm - Mariehamn - Turku service. During winter 1991/92 she was extensively rebuilt and in 1991 renamed the SILJA KARNEVAL; ownership was transferred to *Silja Line*. In 1993 she was sold

Christain IV *(Miles Cowsill)*

to *Color Line* and renamed the COLOR FESTIVAL. She is used on the Oslo - Hirtshals service.

COLOR VIKING Built at Nakskov, Denmark as the PEDER PAARS for *DSB (Danish State Railways)* for their service between Kalundborg (Sealand) and Århus (Jutland). In 1990 purchased by *Stena Line* of Sweden for delivery in 1991. In 1991 renamed the STENA INVICTA and entered service on the *Sealink Stena Line* Dover - Calais service. She was withdrawn from the route in February 1998, before the formation of *P&O Stena Line* but ownership was transferred to that company. In summer 1998, she was chartered to *Silja Line* to operate between Vaasa and Umeå under the marketing name 'WASA JUBILEE'. In autumn 1998 she was laid up at Zeebrugge. She remained there until autumn 1999 when she was chartered to *Stena Line* to operate between Holyhead and Dublin. In 2000 she was chartered to *Color Line* and renamed the COLOR VIKING and in April entered service on the Sandefjord - Strömstad service. In 2002 purchased by *Color Line*.

KRONPRINS HARALD Built at Turku, Finland for *Jahre Line* of Norway for the Oslo - Kiel service. In 1991 ownership was transferred to *Color Line*.

PETER WESSEL Built at Landskrona, Sweden for *Rederi AB Gotland* of Sweden. A sister vessel of the VISBY (see *Destination Gotland*), it was intended that she should be named the GOTLAND. However, she was delivered as the WASA STAR and chartered to *Vaasanlaivat* of Finland and used on their Vaasa - Sundsvall service. In 1982 she was chartered to *Karageorgis Line* of Greece for service between Patras (Greece) and Ancona (Italy). This charter was abruptly terminated in 1983 following a dispute over payment of charter dues. She returned the Baltic and was laid up until February 1984 when she was sold to *Larvik Line*. She was renamed the PETER WESSEL. In 1988 she was lengthened. In 1996 acquired by *Color Line*. She remains on the Larvik - Moss - Frederikshavn route.

PRINSESSE RAGNHILD Built at Kiel, Germany for *Jahre Line* of Norway for the Oslo - Kiel service. In 1991 ownership transferred to *Color Line*. In 1992 rebuilt in Spain with an additional mid-ships section and additional decks.

SILVIA ANA L Bazan Alhambra monohull vessel built at San Fernando, Spain for *Buquebus* of Argentina. Initially operated between Buenos Aires (Argentina) and Piriapolis (Uruguay). In 1997 chartered to *Color Line* to operate between Kristiansand and Hirtshals. During winter 1997/98 she again operated in South America but returned to *Color Line* in spring 1998. This was repeated during winters 1998/9 and 1999/2000 but during winter 2000/2001 she remained laid up in Europe. In 2001 she was sold to *MDFC Aircraft* of the Irish Republic and chartered to *Color Line* for four years.

SKAGEN Vehicle/train ferry built at Aalborg, Denmark as the BORGEN for *Fred. Olsen Lines* of Norway for Norway - Denmark services. In December 1990 acquired by *Color Line* and in 1991 renamed the SKAGEN. Until 1997 she operated mainly between Hirtshals and Kristiansand although in later years rail wagons were longer conveyed. In recent years she also operated between Hirtshals and Moss but this service ceased in 2000 and she then served Kristiansand only. In spring 2001 she was transferred to the Larvik - Frederikshavn service. Although mainly operated for freight, the service is also available to car passengers and a special lower rate is available on most sailings.

Under Construction

10	NEWBUILDING	74600t	04	22.0k	224.0m	2770P	750C	90T	BA2	NO

NEWBUILDING Under construction at Turku Finland for *Color Line* to replace the PRINSESSE RAGNHILD on the Oslo – Kiel service.

DESTINATION GOTLAND

THE COMPANY *Destination Gotland AB* is a Swedish private sector company owned by *Rederi AB Gotland*. It took over the operations of services to Gotland from 1st January 1998 on a six-year concession. Originally jointly owned by *Rederi AB Gotland* and *Silja Line, Silja Line* involvement in the company ceased at the end of 1998.

MANAGEMENT Managing Director Sten-Christer Fursberg, **Marketing Manager** Per-Erling Evensen.

ADDRESS PO Box 1234, 621 23 Visby, Gotland, Sweden.

TELEPHONE Administration +46 (0)498-20 18 00, **Reservations** +46 (0)498-20 10 20.

FAX Administration & Reservations +46 (0)498-20 13 90.

INTERNET Email per-erling.evensen@destinationgotland.se **Website** www.destinationgotland.se *(Swedish, English)*

ROUTES OPERATED Conventional Ferries Visby (Gotland) - Nynäshamn (Swedish mainland) (5 hrs (3), 3 hrs 15 mins (5); *(3,5)*; 1/2 per day), Visby - Oskarshamn (Swedish mainland) (4 hrs (3), 2 hrs 45 mins (5); (3,5); 1/2 per day). **Fast Ferry** Visby - Nynäshamn (2 hrs 50 mins; *(2)*; up to 2 per day), (no fast ferry services after early October 2003).

1»	GOTLAND	5632t	99	35.0k	112.5m	700P	140C	-	A	SW
2F	GUTE	6643t	79	15.0k	118.5m	52P	-	50T	BA	SW
3	THJELVAR	16829t	81	19.0k	140.8m	1500P	440C	84T	BA2	SW
4•	VISBORG	23775t	80	20.0k	146.1m	1800P	510C	60L	BA2	SW
5	VISBY	29000t	03	28.5k	195.8m	1500P	500C	118T	BA	SW

GOTLAND Alstom Leroux Corsair 11500 monohull vessel built at Nantes, France for *Rederi AB Gotland* and chartered to *Destination Gotland.*

GUTE Built at Falkenburg, Sweden for *Rederi AB Gotland* of Sweden. Used on service between Gotland and the Swedish mainland. In 1988 chartered to *Brambles Shipping* of Australia and used between Port Melbourne (Victoria) and Burnie (Tasmania). In 1992 she was renamed the SALLY SUN and chartered to *Sally Ferries*, operating between Ramsgate and Dunkerque. In 1994 she inaugurated a Ramsgate - Vlissingen service, which was later changed to Dartford - Vlissingen. In 1995 she was chartered to *SeaWind Line*, renamed the SEAWIND II and operated between Stockholm and Turku. In 1997 she was chartered to *Nordic Trucker Line* for the Oxelösund - St Petersburg service and in 1998 she returned to *SeaWind Line*. In 1998, after *Rederi AB Gotland* owned *Destination Gotland* regained the franchise to operate to Gotland, she was renamed the GUTE and resumed her summer role of providing summer freight back up to the passenger vessels, but with a number of short charters during the winter. In autumn 2002 chartered to *Amber Lines* for the Karlshamn - Liepaja service. In 2003 chartered to *NATO* for the Iraq crisis. May return to *Destination Gotland* in summer 2003.

THJELVAR Built at Helsinki, Finland as the TRAVEMÜNDE for *Gedser-Travemünde Ruten* of Denmark for their service between Gedser (Denmark) and Travemünde (Germany). In 1986 the company's trading name was changed to *GT Linien* and in 1987, following the take-over by *Sea-Link AB* of Sweden, it was further changed to *GT Link*. The vessel's name was changed to the TRAVEMÜNDE LINK. In 1988 she was purchased by *Rederi AB Gotland* of Sweden, although remaining in service with *GT Link*. Later in 1988 she was chartered to *Sally Ferries* and entered service in December on the Ramsgate - Dunkerque service. She was renamed the SALLY STAR. In 1997 she was transferred to *Silja Line*, to operate between Vaasa and Umeå during the summer period and operated under the marketing name WASA EXPRESS (although not renamed). She returned to *Rederi AB Gotland* in autumn 1997, was renamed the THJELVAR and entered service with *Destination Gotland* in January 1998. Due to be withdrawn in December 2003.

VISBORG Built at Landskrona, Sweden as the VISBY for *Rederi AB Gotland* of Sweden for their services between the island of Gotland and the Swedish mainland. In 1987, the franchise to operate these services was lost by the company and awarded to *Nordström & Thulin* of Sweden. A subsidiary

Visby *(Destination Gotland)*

called *N&T Gotlandslinjen AB* was formed to operate the service. The VISBY was chartered to this company and managed by *Johnson Line*, remaining owned by *Rederi AB Gotland*. In early 1990 she was chartered to *Sealink* and renamed the FELICITY. After modifications at Tilbury, she was, in March 1990, introduced onto the Fishguard - Rosslare route. Later in 1990 she was renamed the STENA FELICITY. In summer 1997 she was returned to *Rederi AB Gotland* for rebuilding, prior to her entering service with *Destination Gotland* in January 1998. She was renamed the VISBY. In late 2002 she was renamed the VISBORG. In March 2003 replaced by the new VISBY and laid up for sale or charter.

VISBY Built at Guangzhou, China for *Rederi AB Gotland* and used on *Destination Gotland* services.

6	NEWBUILDING	29000t	03	28.5k	195.8m	1500P	500C	118T	BA	SW

NEWBUILDING Under construction at Guangzhou, China for *Rederi AB Gotland* and to be used on *Destination Gotland* services. Due to enter service in December 2003.

DFDS SEAWAYS

THE COMPANY *DFDS Seaways A/S* is the passenger division of *DFDS Group*, a Danish private sector company.

MANAGEMENT Managing Director DFDS A/S Thorleif Blok, **Managing Director DFDS Seaways A/S** Thor Johannesen.

ADDRESS Sankt Annæ Plads 30, DK-1295 Copenhagen K, Denmark.

TELEPHONE Administration +45 33 42 33 42, **Reservations** +45 33 42 30 00.

FAX Administration & Reservations +45 33 42 33 41.

INTERNET Website www.dfdsseaways.com *(Danish, Dutch, English, German, Norwegian, Swedish)*

ROUTE OPERATED Copenhagen - Helsingborg (Sweden) - Oslo (Norway) (16 hrs; *(1,3)*; 1 per day), Copenhagen – Trelleborg (Sweden) - Gdansk (Poland) (13 hrs; *(2)*; alternate days). See Section 1 for services operating to Britain.

1	CROWN OF SCANDINAVIA	35498t	94	21.5k	171.0m	2136P	450C	66T	BA	DK
2	DUKE OF SCANDINAVIA	19589t	78	21.0k	152.9m	1120P	416C	60T	BA	DK
3	PEARL OF SCANDINAVIA	40022t	89	21.5k	176.6m	2200P	620C	82T	BA	DK

CROWN OF SCANDINAVIA Launched at Split, Croatia for *Euroway* for their Lübeck - Travemünde - Malmö service as the THOMAS MANN. However, political problems led to serious delays and, before delivery, the service had ceased. She was purchased by *DFDS*, renamed the CROWN OF SCANDINAVIA and introduced onto the Copenhagen - Oslo service.

DUKE OF SCANDINAVIA Built at Aalborg, Denmark as the DANA ANGLIA for the Harwich - Esbjerg service and seldom operated elsewhere. In autumn 2002, renamed the DUKE OF SCANDINAVIA and inaugurated a new Copenhagen - Trelleborg - Gdansk service.

PEARL OF SCANDINAVIA Built at Turku, Finland as the ATHENA for *Rederi AB Slite* of Sweden (part of *Viking Line*) and used on 24 hour cruises from Stockholm to Mariehamn (Åland). In 1993 the company went into liquidation and she was sold to *Star Cruises* of Malaysia for cruises in the Far East. She was renamed the STAR AQUARIUS. Later that year she was renamed the LANGKAPURI STAR AQUARIUS. In February 2001 sold to *DFDS* and renamed the AQUARIUS. After rebuilding, she was renamed the PEARL OF SCANDINAVIA and introduced onto the Copenhagen - Oslo service.

Pearl of Scandinavia *(Soran Bay Hansen)*

Finnclipper *(Ferry Information)*

SECTION 6 – NORTHERN EUROPE

REDERIJ DOEKSEN

THE COMPANY *Rederij G Doeksen & Zonen bv* is a Dutch public sector company. Ferries are operated by subsidiary *Terschellinger Stoomboot Maatschappij*, trading as *Rederij Doeksen*.

MANAGEMENT Managing Director P Melles, **Marketing Manager** C Dekker.

ADDRESS Willem Barentskade 21, Postbus 40, 8880 AA West Terschelling, Netherlands.

TELEPHONE Administration +31 (0)562 442141, **Reservations** +31 (0)562 446111.

FAX Administration & Reservations +31 (0)562 443241.

INTERNET Email info@rederij-doeksen.nl **Website** www.rederij-doeksen.nl *(Dutch)*

ROUTES OPERATED Conventional Ferries Harlingen (Netherlands) - Terschelling (Frisian Islands) (2 hrs; *(1,3)*; up to 6 per day), Harlingen - Vlieland (Frisian Islands) (1 hr 45 mins; *(5)*; 3 per day). **Fast Passenger Ferries** Harlingen - Terschelling (50 mins; *(2,4)*; up to 3 per day), Harlingen - Vlieland (50 mins; *(2,4)*; 2 per day), Vlieland - Terschelling (30 mins; *(2,4)*; 2 per day).

1	FRIESLAND	3583t	89	14.0k	69.0m	1750P	122C	12L	BA	NL
2»p	KOEGELWIECK	439t	92	33.0k	36.7m	317P	0C	0L	-	NL
3	MIDSLAND	1812t	74	15.5k	77.9m	1200P	55C	6L	BA	NL
4»p	NAJADE	164t	99	32.0k	31.8m	184P	0C	0L	-	NL
5	OOST-VLIELAND	1350t	70	15.0k	62.6m	1100P	45C	4L	BA	NL
6F	NOORD-NEDERLAND	-	02	14.0k	45.6m	12P	-	9L	BA	NL

FRIESLAND Built at Krimpen aan den IJssel, Rotterdam, Netherlands for *Rederij Doeksen*. Used on the Harlingen - Terschelling route.

KOEGELWIECK Harding 35m catamaran built at Rosendal, Norway for *Rederij Doeksen* to operate between Harlingen and Terschelling, Harlingen and Vlieland and Terschelling and Vlieland.

MIDSLAND Built at Emden, Germany as the RHEINLAND for *AG Ems* of Germany. In 1993 purchased by *Rederij Doeksen* and renamed the MIDSLAND. Used mainly on the Harlingen - Terschelling route but also used on the Harlingen - Vlieland service. She is now a reserve vessel.

NAJADE SBF Shipbuilders 31m monohull built at Henderson, Australia for *Rederij Doeksen* to operate between Harlingen and Terschelling, Harlingen and Vlieland and Terschelling and Vlieland.

OOST-VLIELAND Built at Emden, Germany as the OSTFRIESLAND for *AG Ems* of Germany. In 1981 purchased by *Rederij Doeksen* and renamed the SCHELLINGERLAND. In 1994 renamed the OOST VLIELAND. Now mainly used on the Harlingen - Vlieland service.

NOORD-NEDERLAND Catamaran built at Harwood, New South Wales, Australia for *Rederij Doeksen*. Used on freight services from Harlingen to Terschelling and Vlieland.

ECKERÖ LINE

THE COMPANY *Eckerö Line Ab Oy* is a Finnish company, 100% owned by *Eckerö Linjen* of Åland, Finland. Until January 1998, the company was called *Eestin-Linjat*.

MANAGEMENT Managing Director Jarl Danielsson, **Marketing Director** Håkan Nordström.

ADDRESS Hietalahdenranta 13, FIN-00180 Helsinki, Finland.

TELEPHONE Administration +358 (0)9 22885421, **Reservations** +358 (0)9 2288544.

FAX Administration & Reservations +358 (0)9 22885222.

INTERNET Email info@eckeroline.fi **Website** www.eckeroline.fi *(Swedish, Finnish, English, German)*

ROUTE OPERATED Helsinki - Tallinn (Estonia) (3 hrs 30 mins; *(1)*; 1 per day).

1	NORDLANDIA	21473t	81	21.0k	153.4m	2048P	530C	40T	BA	FI

NORDLANDIA Built at Bremerhaven, Germany as the OLAU HOLLANDIA for *Olau Line* of Germany for the service between Vlissingen (Netherlands) and Sheerness (England). In 1989 she was replaced by a new vessel of the same name and she was sold to *Nordström & Thulin*. She was renamed the NORD GOTLANDIA and introduced onto *Gotlandslinjen* services between Gotland and the Swedish mainland. In 1997 she was purchased by *Eckerö Linjen* of Åland for delivery in early 1998, following the ending of *Nordström & Thulin's* concession to operate the Gotland services. She was renamed the NORDLANDIA and placed on the *Eckerö Line* Helsinki - Tallinn service, operating day trips.

ECKERÖ LINJEN

THE COMPANY *Eckerö Linjen* is an Åland Islands company.

MANAGEMENT Managing Director Jarl Danielsson, **Marketing Director** Christer Lindman.

ADDRESS Torggatan 2, Box 158, FIN-22100 Mariehamn, Åland.

TELEPHONE Administration +358 (0)18 28000, **Reservations** +358 (0)18 28300.

FAX Administration & Reservations +358 (0)18 28380.

INTERNET Website www.eckerolinjen.fi *(Swedish)*

ROUTE OPERATED Eckerö (Åland) - Grisslehamn (Sweden) (2 hrs; *(1,2)*; 5 per day).

| 1 | ALANDIA | 6754t | 72 | 17.0k | 108.7m | 1320P | 225C | 32T | BA | FI |
| 2 | ROSLAGEN | 6652t | 72 | 18.7k | 109.3m | 1320P | 225C | 32T | BA | FI |

ALANDIA Built at Papenburg, Germany as the DIANA for *Rederi AB Slite* of Sweden for *Viking Line* services. In 1979 she was sold to *Wasa Line* of Finland and renamed the BOTNIA EXPRESS. In 1982 she was sold to *Sally Line* of Finland; later that year she was sold to *Suomen Yritysrahoitus Oy* and chartered back. In 1992 she was sold to *Eckerö Linjen* and renamed the ALANDIA. She has also been used by subsidiary company *Eckerö Line*.

ROSLAGEN Built at Papenburg, Germany as the VIKING 3 for *Rederi AB Sally* and used on *Viking Line* Baltic services. In 1976 she was sold to *Vaasanlaivat* of Finland for their service between Vaasa (Finland) and Umeå/Sundsvall (Sweden) and renamed the WASA EXPRESS. In 1982 *Vaasanlaivat* was taken over by *Rederi AB Sally* and in April 1983 she resumed her original name, was transferred to *Sally Line* and used on the Ramsgate - Dunkerque service. She remained in the Channel during winter 1983/4 on freight-only services. However, in early 1984 she returned to *Vaasanlaivat* and resumed the name WASA EXPRESS. In 1988 she was sold to *Eckerö Linjen* and renamed the ROSLAGEN. During winter 1992/3 she operated between Helsinki and Tallinn for *Estonia New Line* and returned to *Eckerö Linjen* in the spring.

AG EMS

THE COMPANY *AG Ems* is a German public sector company.

MANAGEMENT Managing Director & Chief Executive B W Brons, **Marine Superintendent** J Alberts, **Marketing Manager & Assistant Manager** P Eesmann, **Operating Manager** Konrad Huismann.

ADDRESS Am Aussenhafen, Postfach 1154, 26691 Emden, Germany.

TELEPHONE Administration & Reservations +49 (0)4921 8907-400 or +49 (0)4921 8907-406.

FAX Administration & Reservations +49 (0)4921 8907-405.

INTERNET Email info@ag-ems.de **Website** www.ag-ems.de *(German)*

ROUTES OPERATED Conventional Ferries Emden (Germany) - Borkum (German Frisian Islands) (2 hrs; *(1,3,6)*; up to 4 per day), Eemshaven (Netherlands) - Borkum (55 mins; *(1,3,6)*; up to 4 per day). Fast **Ferries** Emden - Borkum (1 hr; *(2,4)*; up to 4 per day), Eemshaven - Borkum (30 mins; *(2,4)*; 1 per week in summer).

Fjord Norway *(Lars Helge Isdahl)*

Transeuropa *(Philippe Holthof)*

1	MÜNSTERLAND	1859t	86	15.5k	78.7m	1200P	70C	10L	BA	GY
2p»	NORDLICHT	435t	89	33.0k	38.8m	272P	0C	0L	-	GY
3	OSTFRIESLAND	1859t	85	15.5k	78.7m	1200P	70C	10L	BA	GY
4p»	POLARSTERN	636t	00	40.0k	45.0m	405P	0C	0L	-	GY
5p	WAPPEN VON BORKUM	287t	76	11.5k	42.8m	358P	0C	0L	-	GY
6	WESTFALEN	1812t	72	15.5k	77.9m	1200P	65C	10L	BA	GY

MÜNSTERLAND, OSTFRIESLAND Built at Leer, Germany for *AG Ems*.

NORDLICHT Fjellstrand 38m passenger only catamaran built Mandal, Norway for *AG Ems*.

POLARSTERN Oceanfast Ferries (Australia) 45m passenger only catamaran built at Henderson, Australia for another operator as the CARAIBE JET. This order was cancelled before delivery and she was sold to *AG Ems* after a period of lay-up, arriving in 2001.

WAPPEN VON BORKUM Built at Oldersum, Germany as the HANNOVER for *Friesland Fahrlinie* of Germany. In 1979 sold to *AG Ems* and renamed the STADT BORKUM. In 1988 sold to *ST-Line* of Finland, operating day trips from Rauma. In 1994 returned to *AG Ems* and renamed the WAPPEN VON BORKUM.

WESTFALEN Built at Emden, Germany for *AG Ems*. Rebuilt in 1994.

FINNLINES

THE COMPANIES *Finnlines plc* is a Finnish private sector company.

MANAGEMENT President Asser Ahleskog, **Vice-President** Simo Airas.

ADDRESS PO Box 197, Salmisaarenkatu 1, FIN-00180 Helsinki, Finland. *Sales and marketing of Finnlines Passenger Services* Nordic Ferry Center Oy, Lönnrotinkatu 21, FIN-00120 Helsinki, Finland.

TELEPHONE Administration +358 (0)10 34350. **Reservations** *(Nordic Ferry Center Oy)* +358 (0)9-2510 200.

FAX Administration +358 (0)10 3435200, **Reservations** +358 (0)9-2510 2022.

INTERNET *Finnlines* **Email** info@finnlines.fi *Nordic Ferry Center* info@ferrycenter.fi

Website *Finnlines* www.finnlines.fi *(English, Finnish)*

Nordic Ferry Center www.ferrycenter.fi/finnlines/en/index.shtml *(English)*

ROUTES OPERATED All year Helsinki - Travemünde (32 hrs; *(1,2,3,4,5)*; 1/2 per day) **Note** frequencies refer to services which convey passengers. The FINNFELLOW does two return trips a week; the others do a round trip every four days.

1	FINNFELLOW	33796t	00	22.0k	188.3m	452P	-	216T	BA	FI
2	FINNHANSA	32531t	94	21.3k	183.0m	90P	-	236T	A2	FI
3	FINNPARTNER	32534t	94	21.3k	183.0m	90P	-	236T	A2	FI
4	FINNTRADER	32534t	95	21.3k	183.0m	90P	-	236T	A2	FI
5	TRANSEUROPA	32534t	95	21.3k	183.0m	90P	-	236T	A2	GY

FINNFELLOW Ro-pax ferry built as the STENA BRITANNICA at Cadiz Spain for *Stena RoRo* and chartered to *Stena Line bv* to operate between Hoek van Holland and Harwich. In 2003 replaced by a new STENA BRITANNICA, sold to *Finnlines*, renamed the FINNFELLOW and placed on the Helsinki – Travemünde route.

FINNHANSA, FINNPARTNER, FINNTRADER 'Ro-pax' vessels built at Gdansk, Poland for *Finnlines Oy* of Finland to provide a daily service conveying both freight and a limited number of cars and passengers on a previously freight-only route.

TRANSEUROPA 'Ro-pax' vessel built at Gdansk, Poland for *Poseidon Schiffahrt* of Germany to operate on a joint service between Lübeck and Helsinki. In 1997 *Poseidon Schiffahrt* was acquired by *Finnlines* and in 2001 renamed *Finnlines Deutschland AG*.

To be ordered

6	NEWBUIDING 1	-	05	25.0k	225m	400P	-	248T	A2	FI
7	NEWBUIDING 2	-	05	25.0k	225m	400P	-	248T	A2	FI
8	NEWBUIDING 2	-	05	25.0k	225m	400P	-	248T	A2	FI

NEWBUILDING 1, NEWBUILDING 2, NEWBUILDING 3 Likely to be ordered for the Helsinki - Travemünde route.

FINNLINK

FinnLink Oy operates a service between Kapellskär (Sweden) and Naantali (Finland). Until spring 2002 the service was freight only. However passengers were conveyed on some sailings from summer 2002.

THE COMPANY is a subsidiary of *Finnlines*.

MANAGEMENT Managing Director Christer Backman.

ADDRESS Satamatie 11, FIN-21100, Naantali, Finland.

TELEPHONE Administration & Reservations +358 (0)10 436 7620.

FAX Administration & Reservations 358 (0)10 436 7660.

INTERNET Email finnlink@finnlink.fi **Website** www.finnlink.fi *(English, Finnish)*

ROUTE OPERATED Kapellskär (Sweden) - Naantali (Finland) (6 hrs; *(6,7,8)*; 3 per day).

9	FINNCLIPPER	30500t	99	22.0k	188.3m	440P	-	184T	BA	FI
10	FINNEAGLE	30500t	99	22.0k	188.3m	440P	-	176T	BA2	FI
11	FINNSAILOR	20783t	87	20.3k	157.6m	119P	-	146T	A	FI

FINNCLIPPER 'Ro-pax' vessel built at Cadiz, Spain. Ordered by *Stena Ro-Ro* of Sweden and launched as the STENA SEPACER 1. In 1998 sold, before delivery, to *Finnlines* and renamed the FINNNCLIPPER. Entered service on the Helsinki - Travemünde route in 1999. During winter 1999/2000 she was converted to double-deck loading. In late 2002 transferred to *FinnLink*.

FINNEAGLE 'Ro-pax' vessel built at Cadiz, Spain. Ordered by *Stena Ro-Ro* of Sweden and launched as the STENA SEAPACER 2. In 1998 sold, before delivery, to *Finnlines* and renamed the FINNNEAGLE. Although expected to join her sister on the Helsinki - Travemünde route, on delivery in late 1999 she entered service with *FinnLink*. During winter 1999/2000 she was converted to double-deck loading.

FINNSAILOR Built at Gdansk, Poland for *Finnlines* of Finland for freight service between Finland and Germany. In 1996 converted to ro-pax format to inaugurate a new passenger/freight service between Helsinki to Norrköping (Sweden) for subsidiary *FinnLink*. In 1997, this service was transferred to the Kapellskär - Naantali route and passengers (other than lorry drivers) ceased to be conveyed. Later in 1997 she was transferred to the Helsinki - Lübeck route. In 2000 she was chartered to *Nördo Link* to operate between Travemünde and Malmö. In 2002 she returned to *FinnLink*.

FJORD LINE

THE COMPANY *Fjord Line* is 100% owned by *Bergen-Nordhordland Rutelag AS (BNR)*, a Norwegian company.

MANAGEMENT Managing Director Ove Solem, **Marketing Manager** Nils Henrik Geitle.

ADDRESS Skoltegrunnskaien, PO Box 6020, N-5020 Bergen, Norway.

TELEPHONE Administration +47 55 54 87 00, **Reservations** +47 55 54 88 00.

FAX Administration & Reservations +47 55 54 86 01.

INTERNET Email fjordline@fjordline.com **Website** www.fjordline.co.UK *(Norwegian, Danish, English)*

ROUTE OPERATED Bergen - Egersund (Norway) - Hanstholm (Denmark) (15 hrs 30 mins; *(1)*; 3 per week), Egersund - Hanstholm (6 hrs 45 mins; *(1)*; 7 per week in summer). Also UK route - see Section 1.

1	FJORD NORWAY	31356t	86	21.0k	161m	1800P	600C	100T	BA	NO

FJORD NORWAY Built at Bremerhaven, Germany as the PETER PAN for *TT-Line* for the service between Travemünde and Trelleborg. In 1992 sold to *TT Line* of Australia (no connection) for use on their service between Port Melbourne (Victoria) and Hobart (Tasmania) and renamed the SPIRIT OF TASMANIA. In 2002 sold to *Nordsjøferger K/S* of Norway and renamed the SPIR. After modification work she was renamed the FJORD NORWAY and chartered to *Fjord Line*.

HH-FERRIES

THE COMPANY *HH-Ferries* is a Danish/Swedish private sector company. In 2002 it was acquired by *Stena AB* of Sweden, part of the *Stena* Group.

MANAGEMENT Managing Director Lars Meijer, **Marketing Manager** Jon Cavalli-Björkman.

ADDRESS Atlantgatan 2, S-252 25 Helsingborg, Sweden.

TELEPHONE Administration +46 (0)42-26 80 00, **Reservations *Denmark*** +45 49 26 01 55, ***Sweden*** +46 (0)42-19 8000.

FAX Administration & Reservations *Denmark* +45 49 26 01 56, ***Sweden*** +46 (0)42-28 10 70.

INTERNET Email admin@hhferries.se **Website** www.hhferries.se *(Swedish, Danish, English)*

ROUTE OPERATED Helsingør - Helsingborg (20 mins; *(1,2)*; every 30 minutes).

1	MERCANDIA IV	4296t	89	13.0k	95.0m	420P	170C	18L	BA	DK
2	MERCANDIA VIII	4296t	87	13.0k	95.0m	420P	170C	18L	BA	DK

MERCANDIA IV Built at Sunderland, UK as the SUPERFLEX NOVEMBER for *Vognmandsruten* of Denmark. In 1989 sold to *Mercandia* and renamed the MERCANDIA IV. In 1990 she began operating on their *Kattegatbroen* Juelsminde - Kalundborg service. In 1996 she was transferred to their *Sundbroen* Helsingør - Helsingborg service. In 1997 the service and vessel were leased to *HH-Ferries*. In 1999 she was purchased by *HH-Ferries*. She has been equipped to carry dangerous cargo.

MERCANDIA VIII Built at Sunderland, UK as the SUPERFLEX BRAVO for *Vognmandsruten* of Denmark and used on their services between Nyborg and Korsør and Copenhagen (Tuborg Havn) and Landskrona (Sweden). In 1991 she was chartered to *Scarlett Line* to operate on the Copenhagen and Landskrona route. In 1993 she was renamed the SVEA SCARLETT but later in the year the service ceased and she was laid up. In 1996 she was purchased by *Mercandia*, renamed the MERCANDIA VIII and placed on their *Sundbroen* Helsingør - Helsingborg service. In 1997 the service and vessel was leased to *HH-Ferries*. In 1999 she was purchased by *HH-Ferries*.

HURTIGRUTEN

SERVICE The *'Hurtigruten'* is the *'Norwegian Coastal Express Service'*. It is part cruise, part passenger ferry, part cargo line and part car ferry (although this is a fairly minor part of the operation). In recent years the service has been operated by a consortium of two operators - *Ofotens og Vesteraalen Dampskipsselskab* and *Troms Fylkes Dampskipsselskab*. Plans to merge in 2002 to form a new company called *Nord Norges Dampskipsselskap* were dropped.

ADDRESS *Ofotens og Vesteraalen Dampskipsselskab* Postboks 43, 8501 Narvik, Norway, ***Troms Fylkes Dampskipsselskab*** 9005 Tromsø, Norway.

TELEPHONE Administration *Ofotens og Vesteraalen D/S* +47 76 96 76 96, ***Troms Fylkes D/S*** +47 77 64 82 00, **Reservations *Norway*** 810 30 000, ***UK*** +44 (0)20 7371 4011.

FAX Administration & Reservations *Ofotens og Vesteraalen D/S* +47 76 96 76 11, ***Troms Fylkes D/S*** +47 77 64 82 40, ***Reservations (UK)*** +44 (0)20 7371 4070.

INTERNET Email booking@ovds.no booking@tfds.no **Website** www.hurtigruten.no *(English, Norwegian, German, Dutch, Spanish, Finnish, French, Italian and Swedish)*

ROUTE OPERATED Bergen - Kirkenes with many intermediate calls. Daily departures throughout the year. The round trip takes just under 11 days.

1	FINNMARKEN	14000t	02	18.0k	133.0m	647P	50C	OL	SC	NO
2	KONG HARALD	11204t	93	18.0k	121.8m	691P	50C	OL	SC	NO
3	LOFOTEN	2621t	64	16.0k	87.4m	410P	4C	OL	C	NO
4	MIDNATSOL	14000t	03	18.0k	135.7m	626P	50C	-	SC	NO
5●	MIDNATSOL II	6167t	82	18.0k	108.6m	550P	40C	OL	SC	NO
6	NARVIK	6257t	82	18.0k	108.6m	550P	40C	OL	SC	NO
7	NORDKAPP	11386t	96	18.0k	123.3m	691P	50C	OL	SC	NO
8	NORDLYS	11204t	94	18.0k	121.8m	691P	50C	OL	SC	NO
9	NORDNORGE	11384t	97	18.0k	123.3m	691P	50C	OL	SC	NO
10	POLARLYS	11341t	96	18.0k	123.0m	691P	50C	OL	SC	NO
11	RICHARD WITH	11205t	93	18.0k	121.8m	691P	50C	OL	SC	NO
12	TROLLFJORD	14000t	02	18.0k	135.7m	626P	50C	OL	SC	NO
13	VESTERÅLEN	6261t	83	18.0k	108.6m	550P	40C	OL	SC	NO

FINNMARKEN Built at Ulsteinvik, Norway for *Ofotens og Vesteraalen D/S* to replace the LOFOTEN.

KONG HARALD Built at Stralsund, Germany for *Troms Fylkes D/S*.

LOFOTEN Built at Oslo, Norway for *Vesteraalens D/S*. In 1984 she was sold to *Finnmark Fylkesrederi og Ruteselskap*. In 1996 she was sold to *Ofotens og Vesteraalen D/S*. In 2002 she was replaced by the FINNMARKEN but continued to operate cruises and she substituted for the NORDNORGE during winter 2002/3 when she went to South America to operate cruises. This will be repeated during winter 2003/4.

MIDNATSOL Built at Rissa, Norway for *Troms Fylkes D/S*. To replace the existing MIDNATSOL, renamed the MIDNATSOL II.

MIDNATSOL II Built at Ulsteinvik, Norway for *Troms Fylkes D/S* at the MIDNATSOL. Withdrawn in 2003 and renamed the MIDNATSOL II.

NARVIK Built at Trondheim, Norway for *Ofoten D/S*. Since 1984 owned by *Ofotens og Vesteraalen D/S*.

NORDKAPP Built at Ulsteinvik, Norway for *Ofotens og Vesteraalen D/S*.

NORDLYS Built at Stralsund, Germany for *Troms Fylkes D/S*.

NORDNORGE Built at Ulsteinvik, Norway for *Ofotens og Vesteraalen D/S*. During winter 2002/3 operated cruises down the coast to Chile and to Antarctica.

POLARLYS Built at Ulsteinvik, Norway for *Troms Fylkes D/S*.

RICHARD WITH Built at Stralsund, Norway for *Ofotens og Vesteraalen D/S*. In 2002 sold to Norwegian interests and chartered back.

TROLLFJORD Built at Rissa, Norway for *Troms Fylkes D/S* to replace the HARALD JARL (2621t, 1960).

VESTERÅLEN Built at Harstad, Norway for *Vesteraalens D/S*. Since 1984 owned by *Ofotens og Vesteraalen D/S*.

Mercandia VIII *(Martin Jensen)*

Mie Mols *(John May)*

LATLINES/DFDS TOR LINE(JOINT SERVICE)

THE COMPANIES *LatLines* is a Latvian company, a subsidiary of *DFDS Tor Line A/S* of Denmark. *DFDS Tor Line A/S* is a Danish Company, a subsidiary of *DFDS A/S*.

MANAGEMENT *LatLines* **Director** Zigmunds Jankovskis, *DFDS Tor Line* **(see Section 3) Marketing Manager** Aivars Oss.

ADDRESS *Latlines* 1 Zivju str, Riga LV-1015, Latvia. *DFDS Tor Line* **(see Section 3)**

TELEPHONE *Latlines* **Administration** *Latvia* +371 7349527, *Germany* +49 (0)451 7099697, **Reservations** *Latvia* +371 7353523, *Germany* +49 (0)451 7099685. *DFDS Tor Line* **(see Section 3)**

FAX *DFDS Latlines* **Administration** *Latvia* +371 7349575, *Germany* +49 (0)451 7099687, **Reservations** *Latvia* +371 7353071, *Germany* +49 (0)451 7099687. *DFDS Tor Line* **(see Section 3)**

INTERNET *DFDS Latlines* **Email** latlines@latlines.lv **Website** www.latlines.lv *(Latvian, English, German, Russian). DFDS Tor Line* **(see Section 3)**

ROUTE OPERATED Lübeck (Germany) - Riga (Latvia) (32 hrs; *(1,2)*; 4 per week).

1	MERMAID II	13730t	72	17.5k	137.3m	69P	170C	84T	AS	FI
2	TRANSPARADEN	13700t	76	17.0k	135.8m	100P	280C	115T	A	FI

MERMAID II Built at Turku, Finland as the HANZ GUTZEIT and chartered to *Finncarriers* for Finland - Germany service. In 1982 she was sold to *EFFOA* of Finland and renamed the CAPELLA. She continued to be chartered to *Finncarriers* and this charter continued under a number of subsequent owners. In 1986 she was renamed the CAPELLA AV Stockholm. In 1988 she was renamed the FINNMAID. In 1989 she was placed on the *FinnLink* service between Uusikaupunki (Finland) and Hargshamn (Sweden). In 1997, this service was transferred to the Kapellskär - Naantali route. In 1998 she was replaced by the FINNARROW and, after service on *Finncarriers'* Finland - Germany routes, was laid up. In 2000 she was chartered to *VV-Line*. Passenger capacity was raised from 48 to 69. She was owned by *Rederi AB Gustaf Erikson* of Åland but in 2001 purchased by *VV-Line* and renamed the MERMAID II. In 2003 chartered to *DFDS Tor Line* to operate between Kiel and Riga. In March service transferred to Lübeck.

TRANSPARADEN Built at Hamburg, Germany as the TRANSGERMANIA for *Poseidon Schiffahrt OHG* of Germany interests for *Finncarriers-Poseidon* services between Finland and West Germany. In 1991 chartered to *Norse Irish Ferries* and used on their freight service between Liverpool and Belfast. In 1992 she was returned to *Finncarriers* and in 1993 sold to Cypriot interests for use in the Mediterranean and renamed the ROSEBAY. In 1994 chartered to *Stena Line* to inaugurate a new service between Harwich and Rotterdam (Frisohaven). In 1995 the service was switched to Hoek van Holland following the construction of a new linkspan. She also, during the summer, carried cars towing caravans, motor caravans and their passengers. In 1997 she was chartered to *Sally Freight* and renamed the EUROSTAR, operating between Ramsgate and Ostend. Later in 1997 she was renamed the EUROCRUISER. In 1998 she returned on charter to *Stena Line* and resumed the name ROSEBAY. In 1999 she was temporarily transferred to the Irish Sea. In autumn 2000 she was transferred to the Killingholme - Hoek van Holland service but was withdrawn in 2001 when the delivery of the new STENA HOLLANDICA enabled the STENA SEARIDER to replace her. She was then sold to *Rederi AB Engship* of Sweden, renamed the TRANSPARADEN and chartered to *Botnia Link*. In 2002 chartered to *DFDS Tor Line* to operate between Kiel and Riga. In January 2003 transferred to the *Latlines* Lübeck – Riga route.

FAERGERUTEN LANGELAND-KIEL

THE COMPANY *Faergeruten Langeland-Kiel A/S* is a Danish Private sector company.

MANAGEMENT Chairman Troels Kroyer, **Managing Director** Lars Carstensen.

ADDRESS Faergevej 6, DK-5935 Bagenkop, Denmark.

TELEPHONE Administration & **Reservations** +45 62 56 22 22.

FAX Administration & Reservations +45 62 56 26 22.

INTERNET Website www.langeland-kiel.dk *(Danish, German)*

ROUTE OPERATED Bagenkop (Langeland, Denmark) - Kiel (Germany) (2 hours 45 minutes; *(1)*; 2 per day).

1	LANGELAND		4101t	88	13.0k	95.0m	300P	170C	42T	BA	DK

LANGELAND Built at Sunderland, UK as the SUPERFLEX KILO for *Vognmandsruten* of Denmark. In 1989 sold to *Mercandia* and renamed the MERCANDIA I. In 1990 she began operating on the *Kattegatbroen* Juelsminde - Kalundborg service. In 1996 this service ceased and plans to use her on the *Sundbroen* Helsingør - Helsingborg service were blocked by the authorities. In 1997 chartered to *Litorina Line* to inaugurate a new service between Öland and Gotland. In 1998, sold to *Eidsiva Rederi* and renamed the ANJA 11. She inaugurated a new service for subsidiary *Easy Line* between Gedser (Denmark) and Rostock (Germany). In December 2000 the *Easy Line* service ended and she was laid up. Note she initially carried the name 'ANJA #11' but the '#' character did not form part of her registered name and was subsequently removed. In 2003 chartered to *Faergeruten Langeland-Kiel* to operate between Kiel and Bagenkop and renamed the LANGELAND.

LISCO BALTIC SERVICE

THE COMPANY *AB Lisco Baltic Service* is a Lithuanian company, 76% owned by *DFDS Tor Line*; they purchased this holding from Lithuanian Government in 2001. Passenger and cargo services are marketed by *AB Lisco Baltic Service* and ticket sales in Lithuania by *Krantas Shipping*.

ADDRESS 24 J. Janonio Str, KLAIPEDA LT-5813, Lithuania.

TELEPHONE Administration *LISCO Baltic Service (Klaìpeda)* + 370 6 393101, **Reservations** *LISCO (Klaìpeda):* + 370 6 393288, *Krantas (Klaìpeda)* + 370 6 395048, *DFDS Tor Line/LISCO Baltic Service (Karlshamn)* + 46 (0)45433680, *LISCO Baltic Service GmbH (Kiel)* + 49 (0)43120976444 - cargo, + 49 (0)43120976420 - passengers.

FAX Administration *LISCO Baltic Service (Klaìpeda)* + 370 6 393601, *Reservations: LISCO (Klaìpeda)* + 370 6 393287, *Krantas (Klaìpeda):* + 370 6 395041, *DFDS Tor Line/LISCO Baltic Service (Karlshamn)* + 46 (0) 45433689, *LISCO Baltic, Service GmbH (Kiel):* + 49 (0) 43120976555.

INTERNET Email - Administration ml5@lisco.lt **Reservations** *LISCO (Klaìpeda)* booking@lisco.lt *Krantas (Klaìpeda)* Cargo.de@krantas.lt *DFDS Tor Line/LISCO Baltic Service (Karlshamn)* Karlshamn@dfdstorline.com, *LISCO Baltic Service GmbH (Kiel):* cargo@lisco-baltic-service.de passage@lisco-baltic-service.de

Website: www.lisco.lt *(English,German)*

ROUTES OPERATED Klaìpeda (Lithuania) - Kiel (Germany) (21 hrs *(3)*; 6 per week) (joint with *Scandlines Euroseabridge* under the 'Kiel-Klaìpeda-Express' name) , Klaìpeda - Karlshamn (Sweden) (15 hrs *(2)*, 17 hrs; *(5)*; 3 per week), Klaìpeda - Sassnitz (Germany) (18 hrs; *(1)*; 6 per week (joint with *Scandlines Euroseabridge*)).

1	KAUNAS		25606t	89	16.0k	190.9m	214P	460C	116T	A2	LT
2F	KLAIPEDA		21890t	87	16.0k	190.9m	45P	250C	116T	A	LT

3	LISCO GLORIA	20608t	01	22.0k	196.6m	308P	316C	160T	A	LT
4	PALANGA	11630t	79	19.0k	126.5m	126P	300C	70T	A	LT
5F	SIAULIAI	6894t	85	13.0k	125.9m	12P	350C	38T	A	LT
6	VILNIUS	22341t	87	16.0k	190.9m	120P	460C	116T	A2	LT

KAUNAS train ferry built at Wismar, Germany (DDR) for *Lisco* of the former Soviet Union and used by to operate between Klaìpeda and Mukran in Germany (DDR). This was part of series of vessels built to link the USSR and Germany (DDR), avoiding Poland. In 1994 she was modified to increase passenger capacity in order to offer limited passenger facilities and placed on Klaìpeda – Kiel service. In 2003 transferred to the Klaìpeda – Karlshamn route.

KLAIPEDA train ferry as KAUNAS – but not converted to full ro-pax format (although she does carry more than the normal 12 for a ro-ro). Operates on the Klaìpeda –Sassnitz route.

LISCO GLORIA Built in Szczecin, Poland for *Lloyd Sardegna* of Italy as the GOLFO DEI CORALLI for operating between Italy and Sardinia. Due to late delivery the order was cancelled. In 2002 purchased by *DFDS Tor Liine* renamed the Dana Gloria and, in Autumn 2002 placed on the Esbjerg – Harwich service. In June 2003 replaced by modified sister vessel DANA SIRENA (see Section 1) and sold to *Lisco Baltic Service* and renamed the LISCO GLORIA. Operates between Klaìpeda and Kiel.

PALANGA Built at Le Havre, France; rebuilt at in 1992 to increase passengers capacity. In 1996 sold to *Lisco*, renamed the PALANGA; replaced on the Klaìpeda – Karlshamn service in 2003 by the KAUNUS.

SIAULIAI Built in Rostock, Germany (DDR) as the KOMPOZITOR BORODIN for *Lisco*. In 1992 renamed the SIAULIAI. At present she operates on the Klaìpeda – Karlshamn service.

VILNIUS train ferry as KAUNUS. Operated on the Klaìpeda – Kiel service until June 2003.

AB Lisco Baltic Service also own the PANEVEZYS and TOR NERINGA which are currently on charter to *DFDS Tor Line*. They are shown under *DFDS Tor Line* in Section 3.

MOLS-LINIEN

THE COMPANY *Mols-Linien A/S* is a Danish private sector company; previously a subsidiary of *J Lauritzen A/S*, it was, in 1988 sold to *DIFKO No LXII (Dansk Investeringsfond)*. Since 1994 shares in the company have been traded on the stock exchange. In January 1999 a 40% share in the company was acquired by *Scandlines Danmark A/S*. Their *Scandlines Cat-Link* Århus - Kalundborg service became part of *Mols-Linien* in February 1999 and the service was switched from Kalundborg to Odden in April 1999. The Ebeltoft - Odden ro-pax service was transferred to the Århus - Kalundborg route in January 2000.

MANAGEMENT Managing Director Preben Wolff, **Marketing Manager** Christian Hingelberg.

ADDRESS Færgehavnen, DK-8400 Ebeltoft, Denmark.

TELEPHONE Administration +45 89 52 52 00, **Reservations** +45 70 10 14 18.

FAX Administration +45 89 52 52 90, **Reservations** +45 89 52 52 92.

INTERNET Email Mols-Linien@Mols-Linien.dk **Website** www.Mols-Linien.dk *(Danish)*

ROUTES OPERATED Ro-pax Ferries Århus (Jutland) - Kalundborg (Sealand) (2 hr 40 mins; *(2,5)*; 7 per day). **Fast Ferries** Århus - Odden (Sealand) (1 hr 5 mins; *(3)*; every 3 hrs), Ebeltoft (Jutland) - Odden (45 mins; *(1,4)*; hourly).

1»	MAI MOLS	3971t	96	43.4k	76.1m	450P	120C	-	BA	DK
2	MAREN MOLS	14221t	96	19.0k	136.4m	600P	344C	82L	BA2	DK
3»	MAX MOLS	5617t	98	43.0k	91.3m	800P	220C	-	A	DK
4»	MIE MOLS	3971t	96	43.4k	76.1m	450P	120C	-	BA	DK
5	METTE MOLS	14221t	96	19.0k	136.4m	600P	344C	82L	BA2	DK

MAI MOLS Danyard SeaJet 250 catamaran built at Aalborg, Denmark for *Mols-Linien*.

MAREN MOLS, METTE MOLS Ro-pax vessels built at Frederikshavn, Denmark for *Mols-Linien*. Initially operated on the Ebeltoft - Odden route. In January 2000 switched to the Århus - Kalundborg route.

MAX MOLS InCat 91 metre catamaran, built speculatively at Hobart, Tasmania, Australia. In spring 1998, following *InCat's* acquisition of a 50% share in *Scandlines Cat-Link A/S, S*he was sold to that company and named the CAT-LINK IV. In 1999 purchased by *Mols-Linien* and renamed the MAX MOLS. In 2000 chartered to *Marine Atlantic* of Canada to operate between Port aux Basques (Newfoundland) and North Sydney (Nova Scotia). Returned to *Mols-Linien* in autumn 2000. In summer 2002 chartered to *Riga Sea Lines* to operate between Riga and Nynäshamn. Returned to *Mols-Linien* in autumn 2002. Laid up until spring 2003 when she replaced the MADS MOLS (moved to subsidiary *Speed Ferries* on the Dover – Boulogne route) on the Århus – Odden service.

MIE MOLS Danyard SeaJet 250 catamaran built at Aalborg, Denmark for *Mols-Linien*.

REEDEREI NORDEN-FRISIA

THE COMPANY *Aktiengesellschaft Reederei Norden-Frisia* is a German public sector company.

MANAGEMENT President/CEO Dr Stegmann, **Managing Director/CFO** Prok. Graw.

ADDRESS Postfach 1262, 26534 Norderney, Germany.

TELEPHONE Administration +49 (0)4932 9130.

FAX Administration +49 (0)4932 9131310.

INTERNET Email info@reederei-frisia.de **Website** www.reederei-frisia.de *(German)*

ROUTES OPERATED *Car Ferries & Passenger Ferries* Norddeich (Germany) - Norderney (German Frisian Islands) (1 hr; *(2,4,5)*; up to 15 per day), Norddeich - Juist (German Frisian Islands) (1 hr 20 mins; *(3,6)*; up to 15 per day), ***Passenger only fast ferry*** Norderney - Helgoland (1 hr 30 mins; *(1)*), Laugeoog - Helgoland (1 hr 15 min; *(1)*), Waugerooge - Helgoland (1 hr 15 min; *(1)*).

1p»	CAT NO 1	963t	99	40.0k	52.4m	432P	-	-	-	GY
2	FRISIA I	1020t	70	12.3k	63.7m	1500P	53C	-	-	GY
3	FRISIA II	1125t	78	12.0k	63.3m	1340P	53C	-	-	GY
4	FRISIA IV	1600t	02	12.0k	71.0m	1400P	60C	-	-	GY
5	FRISIA V	1007t	65	11.0k	63.8m	1442P	53C	-	-	GY
6	FRISIA VI	768t	68	12.0k	54.9m	1096P	35C	-	-	GY
7F	FRISIA VII	363t	84	12.0k	53.0m	12P	30C	-	-	GY
8p	FRISIA IX	571t	80	11.0k	51.0m	785P	-	-	-	GY
9f	FRISIA X	187t	72	12.0k	36.3m	290P	-	-	-	GY

CAT NO I Built at Fremantle, Western Australia for *Reederei Norden-Frisia* to inaugurate new services to Helgoland.

FRISIA I, FRISIA II, FRISIA V, FRISIA VI Built at Papenburg, Germany for *Reederei Norden-Frisia*. Passenger capacities relate to the summer seasons. Capacity is reduced during the winter.

FRISIA IV Built at Emden, Germany for *Reederei Norden-Frisia* to replace the FRISIA VIII.

FRISIA VI Built at Papenburg, Germany for *Reederei Norden-Frisia*. Conveys freight to Norderney and Juist.

FRISIA IX, FRISIA X Built at Oldersum, Germany for *Reederei Norden-Frisia*. The FRISIA IX was built at to convey 9 cars at the bow end but is now used mainly in passenger only mode. These ships are generally used for excursions.

NORDIC JET LINE

THE COMPANY *Nordic Jet Line* is an international company, registered in Estonia. Main shareholders are *Förde Reederei Seetouristik* of Germany, *Finnmark Fylkesrederi og Ruteselskap* of Norway and *Kværner Investments* of Norway.

MANAGEMENT Managing Director Mikael Granrot, **Deputy Managing Director** Hans Jonasson.

ADDRESS *Estonia* Sadama 25-4, 15051 Tallinn, Estonia, *Finland* Kanavaterminaali K5, 00160 Helsinki, Finland.

TELEPHONE Administration *Estonia* +372 (0)6 137200, *Finland* +358 (0)9 68177150, **Reservations** *Estonia* +372 (0)6 137000, *Finland* +358 (0)9 681770.

FAX Administration & Reservations *Estonia* +372 (0)6 137222, *Finland* +358 (0)9 6817111.

INTERNET Email marketing@njl.fi **Website** www.njl.fi *(English, Finnish, Estonian, German)*

ROUTE OPERATED Helsinki (Finland) - Tallinn (Estonia) (1 hr 30 mins; *(1,2)*; up to 6 per day (all year except during winter ice period)).

1»	BALTIC JET	2273t	99	36.0k	60.0m	430P	52C	-	A	NO
2»	NORDIC JET	2273t	98	36.0k	60.0m	430P	52C	-	A	NO

BALTIC JET, NORDIC JET Kværner Fjellstrand JumboCat 60m catamarans built at Omastrand, Norway for *Nordic Jet Line*. Alternative traffic mix is 38 cars and 2 buses.

NORDÖ LINK

THE COMPANY *Rederi AB Nordö-Link* is a Swedish private sector company, a subsidiary of *Finnlines* of Finland.

MANAGEMENT Managing Director Rüdiger Meyer.

ADDRESS PO Box 106, S-201 21 MALMÖ, Sweden.

TELEPHONE Administration +46 (0)40 72417, **Reservations** +46 (0)40 79603, **Fax:** +46 (0)40 6119849.

INTERNET Website www.nordoe-link.se *(Swedish, German)*

ROUTES OPERATED Malmö - Travemünde (9 hrs; *(1,2,3)*; up to 3 per day but passengers are generally only carried on mid-morning departures).

1	FINNARROW	25996t	96	21.0k	168.0m	200P	800C	154T	BA2	FI
2	LÜBECK LINK	33163t	80	19.0k	194.1m	240P	-	250T	BS	SW
3	MALMÖ LINK	33163t	80	19.0k	194.1m	240P	-	250T	BS	SW

FINNARROW Built at Kodja, Indonesia as the GOTLAND for *Rederi AB Gotland* for charter. In 1997 briefly chartered to *Tor Line* and then to *Nordic Trucker Line*, to operate between Oxelösund and St Petersburg (a ro-ro service). In June 1997 she was chartered to *SeaWind Line*, enabling a twice daily passenger service to be operated. In late 1997 she was sold to *Finnlines* and renamed the FINNARROW. She started operating twice weekly between Helsinki and Travemünde. During summer 1998 she was transferred to *FinnLink*; a bow door was fitted and she was modified to allow for two level loading. In 2003 transferred to *Nordö Link*.

LÜBECK LINK Built at Oskarshamn, Sweden as the FINNROSE for *Finncarriers* of Finland and used on deep sea services. In 1990 sold to *Sea Link AB*, converted to 'ROPax' format with passenger accommodation and rail tracks, and placed on the Malmö - Travemünde service.

MALMÖ LINK Built as the FINNHAWK; otherwise as the LÜBECK LINK.

POLFERRIES

THE COMPANY *Polferries* is the trading name of *Polska Zegluga Baltycka SA (Polish Baltic Shipping Company)*, a Polish state owned company.

MANAGEMENT General Director & President of the Board Jan Warchol, **Shipping Policy Director and Board Member** Grazyna Bak **Financial Director** Wojciech Rogowski **Technical Director** Wlodzimierz Miadowicz.

ADDRESS ul Portowa 41, PL 78-100 Kolobrzeg, Poland.

TELEPHONE Administration +48 (0)94 35 52 103, +48 (0)94 35 52 200, **Passenger Reservations** *Swinoujscie* +48 (0)91 32 16 140, *Gdansk* +48 (0)58 34 31 887, **Freight Reservations** *Swinoujscie* +48 (0)91 3216161, *Gdansk* +48 (0)58 34 30 212.

FAX Administration +48 (0)94 35 52 130, **Passenger Reservations** *Swinoujscie* +48 (0)91 32 16 168, *Gdansk* +48 (0)58 34 36 574, **Freight Reservations** *Swinoujscie* +48 (0)91 32 16 169, *Gdansk* +48 (0)58 34 30 975.

INTERNET Email info@polferries.pl **Passenger Reservations** *Swinoujscie* boas.pax@polferries.pl *Gdansk* pax.gdansk@polferries.pl **Freight Reservations** *Swinoujscie* boas.cargo@polferries.pl, *Gdansk* cargo.gsansk@polferries.pl **Website** www.polferries.pl *(Polish, English, Swedish)*

ROUTES OPERATED Swinoujscie - Ystad (8 hrs; *(1,3)*; 2 per day), Swinoujscie - Copenhagen (9 hrs 45 mins; *(2)*; 5 per week), Swinoujscie - Rønne (6 hrs; *(2)*; 1 per week (seasonal)), Gdansk - Nynäshamn (Sweden) (19 hrs; *(4)*; 3 per week).

1	KAHLEBERG	10271t	83	14.5k	140.1m	79P	-	58T	AS	LB
2	POMERANIA	12087t	78	15.4k	127.7m	1000P	273C	26L	BA	BS
3	ROGALIN	10241t	72	16.5k	126.9m	708P	146C	18L	BA	BS
4	SILESIA	10553t	79	17.0k	127.6m	755P	250C	22L	BA	BS

KAHLEBERG Built at Wismar, Germany (DDR) for *DSR* of Germany (DDR). In 1991 chartered to *TR Line* (joint venture between *TT-Line* and *DSR*) for service between Rostock and Trelleborg. In 1995 *DSR* pulled out of the venture and the service became *TT-Line*. In 1997 she returned to *DSR* to operate for *Euroseabridge* (later *Scandlines Euroseabridge*). She initially operated on the Travemünde - Klaìpeda service. In 1999 she was transferred to the formerly freight only Rostock - Liepaja service. In 2000 transferred to the *Amber Line* Karlshamn - Liepaja route as a ro-pax vessel. In 2003 chartered to *Polferries* to operate between Swinoujscie and Ystad.

POMERANIA Built at Szczecin, Poland for *Polferries*. In 1978 and 1979 she briefly operated between Felixstowe and Swinoujscie via Copenhagen. In recent years she was the regular vessel on the Gdansk - Helsinki service before that service was withdrawn. She was rebuilt in 1997. Currently used on the Swinoujscie - Copenhagen and Swinoujscie - Rønne routes.

ROGALIN Built at Nantes, France as the AALLOTAR for the *EFFOA* of Finland. Used on overnight *Silja Line* services (joint with *Svea Line* of Sweden and *Bore Line* of Finland) between Stockholm and Helsinki. Later used on the Stockholm - Mariehamn - Turku service. In 1978 she was sold to *Polferries*. She was renamed the ROGALIN and operated on various services between Poland, West Germany and Scandinavia. In 1983 she was chartered to *Farskip* of Iceland from the end of May until September, renamed the EDDA and inaugurated a service between Reykjavik (Iceland), Newcastle and Bremerhaven (Germany). In September of that year she returned to *Polferries* and resumed the name ROGALIN. This service was not repeated in 1984 and she continued to operate for *Polferries* until chartered (with crew) by *Swansea Cork Ferries* in 1987. She was renamed the CELTIC PRIDE and inaugurated a new Swansea - Cork service. This service also operated during summer 1988 but during winter 1987/88 and after the 1988 summer season she was returned to *Polferries* and resumed the name ROGALIN, operating on Baltic services. She did not serve with *Swansea Cork Ferries* in 1989 or 1990 but in 1991 she was taken on charter (again with crew) and was again renamed the CELTIC PRIDE. This charter terminated at the end of 1992 and she returned to the Baltic and resumed the name ROGALIN. Currently used on the Swinoujscie – Ystad route.

SILESIA Built at Szczecin, Poland for *Polferries*. rebuilt during winter 1997/98, although not as extensively as the POMERANIA. Currently used on the Gdansk - Nynäshamn route.

RG-LINE

THE COMPANY *RG-Line Oy/Ab* is a Finnish private sector company, named after its owner, Rabbe Grönblom.

ADDRESS Hovioikeudenpuistikko 11, 65100 Vaasa, Finland.

TELEPHONE Administration & Reservations +358 (0)6-3200 300.

FAX Administration & Reservations +358 (0)6-3104 551.

INTERNET Email marketing@rgline.com **Website** www.rgline.com *(Finnish, Swedish)*

ROUTE OPERATED Vaasa (Finland) - Umeå (Sweden) (4 hrs; *(1)*; 1/2 per day).

1	CASINO EXPRESS	10542t	66	18.0k	128.9m	1200P	265C	32T	BA	SW

CASINO EXPRESS Built at Landskrona, Sweden as the FENNIA for *Siljavarustamo-Siljarederiet* of Finland to operate *Silja Line* services between Sweden and Finland. In 1970 she was transferred to *Stockholms Rederi AB Svea*, when *Silja Line* became a marketing organisation. In 1983 she was withdrawn and operated for a short period with *B&I Line* of Ireland between Rosslare and Pembroke Dock. In 1984 she was sold to *Jakob Line*. In 1985 she was sold to *Vaasanlaivat*. In 1992 she was returned to *Jakob Line*. During winter 1992/3 she operated for *Baltic Link* between Norrköping (Sweden) and Riga (Latvia), but returned to *Silja Line* in summer 1993 and was used on the Vaasa - Umeå and Pietarsaari - Skellefteå services. The latter service did not operate in 1999 and, on 1st July, she was transferred to the new *Vaasanlaivat*, a *Silja Line* subsidiary formed to operate the Vaasa - Umeå link. In September 1999 she was replaced by the WASA QUEEN and withdrawn. During summer 2000 she operated freight only services between Stockholm and Turku. In 2001 sold to *RG-Line*, renamed the CASINO EXPRESS and in May re-opened the Vaasa - Umeå route which had been closed by *Silja Line* subsidiary *Vaasanlaivat* in December 2000.

RIGA SEA LINES

THE COMPANY *Riga Sea Lines (Rīgas Jūras Līnija)* is a Latvian company, largely owned by the city of Riga. Services began in summer 2002 using the chartered MAX MOLS of *Mols-Linien*, operating from Riga to Nynäshamn. Service suspended in September and restarted in December as stated below.

MANAGEMENT Managing Director Egils Rozinskis, **Marketing Manager** Galina Fomenko.

ADDRESS A/s Rīgas Jūras Līnija, Eksporta iela 3a, Rīga LV - 1010.

TELEPHONE Administration +371 7205454, **Reservations** *Passenger* +371 7205460, *Cargo* +371 7205464.

FAX Administration +371 7205457, **Reservations** +371 7205461.

INTERNET Email Administration office@rigasealine.lv **Reservations** booking@rigasealine.lv

Website www.rigasealine.lv *(Latvian, English)*

ROUTE OPERATED Riga (Latvia) - Stockholm (Sweden) (17 hrs 30 mins; *(1)*; 3 per week).

1	BALTIC KRISTINA	12281t	73	19.0k	128.0m	512P	50C	30T	BA2	LV

BALTIC KRISTINA Built at Turku, Finland as the BORE 1 for *Ångfartygs AB Bore* of Finland for *Silja Line* services between Turku and Stockholm. In 1980, *Bore Line* left the *Silja Line* consortium and disposed of its passenger ships. She was acquired by *EFFOA* of Finland and continued to operate on *Silja Line* service, being renamed the SKANDIA. In 1983 she was sold to *Stena Line* and renamed the STENA BALTICA. She was then resold to *Latvia Shipping* of the USSR, substantially rebuilt, renamed the ILLICH and introduced onto a Stockholm - Leningrad (now St Petersburg) service trading as *ScanSov Line*. In 1986 operations were transferred to *Baltic Shipping Company*. In 1992 she inaugurated a new service between Stockholm and Riga but continued to also serve St Petersburg. In 1995 the Swedish terminal was changed to Nynäshamn. In late 1995 arrested and laid up in

Stockholm. In 1997, services were planned to restart between Kiel and St Petersburg under the auspices of a German company called *Baltic Line*, with the vessel renamed the ANASTASIA V. However, this did not materialise and she was sold to *Windward Line* of Barbados and renamed the WINDWARD PRIDE. In 1997, she was chartered to *ESCO*, and renamed the BALTIC KRISTINA. In late 1997 she sailed for *EstLine* between Stockholm and Tallinn in a freight-only role. Following a major refurbishment, she entered service with *EstLine* in May 1998, allowing a daily full passenger service to be operated. In 2000 the charter was transferred to *Tallink*. Placed on the Paldiski - Kapellskär service. In late 2002 chartered to *Riga Sea Lines* to inaugurate a service between Riga and Stockholm.

RÖMÖ-SYLT LINIE

THE COMPANY *Römö-Sylt Linie GmbH* is a German company, a subsidiary of *FRS (Förde Reederei Seetouristik)* of Flensburg.

MANAGEMENT Managing Director P Rathke.

ADDRESS *Germany* Am Fähranleger, D-25992 List, Germany, *Denmark* Kilebryggen, DK-6792 Rømø, Denmark.

TELEPHONE Administration (Germany) +49 (0)4651 870475, **Reservations (Denmark)** +45 73 75 53 03.

FAX Administration (Germany) +49 (0)4651 871446, **Reservations (Denmark)** +45 73 75 53 05.

INTERNET Email romo-sylt@post12.tele.dk **Website** www.romo-sylt.dk *(Danish, German)*

ROUTE OPERATED List (Sylt, Germany) - Havneby (Rømø, Denmark) (45 mins; *(1,2)*; variable - half hourly at peaks). Note the island of Rømø is linked to the Danish mainland by a road causeway; the island of Sylt is linked to the German mainland by a rail-only causeway on which cars are conveyed on shuttle wagons.

1	VIKINGLAND	1963t	74	11.0k	68.3m	420P	60C	8L	BA	GY
2	WESTERLAND	1509t	71	11.0k	58.3m	400P	40C	5L	BA	GY

VIKINGLAND, WESTERLAND Built at Husum, Germany for *Römö-Sylt Linie*.

SAAREMAA LAEVAKOMPANII

THE COMPANY *Saaremaa Laevakompanii* is an Estonian company, founded in 1992.

MANAGEMENT General Director Mr. Tõnis Rihvk.

ADDRESS AS Kohtu, 93812 Kuressaare, Estonia.

TELEPHONE Administration +372-45-24350, **Reservations** +372-45-24444.

FAX Administration +372-45-24355, **Reservations** +372-45-24373.

INTERNET Email slk@laevakompanii.ee **Website** www.laevakompanii.ee

ROUTE OPERATED Kuivastu – Virtsu (30 mins; *(3,6,8,11)*; up to 12 per day), Heltermaa (Hiiumaa) – Rohuküla (1 hr 30 mins; *(2,4,5,6)*; 5 per day), Rohuküla – Sviby (45 mins; *(1,4)*; up to 3 per day), Triigi - Sõru (1 hr 5 mins; *(10)*; up to 2 per day).

1	HARILAID	1028t	85	9.9k	49.9m	120P	35C	0L	BA	ES
2	HIIUMAA	1549t	66	10.0k	53.8m	175P	28C	0L	BA	ES
3	KOGUVA	1305t	79	10.6k	55.5m	204P	41C	0L	BA	ES
4	KÖRGELAID	1028t	87	9.9k	49.9m	200P	35C	0L	BA	ES
5	OFELIA	3638t	68	14.4k	74.4m	600P	110C	12L	BA	ES
6	REGULA	1157t	71	14.5k	71.2m	580P	105C	12L	BA	ES
7	SCANIA	3474t	72	14.5k	74.2m	400P	80C	12L	BA	ES
8	ST OLA	4833t	71	16.0k	85.9m	500P	140C	12L	BA	ES

9	TEHUMARDI	1163t	73	10.6k	55.5m	140P	28C	0L	BA	ES
10	VARDO	116t	62	9.0k	27.1m	47P	17C	0L	BA	ES
11	VIIRE	4101t	88	12.7k	95.8m	469P	140C	36L	BA	ES

HARILAID Built at Riga, Latvia (USSR) for *ESCO* of Estonia. In 1992 transferred to *Saaremaa Laevakompanii.*

HIIUMAA Built at Kristiansand, Norway as the TAARS for *Sydfyenske Dampskibsselskab A/S* of Denmark. Initially used on the Spodsbjerg – Nakskov route. In 1975 transferred to the Spodsbjerg – Taars route. Withdrawn in 1984 and in 1985 sold to *ESCO* of Estonia and renamed the HIIUMAA; she was placed on the Heltermaa – Rohuküla route. In 1992 renamed the HIIUMAA 2. In 1992 transferred to *Saaremaa Laevakompanii.* In 1996 renamed the HIIUMAA.

KOGUVA Built at Riga, Latvia (USSR) for *ESCO* of Estonia. In 1992 transferred to *Saaremaa Laevakompanii.*

KÖRGELAID Built at Riga, Latvia (USSR) for *ESCO* of Estonia. In 1992 transferred to *Saaremaa Laevakompanii.*

OFELIA Built at Rendsburg, Germany for *Svenska Rederi-AB Öresund* of Sweden and used on the Limhamn - Dragør service. In 1980 sold to *Scandinavian Ferry Lines*. In 1990 transferred to *SweFerry* and later to *Scandlines AB*. In 1997 sold to *Saaremaa Laevakompanii.*

REGULA Built at Papenburg, Germany for *Stockholms Rederi AB Svea* of Sweden for the service between Helsingborg and Helsingør operated by *Linjebuss International AB* (a subsidiary company). In 1980 she was sold to *Scandinavian Ferry Lines*. During winter 1984/85 she was rebuilt to increase vehicle and passenger capacity. In 1991 ownership was transferred to *SweFerry* and operations to *ScandLines* on the Helsingborg - Helsingør service. Ownership later transferred to *Scandlines AB*. In 1997 sold to *Saaremaa Laevakompanii.*

SCANIA Built at Aalborg, Denmark for *Svenska Rederi-AB Öresund* of Sweden and used on the Limhamn - Dragør service. In 1980 sold to *Scandinavian Ferry Lines*. In 1990 transferred to *SweFerry* and later to Scandlines AB. In 1999 sold to *Saaremaa Laevakompanii.*

ST OLA Built at Papenburg Germany as the SVEA SCARLETT for *Stockholms Rederi AB Svea* of Sweden and used on the *SL (Skandinavisk Linjetrafik)* service between Copenhagen (Tuborg Havn) and Landskrona (Sweden). In 1980 she was sold to *Scandinavian Ferry Lines* of Sweden and *Dampskibsselskabet Øresund A/S* of Denmark (jointly owned). Initially she continued to serve Landskrona but later that year the Swedish terminal became Malmö. In 1981 she operated on the Helsingborg - Helsingør service for a short while, after which she was withdrawn and laid up. In 1982 she was sold to *Eckerö Linjen* of Finland, renamed the ECKERÖ and used on services between Grisslehamn (Sweden) and Eckerö (Åland Islands). In 1991 she was sold to *P&O Scottish Ferries* and renamed the ST OLA. In March 1992 she replaced the previous ST OLA (1345t, 1974) on the Scrabster - Stromness service. In September 2002 withdrawn and sold to *Saaremaa Laevakompanii.* Used on the Kuivastu - Virtsu route.

VIIRE Built as the SUPERFLEX CHARLIE for *Vognmandsruten* of Denmark to establish a new service between Korsør (Fyn) and Nyborg (Sjælland). In 1990 this company was taken over by *DIFKO* and the renamed the DIFKO KORSØR. In 1998, following the opening of the Great Belt road fixed link, the service ceased and she was laid up. In 1999 chartered to *Saaremaa Laevakompanii* and renamed the VIIRE. In 2000, the charter ended and she returned to lay-up in Denmark. In 2001 she was again chartered to *Saaremaa Laevakompanii.* Used on the Kuivastu – Virtsu route.

VARDO Built at Rauma, Finland *ESCO* of Estonia. In 1992 transferred to *Saaremaa Laevakompanii.*

SAGA LINE

THE COMPANY *Saga Line* is a Norwegian Company. No other details available at time of going to press. Start of operations subject to confirmation.

INTERNET Website www.sagaline.dk www.sagaline.no

ROUTE OPERATED Moss (Norway) - Skagen (Denmark) (not known; *(1)*; 1 per day).

1	SAGAFJORD	5678t	65	17.8k	99.5m	1100P	145C	30T	BA	NO

SAGAFJORD Built at Lübeck, Germany as the VIKING III for *Otto Thoresen* of Norway for the *Thoresen Car Ferries* Southampton (England) - Cherbourg and Southampton - Le Havre services. During the winter, until 1970/71, she was chartered to *Lion Ferry* of Sweden for their Harwich - Bremerhaven service. In 1967 the service was acquired by *European Ferries* of Great Britain, trading as *Townsend Thoresen*. She was chartered to this organisation and retained Norwegian registry. During winter 1971/72 and 1972/73 she was chartered to *Larvik Line*. She became surplus to requirements following the delivery of the 'Super Vikings' in 1975 and was the subject of a number of short term charters until 1982 when she was sold to *Da-No Linjen* of Norway, renamed the TERJE VIGEN and used on their Fredrikstad (Norway) - Frederikshavn (Denmark) service. In 1986 she was sold to *KG Line* to operate between Kaskinen (Finland) and Gävle (Sweden) and renamed the SCANDINAVIA. In 1990 she was sold *Johnson Line* and used on *Jakob Line* service, being renamed the FENNO STAR. In 1991 she was sold to *Scandi Line* and renamed the SANDEFJORD but served briefly as the FENNO STAR on the *Corona Line* service between Karlskrona and Gdynia before being introduced onto the Sandefjord - Strömstad service in 1992. In 1999 *Scandi Line* operations were integrated into *Color Line*. In she was 2000 withdrawn and in 2001 sold to *Buquebus Los Cipreses* of Uruguay. However, she was not moved to South America and remained laid up in Norway. In 2003 to be chartered to *Saga Line* and renamed the SAGAFJORD.

SCANDLINES (DENMARK & GERMANY)

THE COMPANY *Scandlines AG* is a German company, 50% owned by *DB Cargo AG*, a subsidiary of *Deutsche Bahn AG (German Railways)* (which is owned by the Federal Government) and 50% owned by the Kingdom of Denmark. In 1998 it took over *DFO (Deutsche Fährgesellschaft Ostsee mbH)* of Germany (renamed *Scandlines Deutschland GmbH*) and *Scandlines A/S* of Denmark (renamed *Scandlines Danmark A/S*). A 50% share in *Euroseabridge GmbH* was acquired in 1998 (by *Scandlines A/S* of Denmark before the merger with *DFO*) and the remaining 50% in 1999; the name was changed to *Scandlines Euroseabridge GmbH*.

Scandlines A/S was formerly *DSB Rederi A/S* and before that the Ferries Division of *DSB (Danish State Railways)*. *DFO* was formed in 1993 by the merging of the Ferries Divisions of *Deutsche Bundesbahn (German Federal Railways)* (which operated in the Federal Republic of Germany) and *Deutsche Reichsbahn (German State Railways)* (which operated in the former DDR).

Stena Line owned *Scandlines AB* of Sweden also trades under this name but remains a separate company. Danish domestic routes are operated by subsidiary company *Scandlines Sydfyenske A/S*, and are marketed as part of the *Scandlines* network.

MANAGEMENT Chairman Bernd Malmström, **Chief Executive** Ole Rendbæk, **Chief Finance Officer** Axel Bertram.

ADDRESS *Denmark* Dampfærgevej 10, DK-2100 Copenhagen Ø, Denmark. *Germany* Hochhaus am Fährhafen, D-18119 Rostock-Warnemünde, Germany.

TELEPHONE Administration *Denmark* +45 33 15 15 15, *Germany* +49 (0)381 5435-0, **Reservations** *Denmark* +45 33 15 15 15, *Germany* +49 (0)1805-7226 354637.

INTERNET Email scandlines@scandlines.dk

Websites www.scandlines.dk *(Danish)* www.scandlines.com *(German, English)*

ROUTES OPERATED Conventional Ferries Helsingør (Sealand, Denmark) - Helsingborg (Sweden) (25 mins; *(5,25)*; every 20 mins) (joint with *Scandlines AB* of Sweden), Rødby (Lolland, Denmark) -

Hamlet *(John May)*

Urd *(Mike Louagie)*

Puttgarden (Germany) (45 mins; *(1,6,13,14,17 (6 road freight only))*; half hourly train/vehicle ferry + additional road freight only sailings), Gedser (Falster, Denmark) - Rostock (Germany) (2 hrs; *(2,7,12)*; every 2 hours (less frequent Dec - Feb), Rostock (Germany) - Trelleborg (Sweden) (5 hrs 45 mins (7 hrs night); *(8)*; 3 per day) (joint with *Scandlines AB* of Sweden), Sassnitz (Germany) - Trelleborg (3 hrs 45 mins; *(16)*; 4-5 per day) (joint with *Scandlines AB* of Sweden), **Summer only** Sassnitz - Rønne (Bornholm, Denmark) (3 hrs 45 mins; *(15)*; 1 or 2 per day.

Danish domestic services operated by subsidiary *Scandlines Sydfyenske A/S (formerly Sydfyenske Dampskibsselskab (SFDS)) and forming part of *Scandlines* network Fynshav (Als) - Bøjden (Fyn) (50 mins; *(23)*; 6-8 per day), Esbjerg (Jutland) - Nordby (Fanø) (12 mins; *(3,9,20)*; every 20-40 mins), Spodsbjerg (Langeland) - Tårs (Lolland) (45 mins; *(4,10,21)*; hourly).

Germany - Latvia & Lithuania routes operated by subsidiary *Scandlines Euroseabridge GmbH* Kiel - Klaìpeda (Lithuania) (20 hrs; *(22, Lisco vessel)*; 6 per week (joint with *Lisco Baltic Service* of Lithuania under the *Kiel-Klaìpeda-Express* name)), Sassnitz (Mukran) (Germany) - Klaìpeda (18 hrs; *(Lisco vessel)*; 3 per week (joint with *Lisco Baltic Service* of Lithuania)), Rostock (Germany) - Liepaja (Latvia) (24 hrs; *(26)*; 2 per week).

Denmark - Lithuania route operated by *Scandlines Balticum Seaways division* Århus (Denmark) - Aabenraa (Denmark) - Klaìpeda (Lithuania) (from 30 hrs; *(18)*; 2 per week from Aabenraa (1 westbound via Århus), 1 per week from Århus via Aabenraa).

Sweden - Latvia route operated by *Amber Line* Karlshamn (Sweden) - Liepaja (Latvia) (17 hrs; *(11,19)*; 3 per week).

1	DEUTSCHLAND	15187t	97	19.0k	142.0m	900P	294C	30Lr	BA2	GY
2	DRONNING MARGRETHE II	10850t	73	16.5k	144.6m	400P	195C	20Lr	BA2	DK
3	FENJA	751t	98	11.5k	49.9m	396P	34C	4L	BA	DK
4	FRIGG SYDFYEN	1676t	84	12.5k	70.1m	338P	50C	8L	BA	DK
5	HAMLET	10067t	97	14.0k	111.2m	1000P	244C	34L	BA	DK
6F	HOLGER DANSKE	2779t	76	14.5k	86.8m	12P	55C	12L	BA	DK
7	KRONPRINS FREDERIK	16071t	81	19.5k	152.0m	1082P	210C	46T	BA	DK
8	MECKLENBURG-VORPOMMERN	36185t	96	20.0k	199.9m	600P	90C	230Tr	A2	GY
9	MENJA	751t	98	11.5k	49.9m	396P	34C	4L	BA	DK
10	ODIN SYDFYEN	1698t	82	12.5k	70.4m	338P	50C	8L	BA	DK
11	PETERSBURG	25353t	86	16k	190.8m	144P	329C	110T	A2	LB
12	PRINS JOACHIM	16071t	80	19.5k	152.0m	1080P	-	46Lr	BA	DK
13	PRINS RICHARD	14621t	97	19.0k	142.0m	900P	294C	36Lr	BA	DK
14	PRINSESSE BENEDIKTE	14621t	97	19.0k	142.0m	900P	294C	36Lr	BA	DK
15	RÜGEN	12289t	72	17.5k	152.2m	850P	235C	30Lr	A2	GY
16	SASSNITZ	21154t	89	19.0k	171.5m	1000P	390C	50Tr	BA2	GY
17	SCHLESWIG-HOLSTEIN	15187t	97	19.0k	142.0m	900P	294C	30Lr	BA2	GY
18F	SEA CORONA	12110t	72	17.0k	137.5m	12P		106T	A	NO
19F	SEA TRADER	8454t	77	16.5k	123.6m	12P	530C	56T	A	MA
20p	SØNDERHO	93t	62	10.0k	26.3m	199P	0C	0L	-	DK
21	SPODSBJERG	958t	72	13.0k	67.3m	225P	40C	9L	BA	DK
22	SVEALAND	25026t	99	21.5k	186.0m	327P	164C	170T	A	MA
23	THOR SYDFYEN	1479t	78	12.0k	71.0m	292P	48C	9L	BA	DK
24F•	TREKRONER	15195t	79	18.0k	198.5m	12P	-	58Tr	A	DK
25	TYCHO BRAHE	11148t	91	14.0k	111.2m	1250P	240C	35Lr	BA	DK
26	URD	13144t	81	17.0k	171.0m	100P	-	104T	AS	DK

DEUTSCHLAND Train/vehicle ferry built at Krimpen aan den IJssel, Rotterdam, Netherlands for *DFO* for the Puttgarden - Rødby service.

DRONNING MARGRETHE II Train/vehicle ferry built at Nakskov, Denmark for *DSB* for the Nyborg - Korsør service. In 1981 transferred to the Rødby - Puttgarden service. An additional vehicle deck was added in 1982. Withdrawn in 1997. In 1998 became a back-up freight-only vessel on the Rødby

- Puttgarden and Gedser - Rostock routes. In 1999 she replaced the fast ferry BERLIN EXPRESS (4675t, 1995) as regular vessel on the Gedser - Rostock route.

FENJA Vehicle ferry built at Svendborg, Denmark for *SFDS A/S* for the Esbjerg - Nordby service.

FRIGG SYDFYEN Vehicle ferry built at Svendborg, Denmark for *Sydfyenske Dampskibsselskab (SFDS)* of Denmark for the service between Spodsbjerg and Tårs. In 1996, this company was taken over by *DSB Rederi* and the company is now *Scandlines Sydfyenske A/S.*

HAMLET Road vehicle ferry built Rauma, Finland for *Scandlines* (50% owned by *Scandlines AG* and 50% owned by *Scandlines AB* of Sweden) for the Helsingør - Helsingborg service. Sister vessel of the TYCHO BRAHE but without rail tracks.

HOLGER DANSKE Built at Aalborg, Denmark as a train/vehicle ferry for *DSB* for the Helsingør - Helsingborg service. In 1991 transferred to the Kalundborg - Samsø route (no rail facilities). In 1997, transferred to subsidiary *SFDS A/S*. Withdrawn at the end of November 1998 when the service passed to *Samsø Linien*. In 1999 began operating between Rødby and Puttgarden as a road freight only vessel, carrying, among others, loads which cannot be conveyed on passenger vessels.

KRONPRINS FREDERIK Train/vehicle ferry built at Nakskov, Denmark for *DSB* for the Nyborg - Korsør service. Withdrawn in 1997. After conversion to car/lorry ferry, she was transferred to the Gedser - Rostock route (no rail facilities).

MECKLENBURG-VORPOMMERN Train/vehicle ferry built at Bremerhaven, Germany for *DFO* for the Rostock - Trelleborg service. During winter 2002/3 modified to increase freight capacity and reduce passenger capacity.

MENJA Built at Svendborg, Denmark for *SFDS A/S* for the Esbjerg - Nordby service.

ODIN SYDFYEN Vehicle ferry built at Svendborg, Denmark for *Sydfyenske Dampskibsselskab (SFDS)* of Denmark for the service between Spodsbjerg and Tårs.

PETERSBURG Built at Wismar, Germany (DDR) as the MUKRAN for *DSR* of Germany (DDR). In 1995 she was rebuilt to introduce road vehicle and additional passenger capacity and was renamed the PETERSBURG. She inaugurated the Travemünde service in 1995 but is now used on the Sassnitz - Klaìpeda service. This service was operated jointly with the *Lisco* vessel KLAIPEDA, a sister vessel which has not been converted to ro-pax format. In 2001 she was transferred to the Kiel - Klaìpeda service, replacing the sister vessel GREIFSWALD whose charter was ended. In 2003 replaced by the SVEALAND and transferred to the *Amber Line* Karlshamn - Liepaja route.

PRINS JOACHIM Train/vehicle ferry, built at Nakskov, Denmark for *DSB* for the Nyborg - Korsør service. Withdrawn in 1997 and laid up. During winter 2000/2001 modified in same way as KRONPRINS FREDERIK and transferred to the Gedser - Rostock route.

PRINS RICHARD, PRINSESSE BENEDIKTE Train/vehicle ferries, built at Frederikshavn, Denmark for *DSB Rederi* for the Rødby - Puttgarden service.

RÜGEN Train/vehicle ferry built at Rostock, Germany (DDR) for *Deutsche Reichsbahn* of Germany (DDR) for services between Trelleborg and Sassnitz. In 1993 ownership was transferred to *DFO*. Since 1989 she has been used on the Sassnitz - Rønne service. In 1998 and 1999 she also operated between Ystad and Rønne but this has not been repeated.

SASSNITZ Train/vehicle ferry built at Frederikshavn, Denmark for *Deutsche Reichsbahn*. In 1993 ownership transferred to *DFO*. Used on the Sassnitz - Trelleborg service.

SCHLESWIG-HOLSTEIN Train/vehicle ferry built at Krimpen aan den IJssel, Rotterdam, Netherlands for *DFO* for the Puttgarden - Rødby service.

SEA CORONA Built at Rauma, Finland as the ANTARES for *Finska Ångfartygs A/B* of Finland and used on services between Finland and Germany. In 1975 she was chartered to DG Hansa of Germany and renamed the RHEINFELS. In 1977 she was sold to *Nedlloyd* of the Netherlands and renamed the NEDLLOYD ROCKANJE. In 1977 she was chartered to *Constellation Line* of the USA for services between the USA and Europe. In 1983 she was sold to *Kotka Line* of Finland, renamed the KOTKA LILY and used on their services between Finland, UK and West Africa. In 1985 she was chartered to

Jahre Line of Norway, renamed the JALINA and operated freight services between Oslo and Kiel. Two years later, she returned to Baltic waters, being chartered to *Finncarriers* and renamed the FINNROVER. In 1988 she was chartered to *Kent Line*, renamed the SEAHORSE and used on their Dartford - Zeebrugge service. In 1991 she was chartered to *DFDS* and in 1992 she was renamed the DANA CORONA. She was initially used on the service between the Immingham and Cuxhaven (Germany) but in 1995 she was transferred to the Fredericia - Copenhagen - Klaìpeda (Lithuania) service. In 2001 the charter was ended and she returned to owners, being renamed the SEA CORONA. She was chartered to *Scandlines AG* and placed on the *Scandlines Balticum Seaways* Århus - Aabenraa - Klaìpeda route.

SEA TRADER Built at Hollming, Finland for *Latvian Shipping Company* of the USSR as the MEKHANIK GERASIMOV. In 1998 sold to the *Mekhanikis Gerasimovs Shipping Co* of Malta and chartered to Color Line as the COLOR TRADER. On conclusion of the charter she was rename the MEKHANIKIS GERASIMOVS. In 1999 chartered to *CCTL* and operated between Hull and Hamburg. She was later renamed the SEA TRADER. In 2002 chartered to *TransRussiaExpress* and operated on their Kiel - Kaliningrad - St Petersburg route. In 2003 chartered to *Scandlines AG* and placed on their *Amber Line* Karlshamn - Liepaja service.

SØNDERHO Passenger only ferry built at Esbjerg, Denmark for *Post & Telegrafvasenet* (Danish Post Office). In 1977 taken over by *DSB*. Used on extra peak sailings and late night and early morning sailings between Esbjerg and Nordby.

SPODSBJERG Vehicle ferry built at Husum, Denmark as the ÆRØ-PILEN for *Øernes D/S* of Denmark for services to the island of Ærø. In 1974 sold to *Sydfyenske Dampskibsselskab (SFDS)* for the service between Spodsbjerg and Tårs.

SVEALAND Ro-pax vessel built at Donada, Italy as the ALYSSA for *Levantina Transporti* of Italy for charter. She was initially chartered to *CoTuNav* of Tunisia for service between Marseilles, Genoa and Tunis and in 2000 to *Trasmediterranea* of Spain for service between Barcelona and Palma de Majorca. In 2001 chartered to *Stena Line Scandinavia AB*, renamed the SVEALAND and placed as second vessel on the *Scandlines AB* freight only Trelleborg - Travemünde service. In 2003 sub-chartered to *Scandlines AG* and placed on the Kiel - Klaìpeda route, replacing the ASK and PETERSBURG.

THOR SYDFYEN Vehicle ferry built at Århus, Denmark for *Sydfyenske Dampskibsselskab (SFDS)* of Denmark (now *Scandlines Sydfyenske A/S*) for the service between Spodsbjerg and Tårs. In 1998 she was transferred to the Fynshav - Bøjden route.

TREKRONER Built at Florø, Norway as the MILORA for *Yngvar Hvistendal* of Norway and chartered to *Foss Line* for services between Europe and Saudi Arabia. In 1983 sold to *Saleninvest* of Sweden and renamed the SCANDIC WASA. In 1985 she was sold to *DSB*. During 1986 she was lengthened and converted into a train ferry. She was re-delivered in late 1986 as the TREKRONER and, in early 1987, entered service on the 'DanLink' train ferry service ferry between Copenhagen and Helsingborg. Withdrawn in July 2000 and laid up.

TYCHO BRAHE Train/vehicle ferry, built at Tomrefjord, Norway for *DSB* for the Helsingør - Helsingborg service.

URD Built at Venice, Italy as the EASY RIDER, a ro-ro freight ferry, for *Delpa Maritime* of Greece and used on Mediterranean services. In 1985 she was acquired by *Sealink British Ferries* and renamed the SEAFREIGHT HIGHWAY to operate freight-only service between Dover and Dunkerque. In 1988 she was sold to *SOMAT* of Bulgaria for use on *Medlink* services in the Mediterranean and renamed the BOYANA. In 1990 she was sold to *Blæsbjerg* of Denmark, renamed the AKTIV MARINE and chartered to *DSB*. In 1991 she was converted into ro-pax vessel, renamed the URD and introduced onto the Århus - Kalundborg service. Purchased by *Scandlines* in 1997. Withdrawn at the end of May 1999 and, after modification, transferred to the *Balticum Seaways* (later *Scandlines Balticum Seaways*) Århus - Aabenraa - Klaìpeda route. In 2001 lengthened moved to the Rostock - Liepaja route.

SCANDLINES (SWEDEN)

THE COMPANY *Scandlines AB* (formerly *SweFerry*) is a Swedish company, a subsidiary of *Stena Line Scandinavia AB* of Sweden.

MANAGEMENT Managing Director Gunnar Blomdahl.

ADDRESS Knutpunkten 43, S-252 78 Helsingborg, Sweden.

TELEPHONE Administration +46 (0)42-18 60 00, **Reservations** *Helsingborg* +46 (0)42-18 61 00, *Trelleborg* +46 (0)410-65 000.

FAX Administration +46 (0)42-18 60 49, **Reservations** *Helsingborg* +46 (0)42-18 74 10, *Trelleborg* +46 (0)410-65 001.

INTERNET Email kundservice@scandlines.se **Website** www.scandlines.se *(Swedish)*

ROUTES OPERATED Conventional Ferries Helsingborg (Sweden) - Helsingør (Denmark) (25 mins; *(1)*; every 20 mins), Trelleborg (Sweden) - Rostock (Germany) (6 hrs; *(3)*; 4 per day), Trelleborg - Sassnitz (Germany) (3 hrs 30 mins; *(5)*; 3 per day), Trelleborg (Sweden) - Travemünde (Germany) (8 hrs; *(2,4)*; 2 per day - freight-only). All routes are joint with *Scandlines AG* except Trelleborg - Travemünde.

1	ASK	13294t	82	18.0k	171.0m	186P	-	104T	AS	DK
2	AURORA AF HELSINGBORG	10918t	92	14.9k	111.2m	1250P	240C	35r	BA	SW
3	GÖTALAND	18060t	73	18.5k	183.1m	400P	118C	94Tr	AS2	SW
4	SKÅNE	42558t	98	21.0k	200.2m	600P	-	240Tr	AS2	SW
5	TRELLEBORG	20028t	82	21.0k	170.2m	900P	108C	48Tr	A2	SW

ASK Built at Venice, Italy as the LUCKY RIDER, a ro-ro freight ferry, for *Delpa Maritime* of Greece. In 1985 she was acquired by *Stena Line* and renamed the STENA DRIVER. Later that year she was acquired by *Sealink British Ferries* and renamed the SEAFREIGHT FREEWAY to operate freight-only services between Dover and Dunkerque. In 1988 she was sold to *SOMAT* of Bulgaria for use on *Medlink* services in the Mediterranean and renamed the SERDICA. In 1990 she was sold and renamed the NORTHERN HUNTER. In 1991 she was sold to *Blæsbjerg* of Denmark, renamed the ARKA MARINE and chartered to *DSB*. She was then converted into a ro-pax vessel, renamed the ASK and introduced onto the Århus - Kalundborg service. Purchased by *Scandlines AS* of Denmark in 1997. In 1999 she was, after some modification, transferred to *Scandlines Euroseabridge* and placed on the Travemünde - Klaìpeda route. In 2000 she was transferred to the Rostock - Liepaja route. Lengthened by 20m in 2001 and, in late 2001, chartered to *Nordö Link* to operate between Travemünde and Malmö. In late 2002 replaced by the FINNARROW and returned to *Scandlines*. She was transferred to the Rostock - Trelleborg route whilst the MECKLENBURG-VORPOMMERN was being rebuilt. She was then transferred to the Kiel - Klaìpeda route. In 2003 chartered to *Scandlines AB* to operate on the Trelleborg - Travemünde route.

AURORA AF HELSINGBORG Train/vehicle ferry built at Tomrefjord, Norway for *SweFerry* for *ScandLines* joint *DSB/SweFerry* service between Helsingør and Helsingborg. Owned by *Aurora 93 Trust* of the USA and chartered to *Scandlines*.

GÖTALAND Train/vehicle ferry built at Nakskov, Denmark for *Statens Järnvägar (Swedish State Railways)* for freight services between Trelleborg and Sassnitz. In 1990 transferred to *SweFerry*. In 1992 modified to increase passenger capacity in order to run in passenger service. She is was on the Trelleborg - Rostock service until autumn 1998 when she was replaced by the SKÅNE. She then inaugurated a new freight-only Trelleborg - Travemünde service.

SKÅNE Train/vehicle ferry built at Cadiz, Spain for an American trust and chartered to *Scandlines*. She is used on the Trelleborg - Rostock service.

TRELLEBORG Train/vehicle ferry built at Landskrona, Sweden for *Svelast* of Sweden (an *SJ* subsidiary). In 1990 ownership transferred to *SweFerry*. She is used on the Trelleborg - Sassnitz service.

SEA ADMINISTRATION OF ST PETERSBURG

THE COMPANY *Sea Administration of St Petersburg* is an agency of the Russian government.

ROUTE OPERATED St Petersburg (Russia) - Baltijsk (Kaliningrad) (36 hrs; *(1)*; 2 per week).

1	GEORG OTS	12549t	80	17.0k	136.8m	250P	107C	15T	BA	RU

GEORG OTS Built at Gdansk, Poland for *Estonian Shipping Company (ESCO)*, then of the USSR, to operate between Tallinn and Helsinki. Later chartered to *Tallink* (which was at the time partly owned by *ESCO*). Rebuilt in 1993 to increase car capacity from 14 to 110 and bring up to modern standards. In 2000 charter ended and she was returned to *ESCO*. In 2002 sold to *Sea Administration St Petersburg* and placed on the St Petersburg - Baltijsk service.

SEAWIND LINE

THE COMPANY *SeaWind Line* is a Swedish private sector company owned by *Silja Service Oy*.

MANAGEMENT Managing Director Mats Rosin **Sales Manager** Anders Levin.

ADDRESS Linnankatu 84, FIN-20100 Turku, Finland.

TELEPHONE Administration & Reservations +358 (0)2 2102 800.

FAX Administration & Reservations +358 (0)2 2102 810.

INTERNET Website www.seawind.fi *(English, Swedish, Finnish)*

ROUTE OPERATED Stockholm (Sweden) - Långnäs (Åland) - Turku (Finland) (10 hrs 45 mins; *(1,2)*; 2 per day), Helsinki - Tallinn) (10 hrs 45 mins; *(3)*; 2 per day).

1	SEA WIND	15879t	71	18.0k	154.9m	260P	60C	88Tr	BAS	SW
2	SKY WIND	16925t	86	15.0k	188.4m	-	-	130Tr	A	SW
3	STAR WIND	13788t	77	18.0k	158.6m	119P	100C	66Tr	A	SW

SEA WIND Train/vehicle ferry built at Helsingør, Denmark as the SVEALAND for *Stockholms Rederi AB Svea* and used on the *Trave Line* Helsingborg (Sweden) - Copenhagen (Tuborg Havn) - Travemünde freight service. Later she operated between Travemünde and Malmö, first for *Saga Line* and then for *TT-Saga Line*. In 1984 she was rebuilt to increase capacity and renamed the SAGA WIND. In 1989 she was acquired by *SeaWind Line*, renamed the SEA WIND and inaugurated a combined rail freight, trailer and lower priced passenger service between Stockholm and Turku.

SKY WIND Train/vehicle ferry built at Moss, Norway as the ÖRESUND for *Statens Järnvägar* (*Swedish State Railways*) for the 'DanLink' service between Helsingborg and Copenhagen. Has 817 metres of rail track. Service ceased in July 2000 and vessel laid up. In 2001 sold to *Sea Containers Ferries* and, in 2002 is being converted at Gdansk, Poland to passenger ferry. She was chartered to *SeaWind Line* and, in autumn 2002, replaced the STAR WIND on the Stockholm - Turku service.

STAR WIND Train/vehicle ferry built at Bergen, Norway as the ROSTOCK for *Deutsche Reichsbahn* of Germany (DDR). Used on freight services between Trelleborg and Sassnitz. In 1992 modified to increase passenger capacity in order to run in passenger service. In 1993 ownership transferred to *DFO* and in 1994 she opened a new service from Rostock to Trelleborg. In 1997 she was used when winds preclude the use of the new MECKLENBURG-VORPOMMERN. Following modifications to this vessel in late 1997, the ROSTOCK continued to operate to provide additional capacity until the delivery of the SKÅNE of *Scandlines AB*, after which she was laid up. In 1999 she was sold to *SeaWind Line*, renamed the STAR WIND and operated in freight-only mode. Initial plans to bring her passenger accommodation up to the standards required for Baltic service were dropped. Later in 2002 replaced by the SKY WIND and transferred to the Helsinki - Tallinn route. She now carries a limited number of ordinary passengers on some sailings.

Prins Joachim *(Mike Louagie)*

Stena Carrier *(Mike Louagie)*

SILJA LINE

THE COMPANY *Silja Oyj Abp*, based in Finland, is a wholly owned subsidiary of *Sea Containers Ltd.* The company has marketing organisations in Sweden, Estonia and Germany.

MANAGEMENT President Antti Pankakoski, **Senior Vice-President, Passenger Services** Pekka J Helin, **Senior Vice President Cargo Services** Sören Lindman, **Senior Vice President, Ship Management** Christian Grönvall, **Senior Vice President, Corporate Communications** Tuomas Nylund, **CFO** Steven G Robson.

ADDRESS POB 880, Bulevardi 1, FIN-00101 Helsinki, Finland.

TELEPHONE Administration *Finland* +358 (0)9 18041, **Reservations** *Finland* +358 (0)9 1804 422, *Sweden* +46 (0)8-222 140.

FAX Administration & Reservations *Finland* +358 (0)9 1804 279, *Sweden* +46 (0)8-667 8681.

INTERNET Email info@silja.com **Website** www.silja.com *(English, Finnish and Swedish)*

ROUTES OPERATED Conventional Ferries *All year* Helsinki (Finland) - Mariehamn (Åland) - Stockholm (Sweden) (16 hrs; *(5,6)*; 1 per day), Turku (Finland) - Mariehamn (Åland) (day)/Långnäs (Åland) (night) - Stockholm (11 hrs; *(2,3)*; 1 or 2 per day), *Winter only* Helsinki - Tallinn (Estonia) (3 hrs 30 mins (4 hrs 30 mins in ice period); *(1)*; 1 per day), *Winter, Spring and Autumn only* Turku (Finland) - Mariehamn (day)/Långnäs (night) - Kapellskär (Sweden) (11 hrs; *(2)*; 1 per day), *Summer only* Helsinki - Tallinn - Rostock (Germany) (24 hrs (Helsinki - Tallinn, 2 hr 30 min, Tallinn - Rostock, 19 hrs)); *(1)*; 3 per week). **Fast Ferry (Operated by *Sea Containers* and marketed by *Silja Line*)** Helsinki - Tallinn (1 hr 30 mins; *(7,8)*; up to 7 per day). **Cruise Service** Helsinki - Tallinn - Visby (Gotland), Helsinki - Riga (Latvia) and other destinations *(4)*.

1	FINNJET	32940t	77	31.0k	214.9m	1790P	374C	44T	BA	FI
2	SILJA EUROPA	59912t	93	21.5k	201.8m	3000P	400C	68T	BA	FI
3	SILJA FESTIVAL	34414t	85	22.0k	170.7m	2000P	400C	80T	BA	SW
4p	SILJA OPERA	25076t	92	21.0k	158.9m	1400P	0C	0T	-	SW
5	SILJA SERENADE	58376t	90	21.0k	203.0m	2641P	450C	70T	BA	FI
6	SILJA SYMPHONY	58377t	91	21.0k	203.0m	2641P	450C	70T	BA	SW
7»	SUPERSEACAT THREE	4697t	99	38.0k	100.0m	800P	175C	-	A	IT
8»	SUPERSEACAT FOUR	4697t	99	38.0k	100.0m	752P	164C	-	A	IT

FINNJET Built at Helsinki, Finland for *Finnlines* to operate between Helsinki and Travemünde, replacing several more vessels with intermediate calls. Her exceptionally fast speed was achieved by the use of gas turbine engines. During winter 1981/82 she was equipped with diesel engines for use during periods when traffic did not justify so many crossings per week. Later the trading name was changed to *Finnjet Line*. In 1986 the company was acquired by *EFFOA* and the trading name changed to *Finnjet Silja Line*. In winter 1997/98 she operated between Helsinki and Tallinn (Muuga Harbour). In summer 1998 she operated a weekly Travemünde - Tallinn - Helsinki - Travemünde triangular service in addition to two weekly Travemünde - Helsinki round trips. In autumn 1998 she resumed operating between Helsinki and Tallinn and since summer 1999 she has operated Helsinki - Tallinn - Rostock.

SILJA EUROPA Built at Papenburg, Germany. Ordered by *Rederi AB Slite* of Sweden for *Viking Line* service between Stockholm and Helsinki and due to be called EUROPA. In 1993, shortly before delivery was due, the order was cancelled. A charter agreement with her builders was then signed by *Silja Line* and she was introduced onto the Stockholm - Helsinki route as SILJA EUROPA. In early 1995 she was transferred to the Stockholm - Turku service. During off peak period she now operates between Turku and Kapellskär.

SILJA FESTIVAL Built at Helsinki, Finland as the WELLAMO for *EFFOA* for the *Silja Line* Stockholm - Mariehamn - Turku service. In 1990, following the sale of the FINLANDIA to *DFDS*, she was transferred to the Stockholm - Helsinki service until the SILJA SERENADE was delivered later in the year. During winter 1991/92 she was extensively rebuilt and in 1991 renamed the SILJA FESTIVAL; ownership was transferred to *Silja Line*. In 1993 she was transferred to the Malmö - Travemünde service of *Euroway*, which was at this time managed by *Silja Line*. This service ceased in 1994 and she was transferred to the Vaasa - Sundsvall service. In 1994 and 1995 she operated on this route during the peak summer period and on the Helsinki - Tallinn route during the rest of the year. The Vaasa - Sundsvall service did not operate in summer 1996 and she continued to operate between Helsinki and Tallinn. In 1997 she was transferred to the Stockholm - Turku route replacing the SILJA SCANDINAVIA (see the GABRIELLA, *Viking Line*).

SILJA OPERA Built as the SALLY ALBATROSS at Rauma, Finland for *Rederi AB Sally* of Finland, a subsidiary of *EffJohn International* to operate cruises from Helsinki. She was built on the lower portions of the previous SALLY ALBATROSS, which had been declared a total constructive loss following a fire when being refitted at a Stockholm shipyard in 1991. (This vessel had been built in 1980 at Turku for *Rederi AB Sally* (at that time part of *Viking Line*) as the VIKING SAGA and was used on the Helsinki - Stockholm service. In 1986 she was replaced by the OLYMPIA (now PRIDE OF BILBAO), modified to a cruising role and renamed the SALLY ALBATROSS). In spring 1994 she grounded whilst on a winter cruise and was badly damaged. Her cruise programme was cancelled and, when she had been repaired and modified, she was renamed the LEEWARD and chartered to *Norwegian Cruise Line* for Caribbean cruising. In 1999 she was chartered to *Star Cruises* of Singapore and renamed the SUPERSTAR TAURUS. She was used on cruises in the Far East. In 2002 returned to *Silja Line* and renamed the SILJA OPERA. She is used on cruises from Helsinki to various destinations, including Tallinn, Visby (Gotland) and Riga (Latvia).

SILJA SERENADE, SILJA SYMPHONY Built at Turku, Finland for *Silja Line* for the Stockholm - Helsinki service. In 1993, SILJA SERENADE was transferred to the Stockholm - Turku service but in early 1995 she was transferred back to the Helsinki route.

SUPERSEACAT THREE Fincantieri MDV1200 monohull vessel built at La Spézia, Italy. In 1999 operated on the Liverpool - Dublin service, operated by *Sea Containers Ferries Scotland*, replacing the SUPERSEACAT TWO. In 2000 she also operated on the Liverpool - Douglas service. In summer 2001 she operated between Dover and Calais and Dover and Ostend; in summer 2002 she operated from Liverpool to Dublin and Douglas. In 2003 she will operate between Helsinki and Tallinn.

SUPERSEACAT FOUR Fincantieri MDV1200 monohull vessel built at Riva Trigoso, Italy. Laid-up following delivery. In 2000 transferred to an Estonian subsidiary of *Sea Containers* to operate between Helsinki and Tallinn under the *Silja Line SeaCat* branding. The service was marketed by *Silja Line*. She operates on the route during the ice free season.

STENA LINE

THE COMPANY *Stena Line Scandinavia AB* is a Swedish private sector company.

MANAGEMENT Managing Director & Chief Operational Officer Gunnar Blomdahl, **Marketing Manager** Elisabeth Strömberg, **Ship Management Director** Håkan Siewers, **Communication Director** Joakim Kenndal.

ADDRESS S-405 19 Gothenburg, Sweden (***Visitors' address*** Danmarksterminalen, Masthuggskajen).

TELEPHONE Administration +46 (0)31-85 80 00, **Reservations** +46 (0)31-704 00 00.

FAX Administration & Reservations +46 (0)31-24 10 38.

INTERNET Email info@stenaline.com **Website** www.stenaline.com (*English, Swedish*)

ROUTES OPERATED Conventional Ferries Gothenburg (Sweden) - Frederikshavn (Denmark) (3 hrs 15 mins; *(4,7)*; up to 6 per day), Gothenburg - Kiel (Germany) (14 hrs; *(6,10)*; 1 per day), Frederikshavn - Oslo (Norway) (8 hrs 45 mins; *(9)*; 1 per day), Varberg (Sweden) - Grenaa (Denmark) (4 hrs; *(8)*; 2 per day), Karlskrona (Sweden) - Gdynia (Poland) (10 hrs 30 mins; *(1,12)*; 2 per day). **Fast Ferry** Gothenburg - Frederikshavn (2 hrs; *(2)*; 4 per day). **Freight Ferries** Gothenburg - Frederikshavn (Train Ferry) (3 hrs 45 mins; *(11)*; 2 per day), Gothenburg - Travemünde (15 hrs; *(3,5)*; 1 per day).

1	STENA BALTICA	31189t	86	20.0k	161.8m	1800P	500C	72T	BA	SW
2»	STENA CARISMA	8631t	97	40.0k	88.0m	900P	210C	-	A	SW
3F	STENA CARRIER	8698t	78	18.0k	156.0m	12P	510C	124T	A	SW
4	STENA DANICA	28727t	83	19.5k	154.9m	2274P	555C	120T	BAS2	SW
5F	STENA FREIGHTER	8800t	77	18.0k	156.0m	12P	510C	124T	A	SW
6	STENA GERMANICA	38772t	87	20.0k	175.4m	2400P	550C	120T	BAS2	SW
7	STENA JUTLANDICA	29691t	96	21.5k	183.7m	1500P	550C	156T	BAS2	SW
8	STENA NAUTICA	19763t	86	19.4k	134.0m	700P	330C	70T	BA2	SW
9	STENA SAGA	33750t	81	22.0k	166.1m	1900P	510C	76T	BA	SW
10	STENA SCANDINAVICA	38756t	88	20.0k	175.4m	2400P	550C	120T	BAS2	SW
11F	STENA SCANRAIL	7504t	73	16.5k	142.4m	65P	-	64Tr	A	SW
12	STENA TRAVELLER	18332t	92	18.0k	153.6m	250P	-	132T	BA2	SW

STENA BALTICA Built at Krimpen aan den IJssel, Rotterdam, Netherlands as the KONINGIN BEATRIX for *Stoomvaart Maatschappij Zeeland* of The Netherlands for their Hoek van Holland - Harwich service (trading as *Crown Line*). In 1989 transferred to *Stena Line bv*. In June 1997 chartered by *Stena Line bv* to *Stena Line Ltd* and used on the Fishguard - Rosslare service. In August 1997, transferred to the British flag. In 2002 renamed the STENA BALTICA and transferred to the Karlskrona - Gdynia service.

STENA CARISMA Westamarin HSS 900 craft built at Kristiansand, Norway for *Stena Line* for the Gothenburg - Frederikshavn service. Work on a sister vessel, approximately 30% completed, was ceased.

STENA CARRIER Built at Ulsan, South Korea as the IMPARCA EXPRESS I for *Stena AB* and chartered to *Imparca Line* and used on Caribbean services. In 1980 renamed the STENA CARRIER. Later that year she was renamed the IMPARCA MIAMI. In 1981 she reverted to the name STENA CARRIER. In 1981 she was chartered to *Ignazio Messina* of Italy and renamed the JOLLY BRUNO. In 1982 renamed the JOLLY SMERALDO and in 1983 this charter ended and she resumed the name STENA CARRIER. In 1988 she was transferred to *Stena Line* and placed on the Gothenburg - Travemünde service.

STENA DANICA Built at Dunkerque, France for *Stena Line* for the Gothenburg - Frederikshavn service. Sister vessel STENA JUTLANDICA was transferred to the Dover - Calais service in July 1996 and renamed the STENA EMPEREUR (now the PRIDE OF PROVENCE of *P&O Ferries*). This vessel is listed in Section 1.

STENA FREIGHTER Built at Ulsan, South Korea as the MERZARIO AUSONIA for *Stena AB*, chartered to *Merzario Line* of Italy and used on services between Italy and the Middle East. In 1981 she was renamed the STENA FREIGHTER. In 1982 she was chartered to *Ignazio Messina* of Italy and renamed the JOLLY GIALLO; later that year she was renamed the JOLLY TURCHESE. In 1983 this charter ended and she resumed the name STENA FREIGHTER. In 1988 she was transferred to *Stena Line* and placed on the Gothenburg - Travemünde service.

STENA GERMANICA, STENA SCANDINAVICA Built at Gdynia, Poland for *Stena Line* for the Gothenburg - Kiel service. Names were swapped during construction in order that the STENA GERMANICA should enter service first. There were originally intended to be four vessels. Only two were delivered to *Stena Line*. The third (due to be called the STENA POLONICA) was sold by the builders as an unfinished hull to *Fred. Olsen Lines* of Norway and then resold to *ANEK* of Greece who had her completed at Perama and delivered as EL VENIZELOS for service between Greece and Italy. The fourth hull (due to be called the STENA BALTICA) was never completed. During the summer period, the vessel arriving in Gothenburg overnight from Kiel operates a round trip to Frederikshavn before departing for Kiel the following evening. During winter 1998/99 they were modified to increase freight capacity and reduce the number of cabins.

STENA JUTLANDICA Train/vehicle 'ro-pax' vessel built at Krimpen aan den IJssel, Rotterdam, Netherlands for *Stena Line* to operate between Gothenburg and Frederikshavn. She was launched as the STENA JUTLANDICA III and renamed on entry into service. During winter she has operated in 'freight-only' mode. However, during winter 2000/1 she continued to provide a full passenger service and this was repeated in winter 2001/2.

STENA NAUTICA Built at Nakskov, Denmark as the NIELS KLIM for *DSB (Danish State Railways)* for their service between Århus (Jutland) and Kalundborg (Sealand). In 1990 she was purchased by *Stena Rederi* of Sweden and renamed the STENA NAUTICA. In 1992 she was chartered to *B&I Line*, renamed the ISLE OF INNISFREE and introduced onto the Rosslare - Pembroke Dock service, replacing the MUNSTER (8093t, 1970). In 1993 she was transferred to the Dublin - Holyhead service. In early 1995 she was chartered to *Lion Ferry*. She was renamed the LION KING. In 1996 she was replaced by a new LION KING and renamed the STENA NAUTICA. During summer 1996 she was chartered to *Trasmediterranea* of Spain but returned to *Stena RoRo* in the autumn and remained laid up during 1997. In December 1997 she was chartered to *Stena Line* and placed on the Halmstad - Grenaa route. This route ended on 31st January 1999 and she was transferred to the Varberg - Grenaa route. During winter 2001/2 rebuilt to heighten upper vehicle deck and allow separate loading of load vehicle decks; passenger capacity reduced.

STENA SAGA Built at Turku, Finland as the SILVIA REGINA for *Stockholms Rederi AB Svea* of Sweden. She was registered with subsidiary company *Svea Line* of Turku, Finland and was used on *Silja Line* services between Stockholm and Helsinki. In 1981 she was sold to *Johnson Line* and in 1984 sold to a Finnish Bank and chartered back. In 1990 she was purchased by *Stena RoRo* of Sweden for delivery in 1991. In 1991 she was renamed the STENA BRITANNICA and took up service on the Hoek van Holland - Harwich service for Dutch subsidiary *Stena Line bv*, operating with a British crew. In 1994 she was transferred to *Stena Line's* Oslo - Frederikshavn route and renamed the STENA SAGA. During winter 2002/3 rebuilt to increase passenger capacity by 200.

STENA SCANRAIL Built at Capelle an der IJssel, Rotterdam, Netherlands. Launched as the STENA SEATRADER for *Stena AB* and entered service as the SEATRADER. In 1976 she was lengthened and then demise chartered to *Bahjah Navigation* of Cyprus and renamed the BAHJAN. In 1981 charter ended and she was renamed the STENA SEARIDER. In 1983 chartered to *Snowdrop Shipping* of Cyprus and renamed the SEARIDER. The charter ended the following year and she renamed the name STENA SEARIDER. Later in 1984 she was renamed the TRUCKER and in 1985 again reverted to the name STENA SEARIDER. In 1987 she was converted to a train ferry to operate between Gothenburg and Frederikshavn, chartered to *Stena Line* and renamed the STENA SCANRAIL.

STENA TRAVELLER Ro-pax vessel built at Fevaag, Norway for *Stena RoRo*. After a short period with *Stena Line* on the Hoek van Holland - Harwich service, she was chartered to *Sealink Stena Line* for their Southampton - Cherbourg route, initially for 28 weeks. At the end of the 1992 summer season she was chartered to *TT-Line* to operate between Travemünde and Trelleborg and was renamed the TT-TRAVELLER. In late 1995, she returned to *Stena Line*, resumed the name STENA TRAVELLER and inaugurated a new service between Holyhead and Dublin. In autumn 1996 she was replaced by the STENA CHALLENGER (18523t, 1991). In early 1997 she was again chartered to *TT-Line* and renamed the TT-TRAVELLER. She operated on the Rostock - Trelleborg route. During winter 1999/2000, her passenger capacity was increased to 250 and passenger facilities renovated. In early 2002 the charter ended and she was renamed the STENA TRAVELLER, chartered to *Stena Line* and placed on their Karlskrona - Gdynia service.

SUPERFAST FERRIES

THE COMPANY *SuperFast Ferries* is a Greek company, owned by *Attica Enterprises*.

MANAGEMENT Managing Director Alexander P Panagopulos, **Corporate Marketing Director** Yannis B Criticos, **General Manager, Germany of Attica Premium SA** Jens-Peter Berg.

ADDRESS *Greece* 157 Alkyonidon Avenue, Voula, GR-16673 Athens, Greece, ***Northern Europe*** Hermann-Lange-Strasse 1, DE-23558 Lübeck, Germany.

TELEPHONE Administration (Greece) +30 (0)210 891 9500, **Administration (Germany)** +49 (0)451 88006130, **Reservations** +49 (0)451 88006130.

FAX Administration (Greece) +30 (0)210 891 9509, **Administration & Reservations (Germany)** +49 (0)451-8800629.

INTERNET Email criticos@superfast.com **Website** www.superfast.com *(English, German, Finnish, Swedish)*

Stena Nautica *(Claus Carlsen)*

Stena Germanica *(Philippe Holthof)*

ROUTES OPERATED Rostock (Germany) - Hanko (Finland) (21 hrs; *(1,2)*; 1 per day).

1	SUPERFAST VII	29800t	01	29.2k	203.3m	626P	1000C	140T	BA2	GR
2	SUPERFAST VIII	29800t	01	29.2k	203.3m	626P	1000C	140T	BA2	GR

SUPERFAST VII, SUPERFAST VIII Built at Kiel, Germany for *Attica Enterprises* for use by *SuperFast Ferries* between Rostock and Hanko.

TALLINK

THE COMPANY *AS Tallink Grupp*, (formerly *AS Hansatee Grupp* trading as *Tallink*), is an Estonian company owned by the *AS Infortar* (86.0%) and others. Services are marketed outside Estonia by *Tallink Finland Oy*.

MANAGEMENT Director, Tallink Finland Oy Keijo Mehtonen.

ADDRESS PO Box 195, 00181 Helsinki, Finland.

TELEPHONE Administration +358 (0)9 228211, **Reservations** +358 (0)9 228311.

FAX Administration & Reservations +358 (0)9 228 21242.

INTERNET Email keijo.mehtonen@tallink.fi **Websites** www.tallink.ee *(Finnish, Estonian, English)*

Also www.tallink.se *(Swedish)* www.tallink.fi *(Finnish)*.

ROUTES OPERATED Conventional Ferries Helsinki - Tallinn (3 hrs 30 mins; *(3,4)*; up to 3 per day), Stockholm - Tallinn (14 hrs; *(1,4)*; daily), Kapellskär - Paldiski (9 hrs - 11 hrs; *(2,8)*; 2 per day). **Fast Ferries** Helsinki - Tallinn (1 hr 30 mins; *(6,7)*; up to 6 per day).

1	FANTAASIA	16630t	79	21.3k	136.1m	1700P	549C	46T	BA2	ES
2	KAPELLA	‡2794t	74	14.5k	110.1m	50P	-	42T	A	ES
3	MELOODIA	17955t	79	21.0k	138.8m	1500P	480C	52T	BA2	ES
4	REGINA BALTICA	18345t	80	21.3k	145.2m	1450P	500C	68T	BA	ES
5	ROMANTIKA	40000t	02	22.0k	193.8m	2178P	300C	83T	BA	ES
6»	TALLINK AUTOEXPRESS	4859t	95	32.0k	78.6m	586P	150C	-	BA	ES
7»	TALLINK AUTOEXPRESS 2	5419t	97	37.0k	82.3m	700P	175C	-	A	ES
8	VANA TALLINN	10002t	74	18.0k	153.7m	1500P	300C	44L	BAS	ES

FANTAASIA Built at Turku, Finland as the TURELLA for *SF Line* of Finland for the *Viking Line* Stockholm - Mariehamn - Turku service and later moved to the Kapellskär - Mariehamn - Naantali service. In 1988 she was sold to *Stena Line*, renamed the STENA NORDICA and placed onto the Frederikshavn - Moss (night) and Frederikshavn - Gothenburg (day) service. In 1996 the Frederikshavn - Moss service ceased and she was transferred to subsidiary *Lion Ferry* and renamed the LION KING. She operated between Halmstad and Grenaa. In December 1997 she was sold to *Tallink Line Ltd* of Cyprus and renamed the FANTAASIA. In February 1998, after substantial modification, she was placed on the *Tallink* service between Helsinki and Tallinn. In June 2002 moved to the Tallinn - Stockholm route, enabling a daily service to be reinstated.

KAPELLA Built at Kristiansand, Norway for *A/S Larvik-Frederikshavnferjen* of Norway as DUKE OF YORKSHIRE. In 1978 she was chartered to (and later purchased by) *CN Marine* of Canada (from 1986 *Marine Atlantic*) and renamed the MARINE EVANGELINE. She was used on services between Canada, USA and Newfoundland. In 1992 she was chartered to *Opale Ferries* of France and inaugurated a new Boulogne - Folkestone freight service. In 1993 the company went into liquidation and the service and charter were taken over by *Meridian Ferries*, a British company. She was renamed the SPIRIT OF BOULOGNE. In spring 1995, *Meridian Ferries* went into liquidation and she returned to her owners, resuming the name MARINE EVANGELINE. After a period of lay up she was chartered to *Stena Sealink Line*. She spent the summer on the Newhaven - Dieppe service and was then transferred to the Stranraer - Larne (from November 1995 Stranraer - Belfast) route. She returned to Newhaven in summer 1996 but was laid up during most of 1997. In late 1997 she was chartered to *Hansatee* and inaugurated a new ro-pax service between Paldiski and Kapellskär. She was renamed the KAPELLA.

MELOODIA Built at Papenburg, Germany as DIANA II for *Rederi AB Slite* for *Viking Line* services between Stockholm and Turku, Mariehamn, Kapellskär and Naantali. In 1992 sold to a *Nordbanken* and, in 1993, chartered to *TR-Line* of Germany (joint venture between *TT-Line* and *DSR*) for service between Trelleborg and Rostock. In 1994 sold to *ESCO* and chartered to *EstLine* and renamed the MARE BALTICUM. During winter 1994/95 she was completely renovated. In 1996, following the delivery of the REGINA BALTICA, she was chartered to *Tallink*, renamed the MELOODIA and placed on the Tallinn - Helsinki service.

REGINA BALTICA Built at Turku, Finland as the VIKING SONG for *Rederi AB Sally* of Finland and used on the *Viking Line* service between Stockholm and Helsinki. In 1985 replaced by the MARIELLA of *SF Line* and sold to *Fred. Olsen Lines*. She was named BRAEMAR and used on services between Norway and Britain as well as Norway and Denmark. Services to Britain ceased in June 1990 and she continued to operate between Norway and Denmark. She was withdrawn in 1991 and sold to *Rigorous Shipping* of Cyprus (a subsidiary of *Fred. Olsen Lines*). She was chartered to the *Baltic Shipping Company* of Russia, renamed the ANNA KARENINA and inaugurated a service between Kiel and St Petersburg. In 1992 a Nynäshamn call was introduced. In 1996 the service ceased and she was returned to her owners and renamed the ANNA K. Later in 1996 she was sold to *Empremare Shipping Co Ltd* of Cyprus (a company jointly owned by *Nordström & Thulin* and *Estonian Shipping Company*), chartered to *EstLine* and renamed the REGINA BALTICA. In 2000 charter transferred to *Tallink*. Continues to operate between Stockholm and Tallinn. Purchased by *Tallink* in 2002.

ROMANTIKA Built at Rauma, Finland for *Tallink Grupp* to operate for *Tallink* between Tallinn and Helsinki.

TALLINK AUTOEXPRESS Austal Ships Auto Express 79 catamaran ordered by *Sea Containers* and launched at Fremantle, Western Australia as the AUTO EXPRESS 96. On completion she was renamed the SUPERSEACAT FRANCE. However, due to a dispute between *Sea Containers* and the builders, delivery was not taken and it was announced that she was to be sold to *Stena Rederi* of Sweden, renamed the STENA LYNX IV and chartered to *Stena Line (UK)*, inaugurating a Newhaven - Dieppe service in February 1996. This did not happen and she was instead sold to *DSB Rederi* (now *Scandlines Danmark A/S*) and, in summer 1996, she was chartered to *Cat-Link* and renamed the CAT-LINK III. In 1999 she was sold to *Tallink* and renamed the TALLINK AUTOEXPRESS. Operates between Tallinn and Helsinki.

TALLINK AUTOEXPRESS 2 Austal Ships Auto Express 82 catamaran built at Fremantle, Western Australia as the BOOMERANG for *Polferries* and used on the Swinoujscie - Malmö route. In autumn 1999 she withdrawn and it was anticipated that she would no longer operate for *Polferries*. However in summer 2000 she returned to the Swinoujscie - Malmö route. She was laid up again in the autumn and in May 2001 was sold to Tallink and renamed the TALLINK AUTOEXPRESS 2. Operates between Tallinn and Helsinki.

VANA TALLINN Built at Helsingør, Denmark as the DANA REGINA for *DFDS* and used on their Esbjerg - Harwich service until 1983 when she was moved to the Copenhagen - Oslo route. In 1990 she was sold to *Nordström & Thulin* of Sweden, renamed the NORD ESTONIA and used on the *EstLine* Stockholm - Tallinn service. In 1992 she was chartered to *Larvik Line* to operate as a second vessel between Larvik and Frederikshavn and renamed the THOR HEYERDAHL. In 1994 she was sold to *Inreko Ships Ltd*, chartered to *Tallink* and renamed the VANA TALLINN. In November 1996 she was withdrawn and in December 1996 she was chartered to a new company called *TH Ferries* and resumed sailings between Helsinki and Tallinn. In January 1998 she was sold to *Hansatee* subsidiary *Vana Tallinn Line Ltd* of Cyprus and placed on *Tallink* service between Helsinki and Tallinn. *TH Ferries* then ceased operations. In autumn 2002 moved to the Paldiski - Kapellskär route, replacing the BALTIC KRISTINA.

Under Construction

9	NEWBUILDING	40000t	04	22.0k	193.8m	2500P	300C	83T	BA	ES

NEWBUILDING Under construction at Rauma, Finland for *Tallink*. To operate between Tallinn and Stockholm.

TESO

THE COMPANY *TESO* is a Dutch public sector company. Its full name is *Texels Eigen Stoomboot Onderneming.*

MANAGEMENT Managing Director R Wortel.

ADDRESS Pontweg 1, 1797 SN Den Hoorn, Texel, Netherlands.

TELEPHONE Administration +31 (0)222 369600, **Reservations** n/a.

FAX Administration & Reservations +31 (0)222 369659.

INTERNET Email info@teso.nl **Website** www.teso.nl *(Dutch, English, German, French)*

ROUTES OPERATED Den Helder (Netherlands) - Texel (Dutch Frisian Islands) (20 minutes; *(1,2)*; hourly).

1	MOLENGAT	6170t	80	13.0k	88.8m	1200P	126C	19L	BA2	NL
2	SCHULPENGAT	8311t	90	13.6k	110.4m	1750P	156C	25L	BA2	NL

MOLENGAT, SCHULPENGAT Built at Heusden, Netherlands for *TESO*.

TT-LINE

THE COMPANY *TT-Line GmbH & Co* is a German private sector company.

MANAGEMENT Managing Director Hanns Heinrich Conzen & Dr Arndt-Heinrich von Oertzen, **Sales Manager** Dirk Lifke.

ADDRESS Mattentwiete 8, D-20457 Hamburg, Germany.

TELEPHONE Administration *Hamburg* +49 (0)40 3601 372, *Rostock* +49 (0)381 6707911, **Reservations** *Hamburg* +49 (0)40 3601 442, *Rostock* +49 (0)381 670790.

FAX Administration & Reservations *Hamburg* +49 (0)40 3601 407, *Rostock* +49 (0)381 6707980.

INTERNET Email info@TTLine.com **Website** www.TTLine.com *(German, English)*

ROUTES OPERATED Passenger Ferries Travemünde (Germany) - Trelleborg (Sweden) (7 hrs 30 mins; *(3,4)*; 2 per day). **Ro-pax Ferries** Travemünde (Germany) - Trelleborg (Sweden) (7 hrs 30 mins; *(2,5)*; 2 per day), Rostock (Germany) - Trelleborg (Sweden) (6 hrs; *(1,6)*; 3 per day) **Fast Ferry** Rostock (Germany) - Trelleborg (Sweden) (2 hrs 45 mins; *(7)*; up to 3 per day).

1	HUCKLEBERRY FINN	30740t	88	20.0k	177.2m	400P	280C	146T	BAS	SW
2	NILS DACKE	26790t	95	21.0k	179.6m	308P	-	157T	BA	BS
3	NILS HOLGERSSON	36000t	01	22.0k	190.0m	744P	-	174T	BA2	GY
4	PETER PAN	36000t	01	22.0k	190.0m	744P	-	174T	BA2	SW
5	ROBIN HOOD	26800t	95	21.0k	179.6m	308P	-	157T	BA	GY
6	TOM SAWYER	30740t	89	20.0k	177.0m	400P	280C	146T	BAS	GY
7»	TT-DELPHIN	5333t	96	37.5k	82.3m	600P	175C	-	A	SW

HUCKLEBERRY FINN Built at Bremerhaven, Germany as the NILS DACKE, a ro-pax vessel. During summer 1993 rebuilt to transform her into a passenger/car ferry and renamed the PETER PAN, replacing a similarly named vessel (31356t, 1986). On arrival of the new PETER PAN in autumn she was renamed the PETER PAN IV. She was then converted back to ro-pax format, renamed the HUCKLEBERRY FINN and, in early 2002, transferred to the Rostock -Trelleborg route.

NILS DACKE, ROBIN HOOD Ro-pax vessels built at Rauma, Finland for *TT-Line*. Primarily freight vessels but accompanied cars - especially camper vans and cars towing caravans - are conveyed.

NILS HOLGERSSON, PETER PAN Built at Bremerhaven, Germany for *TT-Line* for the Travemünde - Trelleborg route.

Nils Holgersson *(TT Line)*

TOM SAWYER Built at Bremerhaven, Germany as the ROBIN HOOD, a ro-pax vessel. During winter 1992/93 rebuilt to transform her into a passenger/car ferry and renamed the NILS HOLGERSSON, replacing a similarly named vessel (31395t, 1987) which had been sold to *Brittany Ferries* and renamed the VAL DE LOIRE. In 2001 converted back to ro-pax format and renamed the TOM SAWYER. Transferred to the Rostock - Trelleborg route.

TT-DELPHIN Austal Ships Auto Express 82 catamaran built as the DELPHIN at Fremantle, Western Australia for *TT-Line* to operate between Rostock and Trelleborg. In 2002 renamed the TT-DELPHIN.

UNITY LINE

THE COMPANY *Unity Line* is a Polish company, jointly owned by *Polish Steamship Company* and *Euroafrica Shipping Lines.*

MANAGEMENT Chairman of the Board Krzysztof Rodzoch, **Managing Director** Ronald Stone.

ADDRESS Poland, 70-419 Szczecin, Plac Rodla 8.

TELEPHONE Administration +48 (0)91 35 95 795, **Reservations** +48 (0)91 35 95 692, (0)91 35 95 755.

FAX Administration +48 (0)91 35 95 885, **Reservations** +48 (0)91 35 95 673.

INTERNET Email unity@unityline.pl **Website** www.unityline.pl *(Polish, Swedish)*

ROUTE OPERATED Swinoujscie (Poland) - Ystad (Sweden) (6 hrs 30 mins (day), 9 hrs (night); *(1)*; 1 per day).

1	POLONIA	29875t	95	17.2k	169.9m	920P	860C	160Tr	BA	BS

POLONIA Train/vehicle ferry built at Tomrefjord, Norway for *Polonia Line Ltd* and chartered to *Unity Line.*

VIKING LINE

THE COMPANY *Viking Line AB* is an Åland (Finland) company (previously *SF Line*, trading (with *Rederi AB Slite* of Sweden) as *Viking Line*). Services are marketed by subsidiary company *Viking Line Marketing AB OY* of Finland and Sweden; this dates from the time that *Viking Line* was a consortium of three operators.

MANAGEMENT Managing Director *(Viking Line AB)* Nils-Erik Eklund, **Managing Director *(Viking Line Marketing AB OY)*** Boris Ekman.

ADDRESS *Viking Line AB* Norragatan 4, FIN-22100 Mariehamn, Åland, ***Viking Line Marketing AB OY*** PO Box 35, FIN-22101 Mariehamn, Åland.

TELEPHONE Administration +358 (0)18 26011, **Reservations** +358 (0)9 12351.

FAX Administration & Reservations +358 (0)9 1235292.

INTERNET Email incoming@vikingline.fi **Websites** www.vikingline.fi *(Finnish, Swedish, English)* www.vikingline.se *(Swedish, English)* www.vikingline.de *(German)*

ROUTES OPERATED *All year* Stockholm (Sweden) - Mariehamn (Åland) - Helsinki (Finland) (14 hrs; *(4,6)*; 1 per day), Stockholm - Mariehamn (day)/Långnäs (Åland) (night) - Turku (Finland) (9 hrs 10 mins; *(2,5)*; 2 per day), Kapellskär (Sweden) - Mariehamn (Åland) (2 hrs 15 mins; *(1)*; up to 3 per day), ***Until September 2003*** cruises from Helsinki to Tallinn (Estonia) (20 hrs - 21 hrs round trip; *(3)*; 1 per day) (freight vehicles are conveyed on this service but not private cars; only 1 hr 30 minutes is spent in port), ***From September 2003*** Helsinki - Tallinn (3 hrs; *(7)*; 2 per day), ***Summer peak period:*** Kapellskär (Sweden) - Mariehamn (Åland) - Turku (Finland) (8 hrs 45 mins; *(7)*; 1 per day), ***Except summer peak period*** Cruises from Stockholm to Mariehamn (21 hrs - 24 hrs round trip (most 22 hrs 30 mins); *(7 until June 2003, 3 from September 2003)*; 1 per day).

1	ÅLANDSFÄRJAN	6172t	72	17.0k	104.6m	1004P	185C	26T	BA	SW

2	AMORELLA	34384t	88	21.5k	169.4m	2480P	450C	70T	BA	FI
3	CINDERELLA	46398t	89	21.5k	190.9m	2500P	340C	82T	BA	SW
4	GABRIELLA	35492t	92	21.5k	171.0m	2420P	420C	70T	BA	FI
5	ISABELLA	34386t	89	21.5k	169.4m	2480P	364C	70T	BA	FI
6	MARIELLA	37799t	85	22.0k	177.0m	2500P	480C	82T	BA	FI
7	ROSELLA	16850t	80	21.3k	136.2m	1700P	340C	52T	BA	FI

ÅLANDSFÄRJAN Built at Helsingør, Denmark as the KATTEGAT for *Jydsk Færgefart* of Denmark for the Grenaa - Hundested service. She was used on this route until 1978 when the service became a single ship operation. She was then sold to *P&O Ferries*, renamed the N F TIGER and introduced as the second vessel on the Dover - Boulogne service. Sold to *European Ferries* in 1985 and withdrawn in June 1986. In 1986 sold to *Finlandshammen AB*, Sweden, renamed the ÅLANDSFÄRJAN and used on *Viking Line* summer service between Kapellskär and Mariehamn. This service now operates all year round.

AMORELLA Built at Split, Yugoslavia for *SF Line* for the Stockholm - Mariehamn - Turku service.

CINDERELLA Built at Turku, Finland for *SF Line*. Until 1993 provided additional capacity between Stockholm and Helsinki and undertook weekend cruises from Helsinki. In 1993 she replaced the OLYMPIA (a sister vessel of the MARIELLA) as the main Stockholm - Helsinki vessel after the OLYMPIA had been chartered to *P&O European Ferries* and renamed the PRIDE OF BILBAO. In 1995 switched to operating 20 hour cruises from Helsinki to Estonia in the off peak and the Stockholm - Mariehamn - Turku service during the peak summer period (end of May to end of August). Since 1997 she has remained cruising throughout the year. In 2003 transferred to Swedish flag. During summer 2003 to also operate nine cruises from Helsinki to Riga (Latvia). In autumn 2003 to be transferred to Stockholm - Mariehamn cruises.

GABRIELLA Built at Split, Croatia as the FRANS SUELL for *Sea-Link AB* of Sweden to operate for subsidiary company *Euroway AB*, who established a service between Lübeck, Travemünde and Malmö. In 1994 this service ceased and she was chartered to *Silja Line*, renamed the SILJA SCANDINAVIA and transferred to the Stockholm - Turku service. In 1997 she was sold to *Viking Line* to operate between Stockholm and Helsinki. She was renamed the GABRIELLA.

ISABELLA Built at Split, Yugoslavia for *SF Line*. Used on the Stockholm - Naantali service until 1992 until she was switched to operating 24 hour cruises from Helsinki and in 1995 she was transferred to the Stockholm - Helsinki route. During 1996 she additionally operated short cruises to Muuga in Estonia during the 'layover' period in Helsinki. In 1997 she was transferred to the Stockholm - Turku route.

MARIELLA Built at Turku, Finland for *SF Line*. Used on the Stockholm - Helsinki service. During 1996 additionally operated short cruises to Muuga in Estonia during the 'layover' period in Helsinki but this has now ceased.

ROSELLA Built at Turku, Finland for *SF Line*. Used mainly on the Stockholm - Turku and Kapellskär - Naantali services until 1997. Since 1997 operated 21-24 hour cruises from Stockholm to Mariehamn under the marketing name 'The Dancing Queen', except in the peak summer period when she operated between Kapellskär and Turku. In autumn 2003 to be transferred to a new twice daily Helsinki – Tallinn ferry service. She also operates as a reserve vessel for the larger ships.

VV-LINE

THE COMPANY *VV-Line* is the trading name of *Västervik – Ventspils Färjelinje AB*, a Swedish company whose main owner is *Scandia Liv Ltd.*

MANAGEMENT Managing Director Vacant.

ADDRESS *Sweden* Lucernahamnen, Västervik Färjevägen 10, S-593 50 Västervik, Sweden, *Latvia* 7 Plostu Iela, Ventspils, LV 3600 Latvia.

TELEPHONE Administration & Reservations *Sweden* +46 (0)490 258080, *Latvia* +371 (0)36 07 358.

FAX Administration & Reservations *Sweden* +46 (0)490 258089, *Latvia* +371 (0)36 07 355.

INTERNET Email office@vvline.com **Website** www.vvline.com *(Swedish, English)*

ROUTE OPERATED Nynäshamn (Sweden) – Ventspils (Latvia) (10 hrs; *(1)*; 6 per week).

1	FELLOW	14297t	73	18.0k	137.3m	64P	170C	84T	AS	FI

FELLOW Built in Turku, Finland for *Finncarriers* as the FINNFELLOW. In 1989 transferred to *FinnLink*. In 2002 chartered to *VV-Line* and renamed the FELLOW.

WAGENBORG PASSAGIERSDIENSTEN

THE COMPANY *Wagenborg Passagiersdiensten BV* is a Dutch public sector company.

MANAGEMENT Managing Director G van Langen.

ADDRESS Postbus 70, 9163 ZM Nes, Ameland, Netherlands.

TELEPHONE Administration & Reservations +31 (0)519 546111.

FAX Administration & Reservations +31 (0)519 542905.

INTERNET Email info@wpd.nl **Website** www.wpd.nl *(Dutch, German, English)*

ROUTES OPERATED Ameland (Netherlands) - Holwerd (Frisian Islands) (45 minutes; *(2,3,4)*; up to 10 per day), Lauwersoog (Netherlands) - Schiermonnikoog (Frisian Islands) (45 minutes; *(5)*; up to 6 per day).

1	BRAKZAND	450t	67	10.5k	50.0m	1000P	20C	-	A	NL
2	OERD	1121t	85	12.2k	58.0m	1000P	46C	9L	BA	NL
3	OERD	c2300t	03	11.2k	73.2m	1200P	72C	22L	BA	NL
4	SIER	2286t	95	11.2k	73.2m	1200P	72C	22L	BA	NL
5	ROTTUM	1121t	85	12.2k	58.0m	1140P	46C	9L	BA	NL

BRAKZAND Built at Hoogezand, Netherlands for *Wagenborg Passagiersdiensten BV*. Now a spare vessel.

OERD (1985) Built at Hoogezand, Netherlands for *Wagenborg Passagiersdiensten BV*. On delivery of the new OERD she is to be renamed.

OERD (2003) Built at Lemmer, Netherlands for *Wagenborg Passagiersdiensten BV*. Used on the Ameland - Holwerd route.

ROTTUM Built at Hoogezand, Netherlands for *Wagenborg Passagiersdiensten BV* as the SIER and used on the Holwerd - Ameland route. In 1995 renamed the ROTTUM and transferred to the Lauwersoog - Schiermonnikoog route.

SIER Built at Wartena, Netherlands for *Wagenborg Passagiersdiensten BV*. Used on the Ameland - Holwerd route.

Silja Symphony (Miles Cowsill)

PURBECK

Purbeck *(John Bryant)*

section **7**
others

The following vessels are, at the time of going to print, not operating and are owned by companies which do not currently operate services. They are therefore available for possible re-deployment, either in the area covered by this book or elsewhere. Withdrawn vessels not yet disposed of owned by operating companies are shown under the appropriate company and marked '•'.

Channel Island Ferries (UK)

1	PURBECK	6507t	78	17.5k	125.5m	58P	-	58T	BA	BS

PURBECK Built at Le Havre, France for *Truckline Ferries* for their Cherbourg - Poole service. In 1986 she was lengthened to increase vehicle capacity by 34%. In 1992 transferred to the Roscoff - Plymouth and Santander - Plymouth services. In 1994 she was sold to *Channel Island Ferries* (parent company of *British Channel Island Ferries*) to operate freight services between Poole and the Channel Islands. Later in 1994, chartered to *Commodore Ferries* following the cessation of *BCIF's* operations. In 1995 she was chartered to *Sally Ferries* for use on their Dartford - Vlissingen service until replaced by the DART 5 later in the year. During summer 1996 she was chartered to *Irish Ferries* to operate supplementary freight services between Dublin and Holyhead. In autumn 1996 she returned to *Sally Ferries* and in 1997 she was transferred to *Holyman Sally Ferries*. In summer 1997 she was chartered to *Truckline Ferries* to operate between Caen and Portsmouth. Later in 1997, she was chartered to *Gaelic Ferries* to inaugurate a new Cork - Cherbourg service. During the French truckers' blockade in late 1997, she operated between Cork and Santander (Spain). In 1998 she was chartered to *Falcon Seafreight* and operated between Folkestone and Boulogne. In summer 1999 she was chartered to *Truckline Ferries* (now *Brittany Ferries Freight*) to operate between Caen and Portsmouth. During summer 2002 she operated between Portsmouth and Cherbourg as well as Caen. Withdrawn in December 2002, following the delivery of the MONT ST MICHEL and laid up for further charter. In 2003 chartered to *TransRail* of New Zealand to operate between Wellington and Picton

Comhairle Nan Eilean Siar

1	EILEAN BHEARNARAIGH	67t	83	7.0k	18.6m	35P	4C	-	B	UK
2	EILEAN NA H-OIGE	69t	80	7.0k	18.6m	35P	4C	-	B	UK

EILEAN BHEARNARAIGH Built at Glasgow, UK for *Western Isles Islands Council* for their Otternish (North Uist) - Berneray service. From 1996 until 1999 she was operated by *Caledonian MacBrayne* in conjunction with the LOCH BHRUSDA on the service between Otternish and Berneray and during the winter she was laid up. Following the opening of a causeway between North Uist and Berneray in early 1999, the ferry service ceased and she became reserve vessel for the Eriskay route. This route ceased in July 2001 following the opening of a causeway and she was laid up. In 2002 she started operating between Eriskay and Barra. In 2003 replaced by the LOCH BHRUSDA of *Caledonian MacBrayne* and laid up.

EILEAN NA H-OIGE Built at Stornoway, UK for *Western Isles Islands Council* (from 1st April 1996 the *Western Isles Council* and from 1st January 1998 *Comhairle Nan Eilean Siar*) for their Ludaig - Eriskay service. From 2000 operated from temporary slipway at the Eriskay causeway. This route ceased in July 2001 following the opening of a causeway and she was laid up. In 2002 she started operating between Eriskay and Barra. In 2003 replaced by the LOCH BHRUSDA of *Caledonian MacBrayne* and laid up.

DIFKO (Denmark)

1	DIFKO FYN	4101t	87	12.7k	95.8m	253P	170C	26L	BA	DK
2	GITTE 3	4296t	87	12.7k	95.0m	300P	170C	20T	BA	DK

DIFKO FYN Built Sunderland, UK at as the SUPERFLEX ECHO for *Vognmandsruten*. She was unused until 1995, when she was renamed the DIFKO FYN (*Vognmandsruten* having meanwhile been acquired by *DIFKO Færger A/S*) and placed on the Nyborg - Korsør service. In 1998, following the opening of the Great Belt fixed link, the service ceased and she was laid up at Helsingborg, initially in the care of *HH-Ferries* and was them to charter at short notice should one of their own vessels be unavailable; this arrangement has now ceased. In summer 2000 operated by *DIFKO* between Langeland (Denmark) and Kiel (Germany). This was not repeated in 2001 and she remains laid up.

GITTE 3 Built at Sunderland, UK as the SUPERFLEX DELTA for *Vognmandsruten*. In 1990 this company was taken over by *DIFKO* and she was renamed the DIFKO STOREBÆLT. In 1998, following the opening of the Great Belt fixed link, the service ceased and she was laid up. In 1999 she was chartered to *Easy Line* renamed the GITTE 3 and operated between Gedser and Rostock. Laid up after August 1999 except for brief periods on charter to *HH-Ferries*.

Far Eastern Shipping (Russia)

1	MIKHAIL SHOLOKHOV	12798t	86	20.0k	139.6m	412P	344C	22T	A	RU
2	RUSS	12798t	86	20.0k	139.6m	409P	344C	45T	A	RU

MIKHAIL SHOLOKHOV Built at Szczecin, Poland for *Far Eastern Shipping* of the Soviet Union and later of Russia. In 1999 started a service from Stockholm to St Petersburg; service ceased at the end of the year. In 2000 began operating for *Mono Line* between Stockholm and Riga (Latvia). In 2001 service ceased and she was laid up.

RUSS Built at Szczecin, Poland as the KONSTANTIN CHERNENKO for *Far Eastern Shipping* of the Soviet Union and later of Russia. She was engaged in cruising. In 1988 renamed the RUSS. In 1996 chartered to *LS Redereja* of Latvia to start a service from Riga to Stockholm (trading as *LS Line*). Permission to convey passengers from Sweden was obtained in April 1997. In 1998 the company changed its name to *Ferry Serviss*. In 1999 the service was taken over by Russian interests; later the serviced ceased and the charter ended and she was laid up.

Reederei F Laeisz (Germany)

1	GREIFSWALD	24084t	88	15.5k	190.9m	120P	100C	116T	A2	LB

GREIFSWALD Built at Wismar, Germany (DDR) as a train ferry for *DSR* of Germany (DDR) to operate on the service between Mukran and Klaìpeda (Lithuania). In 1994 she was rebuilt to introduce road vehicle and additional passenger capacity. In 1996 she was transferred to the new *Euroseabridge* Travemünde - Klaìpeda service. During winter 1998/99 she was chartered to *Stena Line* to operate between Gothenburg and Kiel. She was then chartered to the British *Ministry of Defence* for use in the Balkans. In November 1999 she was transferred to the Kiel - Klaìpeda route. In early 2001 the charter was ended and she was chartered to *Transocean Line* of Denmark and operated between Århus (Denmark) and Halmstad (Sweden). This service ended after a few weeks. In the autumn chartered to *TransRussia Express*. Later in 2001 chartered to *Lisco* for the Klaìpeda - Kiel route. Charter ended in 2003.

british isles and northern europe

DISPOSALS

The following vessels, listed in the *Ferries 2002 - British Isles and Northern Europe* have been disposed of - either to other companies listed in this book or others. Company names are as used in that publication.

ADMIRAL OF SCANDINAVIA *(DFDS Seaways)* In 2002 sold to *Access Ferries*. In 2003 chartered to *Ferries del Caribe* and renamed the CARIBBEAN EXPRESS. She operates between Mayagüez (Puerto Rico) and Santa Domingo (Dominican Republic).

ANJA 11 *(DIFKO)* In 2003 chartered to *Faergeruten Langeland-Kiel* and renamed the LANGELAND.

ASK *(Scandlines Denmark and Germany)* In 2003 chartered to *Scandlines Sweden* to operate between Trelleborg and Travemünde.

BERGEN *(Fjord Line)* In 2003 chartered to *DFDS Seaways* and renamed the DUCHESS OF SCANDINAVIA. Placed on the Harwich - Cuxhaven service.

BORDEN *(ArgoGood)* In 2002 charter ended. Later chartered to *CETAM* and renamed the CETAM VICTORIAE.

CAP AFRIQUE *(Farmers Ferry)* In 2002 charter ended and now operating for *Delom* in the Mediterranean.

CONDOR 9 *(Condor Ferries)* In 2002 sold to a Mexican company and renamed the CORTEZ. Operates between Topolobampo and La Paz (Baja California).

CLAYMORE *(Sea Containers Ferries)* In 2002 sold to *Pentland Ferries*.

DAWN MERCHANT *(NorseMerchant Ferries)* In 2002 chartered to *Norfolkline* to operate between Dover and Dunkerque.

EUROPEAN ENDEAVOUR *(P&O Irish Sea)* In 2002 sold to *Odyssy Maritime Co Ltd* and chartered to *TransEuropa Ferries*. Renamed the GARDENIA.

EUROPEAN FREEWAY *(P&O North Sea Ferries)* In 2002 sold to *Stena Line* and renamed the FREEWAY. In 2003 renamed the STENA PARTNER.

EUROPEAN HIGHWAY *(P&O Stena Line)* In 2002 transferred to *P&O Ferries*. In 2003 rebuilt as a full passenger ship and renamed the PRIDE OF KENT.

EUROPEAN NAVIGATOR *(P&O Irish Sea)* In 2003 sold to *Arab Bridge* of Jordan and renamed the BLACK IRIS.

EUROPEAN PATHFINDER *(P&O Irish Sea)* In 2002 sold to *Abbey Trading SA Trust Co* and chartered to *TransEuropa Ferries*. Renamed the BEGONIA.

EUROPEAN PATHWAY *(P&O Stena Line)* In 2002 transferred to *P&O Ferries*. In 2003 rebuilt as a full passenger ship and renamed the PRIDE OF CANTERBURY.

EUROPEAN TIDEWAY *(P&O North Sea Ferries)* In 2002 sold to *Stena Line* and renamed the IDEWAY.

European Highway *(John May)*

Quiberon *(John May)*

Later renamed the STENA TRANSFER.

FINNBEAVER *(Finnlines)* In 2002 charter ended. Renamed the BORE MARI and chartered to *BornholmsTrafikken* to operate between Rønne and Køge. In 2003 charter ended.

FINNRIVER *(Finnlines)* In 2002 charter ended and renamed the CELIA. Later chartered to *Grupo Boluda* and renamed the CELIA B; operates between Spain and the Canary Islands.

FINNROSE *(Finnlines)* In 2002 charter ended and renamed the CORTIA. Later chartered to *Grupo Boluda* and renamed the CARMEN B; operates between Spain and the Canary Islands.

FINNSEAL *(Finnlines)* At end of 2002 charter ended and renamed the BORE NORDIA. Chartered to *Transfennica*.

FRISIA VIII *(Reederei Norden-Frisia)* In 2003 sold to Costa Rican owners.

GREIFSWALD *(Lisco)* In 2002 charter ended. Now listed in Section 7 under owners *Reederei F Laeisz*.

GEORG OTS *(ESCO)* In 2002 sold to the *Sea Administration of St Petersburg* and inaugurated a new St Petersburg - Baltijsk (Kaliningrad) service. Un-renamed but name now expressed in Cyrillic characters.

HARALD JARL *(Hurtigruten)* In 2002 sold to *Elegant Cruise Line* and renamed the ANDREA.

HINRICH-WILHELM KOPF *(Elbe-Ferry)* In 2002 sold to Egyptian interests and renamed the HEBA. To be used on pilgrim services between Egypt and Saudi Arabia.

IDUN VIKING *(Hovertravel)* In 2002 withdrawn and sold.

JOCHEN STEFFEN *(Elbe-Ferry)* In 2002 sold to Egyptian interests and renamed the MIRIAM. To be used on pilgrim services between Egypt and Saudi Arabia.

KAHLEBERG *(Scandlines Denmark & Germany)* In 2003 chartered to *Polferries* to operate between Swinoujscie and Ystad.

LABURNUM *(TransEuropa Ferries)* In 2003 chartered to *COMANAV* to operate between Genoa and Tangier. Renamed the TADLA.

LYRA *(Cobelfret Ferries)* In 2002 charter ended. In 2003 chartered to the *UK MoD* to convey military materials to the Gulf. On return sold to *StradaBlu Srl* of Italy and renamed the STRADA MAESTRA.

MARTIN CHUZZLEWIT *(Lower Thames & Medway Passenger Boat Co Ltd)* In 2002 charter ended. Returned to the administrators of *White Horse Fast Ferries* and laid up.

MADS MOLS *(Mols-Linien)* In 2003 transferred to subsidiary SpeedFerries to operate between Dover and Boulogne and renamed the SPEED ONE.

MERCHANT VENTURE *(Norse Irish Ferries)* In 2002 chartered to *Norse Island Ferries* to operate between Aberdeen and Lerwick (Shetland)

MERMAID II *(VV-Line)* In 2002 chartered to *Latlines* to operate between Travemünde and Riga (Latvia).

NIEBOROW *(Polferries)* In 2002 sold to *Montenegro Lines* and renamed the SVETI STEFAN II. She operates between Bari (Italy) and Bar (Montenegro).

NORMANDIE EXPRESS *(Emeraude Lines)* In 2003 sold to *Société de Developement de Mooréa* of Tahiti and renamed the MOOREA EXPRESS. She operates between Tahiti and Mooréa.

P&OSL AQUITAINE *(P&O Stena Line)* In 2002 transferred to *P&O Ferries* and renamed the PO AQUITAINE. In 2003 renamed the PRIDE OF AQUITAINE.

P&OSL BURGUNDY *(P&O Stena Line)* In 2002 transferred to *P&O Ferries* and renamed the PO BURGUNDY. In 2003 renamed the PRIDE OF BURGUNDY.

P&OSL CALAIS *(P&O Stena Line)* In 2002 transferred to *P&O Ferries* and renamed the PO CALAIS. In 2003 renamed the renamed the PRIDE OF CALAIS.

P&OSL CANTERBURY *(P&O Stena Line)* In 2002 transferred to *P&O Ferries* and renamed the PO CANTERBURY.

P&OSL DOVER *(P&O Stena Line)* In 2002 transferred to *P&O Ferries* and renamed the PO DOVER. In 2003 renamed the renamed the PRIDE OF DOVER.

P&OSL KENT *(P&O Stena Line)* In 2002 transferred to *P&O Ferries* and renamed the PO KENT.

P&OSL PROVENCE *(P&O Stena Line)* In 2002 transferred to *P&O Ferries* and renamed the PO PROVENCE. In 2003 renamed the renamed the PRIDE OF PROVENCE.

PASEWALK *(CCTL)* In 2003 charter ended. Chartered to the *MoD* for Gulf service.

PORTAFERRY *(Strangford Lough Ferry Service)* In 2002 sold to *Fastnet Shipping* of Waterford, Irish Republic, for uses as a work boat.

PRIDE OF CHERBOURG *(P&O Portsmouth)* In 2002 renamed the PRIDE OF CHERBOURG A. Later sold to *El Salam Maritime* of Egypt and renamed the PRIDE OF EL SALAM II.

PRIDE OF FLANDERS *(P&O North Sea Ferries)* In 2002 sold to *Stena Line* and renamed the FLANDERS. Later renamed the STENA TRANSPORTER.

PRIDE OF HAMPSHIRE *(P&O Portsmouth)* In 2002 sold to *El Salam Maritime* of Egypt and renamed the PRIDE OF EL SALAM III.

PRINS WILLEM-ALEXANDER *(Provinciale Stoombootdiensten in Zeeland)* In 2003 sold to *Amadeus Spa* of Italy to operate between Villa San Giovanni (Calabria) and Messina (Sicily). Renamed the ATOS MATACENA.

PRINSES CHRISTINA *(Provinciale Stoombootdiensten in Zeeland)* In 2003 sold to *Amadeus Spa* of Italy to operate between Villa San Giovanni (Calabria) and Messina (Sicily). Renamed the LADIES MATACENA

PRINSES JULIANA *(Provinciale Stoombootdiensten in Zeeland)* In 2003 sold to *Amadeus Spa* of Italy to operate between Villa San Giovanni (Calabria) and Messina (Sicily). Renamed the AMEDO MATACENA.

PURBECK *(Truckline Ferries)* In 2002 charter ended and laid up. Now listed in Section 7 under owners *Channel Island Ferries*.

QUIBERON *(Brittany Ferries)* In 2003 sold to *Linee Lauro* of Italy to operate for *Euro-Mer Ferries* of France from Sete (France) to Palma De Mallorca, Ibiza and Menorca and renamed GUILIA D'ABUNDO.

SÆLEN *(Scandlines Denmark and Germany)* In 2002 sold to *SNAV* of Italy and renamed the SNAV AQUILA.

SAMMARINA A *(Sammarina Shipping and Trading)* In 2002 service ceased. Vessel laid up at Zeebrugge. Current whereabouts unknown.

SAMMARINA M *(Sammarina Shipping and Trading)* In 2002 service ceased. Vessel never used.

SEA SYMPHONY *(Latlines)* In 2002 charter ceased and vessel returned to the Mediterranean.

SHANNON WILLOW *(Shannon Ferry Ltd)* In 2003 sold to *Lough Foyle Ferry Company* and renamed the FOYLE VENTURE.

SHEARWATER 5 *(Red Funnel Ferries)* In 2002 sold to *Kon-Tiki* of Thailand and renamed the COLONA V.

SHEARWATER 6 *(Red Funnel Ferries)* In 2002 sold to *Kon-Tiki* of Thailand and renamed the COLONA VI.

SJÖBJÖRNEN *(Scandlines Denmark and Germany)* In 2002 sold to *SNAV* of Italy and renamed the SNAV ORION.

SOUND OF SHUNA *(Western Ferries)* In 2002 renamed the SHUNA. In 2003 sold.

Dana Anglia *(John May)*

European Freeway *(John May)*

ST CLAIR *(P&O Scottish Ferries)* In 2002 sold to *Baaboud Trading & Shipping* of Saudi Arabia and renamed the BARAKAT.

ST OLA *(P&O Scottish Ferries)* In 2002 sold to *Saaremaa Lævakompanii* of Estonia. Not renamed.

ST ROGNVALD *(P&O Scottish Ferries)* In August 2002 chartered to *Norse Island Ferries*. Not renamed.

ST SUNNIVA *(P&O Scottish Ferries)* In 2002 sold to *Althuraya* of Dubai, UAE and renamed the FAYE.

STENA FORWARDER *(Stena Line)* In 2003 charter ended. Renamed the CALIFORNIA STAR and Chartered to *Baja Ferries* of Mexico to operate between Topolobampo (Los Mochis) and La Paz (Baja California).

STENA BRITANNICA *(Stena Line)* In 2003 sold to *Finnlines* and renamed the FINNFELLOW. Used on the Helsinki - Travemünde route.

SUPERSEACAT ONE *(Sea Containers Ferries)* In 2003 transferred to *Silja Line* to operate between Helsinki and Tallinn.

SVEALAND *(Scandlines Sweden)* In 2003 charter transferred to *Scandlines AG* and placed on the Kiel - Klaipeda route.

SVALEN *(Scandlines Denmark and Germany)* In 2002 sold to *SNAV* of Italy and renamed the SNAV AURORA.

TANGO *(Ferryways)* In 2002 charter ended. Chartered to *Transfennica* for Baltic service.

TOR ANGLIA *(DFDS Tor Line)* In 2003 sold to *StradaBlu Srl* of Italy.

TRADEN *(Finnlines)* In 2002 Hull - Gdynia service ceased. Charter ended. In 2003 chartered to *Mann Lines* to operate between Turku and Bremerhaven.

TRANSPARADEN *(Botnia Link)* In 2002 charter ended. Chartered to *DFDS Tor Line* to operate between Kiel and Riga (Latvia). In 2003 transferred to the Travemünde - Riga route.

TYCHY *(CCTL)* In 2002 charter ended.

VARBOLA *(NorseMerchant Ferries)* In 2003 chartered to *Dart Line* and placed on the Dartford - Vlissingen service.

WILHELM KAISEN *(Elbe-Ferry)* In 2002 sold to Egyptian interests and renamed the AMNA. To be used on pilgrim services between Egypt and Saudi Arabia.

NAME CHANGES

The following vessels have been renamed without change of operator.

DANA ANGLIA *(DFDS Seaways)* In 2002 transferred to the Copenhagen - Trelleborg – Gdansk route and renamed the DUKE OF SCANDINAVIA. Transferred from section 1 to section 6.

FREJA VIKING *(Hovertravel)* In 2002 renamed the ISLAND EXPRESS.

LOMERVAL *(Cobelfret Ferries)* In 2003 sold and renamed the MARABOU.

MIDNATSOL *(Hurtigruten - TFDS)* In 2003 renamed the MIDNATSOL II.

NORSEA *(P&O North Sea Ferries)* In 2003 renamed the PRIDE OF YORK.

NORSUN *(P&O North Sea Ferries)* In 2003 renamed the PRIDE OF BRUGES.

REDONA and SAPPHIRE *(Ferryways)* In 2003 sold and renamed IPSWICH WAY and OSTEND WAY.

UNITED CARRIER, UNITED EXPRESS, UNITED TRADER *(Finnlines)* In 2002 renamed the BIRKA CARRIER, BIRKA EXPRESS and BIRKA TRADER respectively.

VISBY *(Destination Gotland)* In 2003 renamed the VISBORG.

SECTION 9 – RECENT CHANGES

COMPANY CHANGES

ArgoGood In 2002 the company ceased trading.

Botnia Link In 2002 the company ceased trading.

CCTL Now listed as Seawheel.

Comhairle Nan Eilean Siar In 2003 their service was taken over by *Caledonian MacBrayne* and their two vessels laid up. Now listed in Section 8.

Farmers Ferry Although service resumed in 2002 following the ending of the foot and mouth disease restrictions, a ro-ro ship is no longer used.

P&O Portsmouth In 2002 as part of a re-organisation of the *P&O* Group, merged with *P&O Stena Line* and *P&O North Sea Ferries* as *P&O Ferries*.

P&O North Sea Ferries In 2002 as part of a re-organisation of the *P&O* Group, merged with *P&O Stena Line* and *P&O Portsmouth* as *P&O Ferries*.

P&O Stena Line In 2002 *Stena Line* participation ceased and the company merged with *P&O Portsmouth* and *P&O North Sea Ferries* as *P&O Ferries*.

Provinciale Stoombootdiensten in Zeeland In 2003 ceased operations following the opening of a new road tunnel. Passenger service taken over by *BBA Fast Ferries*.

Sammarina Shipping and Trading In 2002 ceased operations.

Truckline Ferries In 2002 the *Truckline* name was dropped and the company became *Brittany Ferries Freight*.

LATE NEWS

P&O Irish Sea and ***Stena Line*** The two companies have agreed that the Fleetwood - Dublin and Liverpool - Dublin routes are to be transferred to Stena Line along with the EUROPEAN LEADER, EUROPEAN PIONEER, EUROPEAN SEAFARER, NORBANK and NORBAY. The Mostyn - Dublin route is likely to close and EUROPEAN AMBASSADOR and EUROPEAN ENVOY to be time chartered to Stena Line. All these ships are likely to be renamed.

Dart Line/Norse Merchant Ferries In May the VARBOLA and RIVER LUNE exchanged roles. This is noted in the text but the vessels remain listed as they were previously.

Norse Island Ferries This operator ceased trading on 6th June 2003. The MERCHANT VENTURE had already returned to ***NorseMerchant Ferries*** following mechanical failure and the ST ROGNVALD has been chartered to **NorthLink Orkney and Shetland Ferries**.

DFDS Tor Line/Latlines (Joint Service) and LISCO Baltic service In June 2003 VILNIUS of LISCO chartered to DFDS Tor Line/Latlines replacing the TRANSPARADEN.

index I
ferries illustrated

index **2**

ferries a to z